SAN FRANCISCO
AND THE BAY AREA

TU CANY
2 HOUR PARKING
8 A.M. 9 P.M.
MON SAT

DK

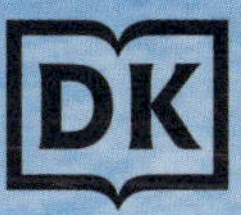

SAN FRANCISCO
AND THE BAY AREA

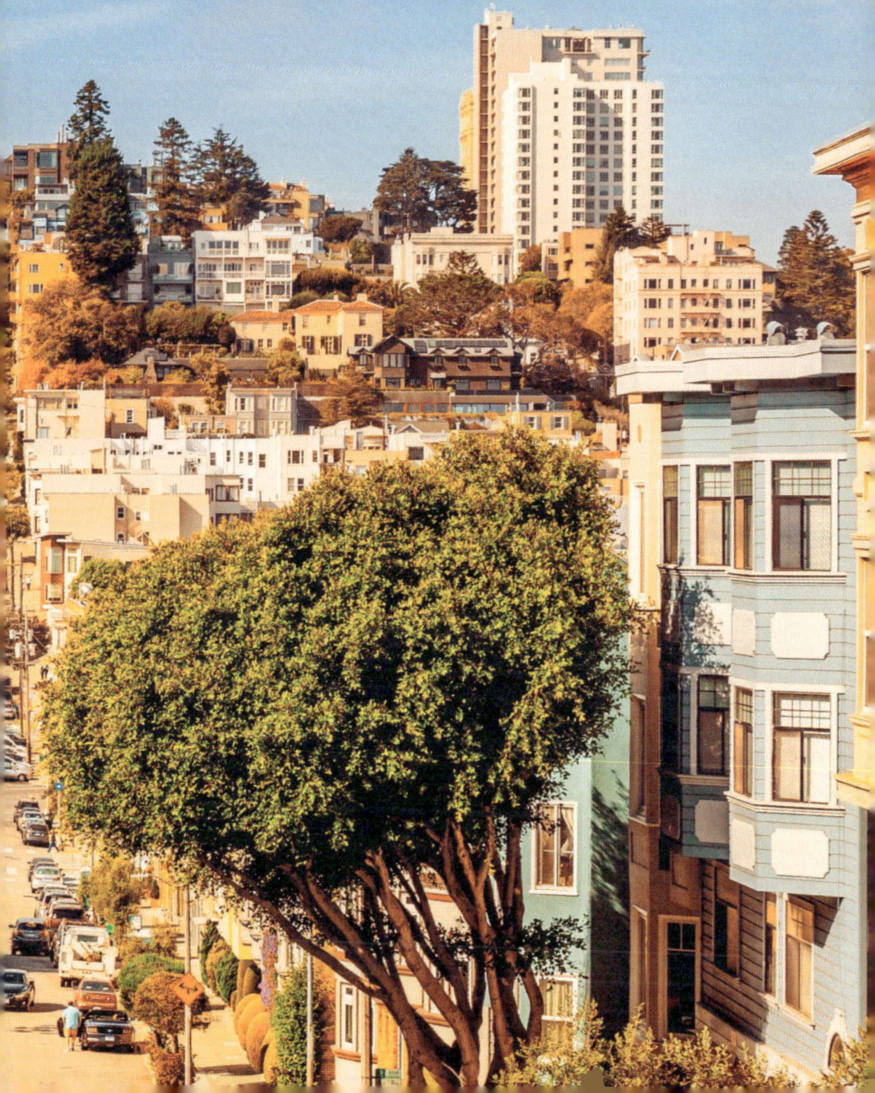

CONTENTS

DISCOVER 6

EXPERIENCE 58

NEED TO KNOW 252

Left: Beautiful fall colors in Napa Valley vineyards
Previous page: View west from Jones Street
Front cover: Majestic Golden Gate Bridge in the evening

DISCOVER

San Francisco skyline at sunset

WELCOME TO SAN FRANCISCO AND THE BAY AREA

Iconic bridges and staggeringly steep streets. Diverse neighborhoods rich with history and accessible public parks. Major museums and teeth-rattling cable cars. Whatever your dream trip to San Francisco includes, this DK travel guide is the perfect companion.

1 Vintage cable car, making its way up one of the city's many hills.

2 PIER 39, still thronged with visitors at sunset.

3 Oakland Bay Bridge, lit up at dusk as it stretches across to San Francisco.

Fingers of fog drift beneath the Golden Gate Bridge, sliding over the hills and welcoming newcomers to the "City by the Bay," as they have since the days when fortune-seekers flocked here during the Gold Rush. But Karl the Fog, as it's affectionately known, can't hide San Francisco's beauty for long; from one of its many steep hills, you'll find yourself confronted with stunning views at almost every turn.

"The City," as it's concisely known to locals, is a place of many nicknames – and many neighborhoods. Track down delicious Italian food in the vibrant North Beach area, or head to Chinatown to experience the spectacular Chinese New Year parade. For those in search of culture, the city's four principal art museums – San Francisco Museum of Modern Art (SFMOMA), the Asian Art Museum, the Legion of Honor, and the de Young Museum – will prove a highlight; if you're looking for nightlife, the Mission District, Lower Nob Hill, and The Castro have great bars.

Down on the water, two iconic bridges and a flotilla of ferries connect to lively bayfront cities such as Oakland and Berkeley. The lush vineyards of California Wine Country also lie within easy reach, while the coastal wonders of the Monterey Peninsula make for breezy weekend getaways.

From the Presidio to Alcatraz, we've broken San Francisco and the Bay Area into easily navigable adventures, with expert local knowledge, detailed itineraries, and colorful, comprehensive maps to help you plan the perfect visit. Whether you're staying for a weekend, or longer, this DK travel guide will ensure that you see the very best that San Francisco has to offer.

REASONS TO LOVE SAN FRANCISCO AND THE BAY AREA

Iconic bridges, multicultural neighborhoods, a world-famous foodie scene, and mild maritime weather. There are so many reasons why San Franciscans love their city. Here are some of our favorite reasons to visit.

1 WINE COUNTRY WEEKENDS

Take a balloon trip above the vineyards, taste the grapes at welcoming wineries, and sink into a hot-springs spa in the Napa and Sonoma valleys.

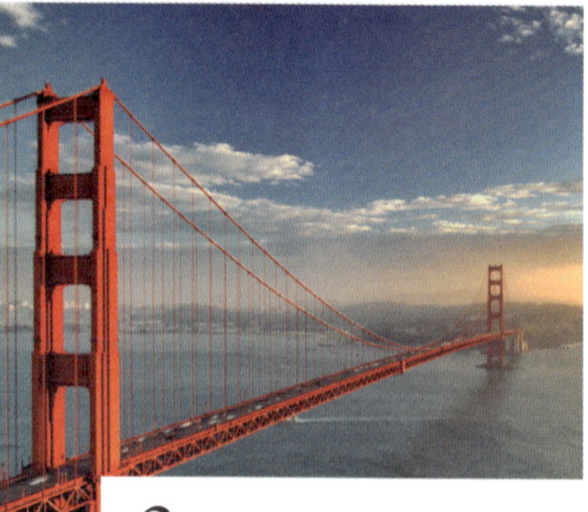

2 FERRY BUILDING MARKETPLACE

Shop for treats at this indoor food hall *(p136)*, located in the Embarcadero. On Tuesdays, Thursdays, and Saturdays, it expands into a lively outdoor farmers' market on the pier.

3 GOLDEN GATE BRIDGE

Every first-time visitor to San Francisco walks or bikes across the red-orange expanse of this suspension bridge *(p64)*, a world-famous gateway to the vast Bay Area.

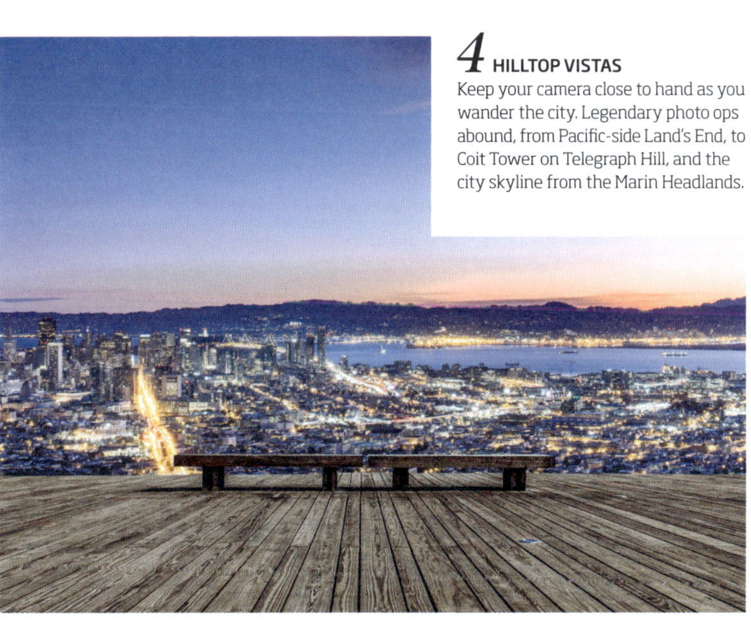

4 HILLTOP VISTAS

Keep your camera close to hand as you wander the city. Legendary photo ops abound, from Pacific-side Land's End, to Coit Tower on Telegraph Hill, and the city skyline from the Marin Headlands.

CABLE-CAR TOURS 5

Climb aboard this National Historic Landmark for an open-air, rattling, and bell-ringing ride, from Fisherman's Wharf, over Nob Hill, and down to Union Square in the heart of the city.

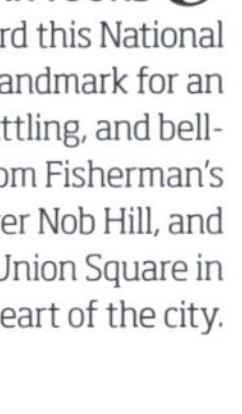

FABULOUS FOOD 6

Discover some of the city's best restaurants amid its vibrant and diverse neighborhoods; choose from French bistros, Italian pasta palaces, Mexican taquerias, and Chinatown dim sum joints.

FIRST-RATE MUSEUMS 7

San Francisco offers a rich museum scene - four major museums (SFMOMA, the Asian Art Museum, the Legion of Honor, and the deYoung) showcase ancient and modern art.

REDWOODS IN MUIR WOODS 8

These woods *(p219)* are one of the world's few remaining stands of old-growth coast redwood trees. For bird's-eye views, hike the Dipsea Trail.

9 PIER 39

A carousel, an arcade, and live outdoor entertainment lure fun-seekers to the most visited attraction in town *(p100)*, complete with basking sea lions only too ready to pose for photos.

10 TREASURES OF GOLDEN GATE PARK

You don't need a plan when you visit Golden Gate Park; just venture in and start exploring. Even a quick walk can turn up everything from world-class museums to wonderful nature.

SAN FRANCISCO PRIDE CELEBRATION 11

San Francisco Pride *(p50)* was first held in 1970 and is now one of the largest LGBTQ+ celebrations in the entire world. It's also the city's largest outdoor event.

HISTORIC HOUSES 12

Having survived the 1906 earthquake, Painted Ladies *(p168)* line Alamo Square and parts of Broadway in Pacific Heights. Some houses can be toured; all can be admired.

EXPLORE SAN FRANCISCO AND THE BAY AREA

This guide divides San Francisco into eight color-coded sightseeing areas, as shown on the map below. Find out more about each area on the following pages. For the Bay Area see p210.

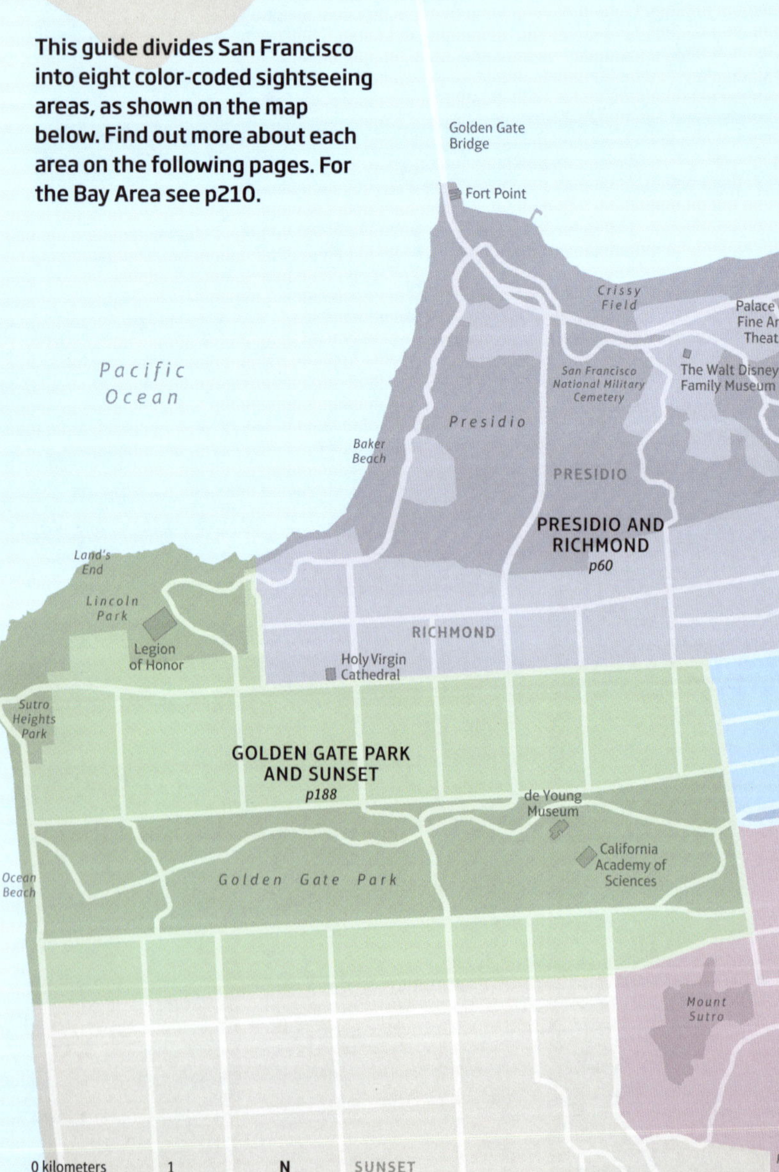

NORTH AMERICA
CANADA
Seattle
USA
Chicago
Boston
New York
SAN FRANCISCO
Washington, DC
Los Angeles
Memphis
Atlantic Ocean
Atlanta
Houston
Miami
Gulf of Mexico
Pacific Ocean
MEXICO
Alcatraz Island
San Francisco Bay
USS Pampanito
PIER 39
FISHERMAN'S WHARF
Fort Mason
MARINA
FISHERMAN'S WHARF AND NORTH BEACH
p90
Coit Tower
Exploratorium
COW HOLLOW
RUSSIAN HILL
NORTH BEACH
Transamerica Pyramid
Ferry Building
PACIFIC HEIGHTS AND THE MARINA
p72
Cable Car Museum
FINANCIAL DISTRICT
CHINATOWN AND NOB HILL
p114
Old St Mary's Cathedral
Salesforce Tower
PACIFIC HEIGHTS
DOWNTOWN
Japantown
THEATER DISTRICT
SFMOMA
Yerba Buena Gardens
St. Mary's Cathedral
CIVIC CENTER
DOWNTOWN AND SOMA
p132
CIVIC CENTER AND HAYES VALLEY
p158
Asian Art Museum
City Hall
SOMA
Oracle Park
HAYES VALLEY
MISSION BAY
LOWER HAIGHT
HAIGHT-ASHBURY
Buena Vista Park
Mission Dolores
GLBT Historical Society Museum
MISSION
POTRERO
HAIGHT-ASHBURY AND THE MISSION
p172
NOE VALLEY

GETTING TO KNOW SAN FRANCISCO AND THE BAY AREA

Known for vibrant neighborhoods, major museums, and waterfront esplanades, San Francisco is the crowning city of the beautiful Bay Area. Visitors get around the seven steep hills by cable car and streetcar, but braving the city on foot can lead to hidden stairways that turn up pocket parks and stunning views. The wider Bay Area offers up even more cityscapes, picturesque towns, and natural wonders to explore.

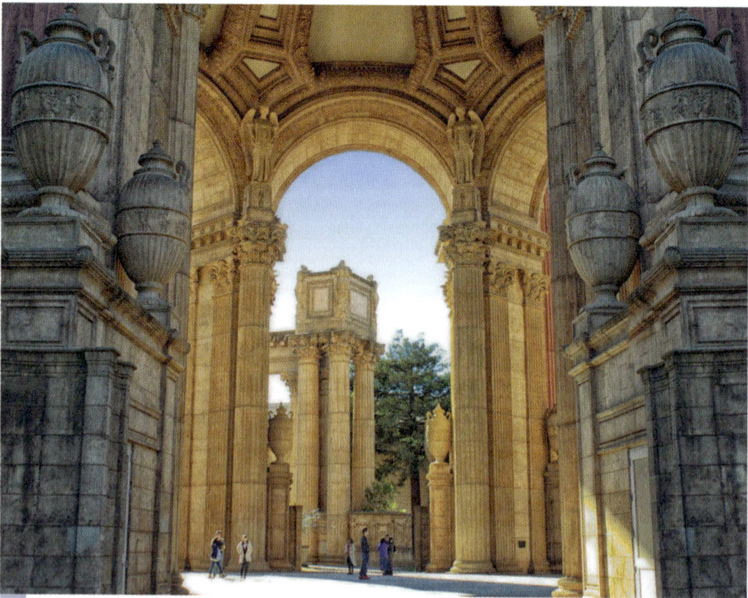

PAGE 60

PRESIDIO AND RICHMOND

Once a major army post, the Presidio is now a National Park bounded by beach, bluff, and stunning views. Thousands of people visit every year to enjoy a vibrant mix of museums, hiking trails, and recreational destinations. The adjacent Richmond district is a multicultural hub where a casual wander will turn up stunning architecture and restaurants serving cuisine from around the world.

Best for
History and outdoor recreation

Home to
Golden Gate Bridge

Experience
Exploring Fort Point and Crissy Field to find the perfect photo op of Golden Gate Bridge

PAGE 72

PACIFIC HEIGHTS AND THE MARINA

Kites fly and wind surfers skim the bay beyond the city's front lawn: Marina Green. Along the waterfront are busy yacht harbors and historic Fort Mason – now a top spot for seeing the sun set over the Pacific. Heading away from the waterfront, you'll find interesting spots like Japantown, as well as beautiful streets recalling past glories in their splendid architecture.

Best for
Architecture and parks

Home to
Fort Mason and Japantown

Experience
A short walk around Pacific Heights to admire the architecture, crowned by the Queen Anne-style Haas-Lilienthal House

PAGE 90

FISHERMAN'S WHARF AND NORTH BEACH

One of the most famous spots in town, PIER 39 at Fisherman's Wharf is loaded with cafés, knick-knack stores, and legendary seafood restaurants. The cultural history of North Beach, also known as "Little Italy," lives on in the Beat Museum and City Lights Bookstore. Nearby are iconic San Francisco sights such as Art Deco Coit Tower, twisting Lombard Street, and the infamous prison on Alcatraz Island.

Best for
Iconic attractions and Italian cuisine

Home to
Alcatraz Island and Exploratorium

Experience
Hopping on a cruise from Pier 33 to explore the iconic Alcatraz Island

→

PAGE 114

CHINATOWN AND NOB HILL

Between Stockton Street and Grant Avenue, the alleys of San Francisco's famous Chinatown are strung with red lanterns, and full of restaurants, Asian markets, and Chinese-inspired architecture. This is also the best place to see the city's historic cable cars trundling through the streets, as they take passengers high above downtown to Nob Hill. Rising above the city here are five iconic hostelries and a towering cathedral, as well as a charming park anchored by an elaborate replica of a 14th-century fountain.

Best for
Skyline views and Asian restaurants

Home to
Cable Car Museum and Grace Cathedral

Experience
A walk around Nob Hill to see its historic hotels, elevated city parks, and boutique stores

PAGE 132

DOWNTOWN AND SOMA

The city's business and financial center has gleaming skyscrapers on either side of Market Street, the main thoroughfare. Nearby Union Square is the city's fashion center, encircled by department stores, shopping malls, and designer boutiques. To the south, SoMa (or the South of Market) is a hotspot for museums, galleries, and nightlife.

Best for
Galleries, theater, and shopping

Home to
Ferry Building, SFMOMA, and Yerba Buena Gardens

Experience
The excellent museums and galleries of SoMa, ending with a drink at Cityscape Bar & Lounge

PAGE 158

CIVIC CENTER AND HAYES VALLEY

The buildings in the civic center are an outstanding example of the Beaux Arts style. It is perhaps the most ambitious and elaborate city center complex in the US and well worth an extended visit. The stunning architecture continues if you head up Fulton Street, which climbs gently to nearby Alamo Square where you'll find the iconic row of late Victorian houses known as the Painted Ladies.

Best for
Architecture and music venues

Home to
Asian Art Museum

Experience
A picnic at Alamo Square as you take in the amazing view of the modern city skyline behind old Victorian houses

PAGE 172

HAIGHT-ASHBURY AND THE MISSION

Vintage clothing, tattoo parlors, and record stores left over from the hippie-era Summer of Love comprise a colorful collage in the Haight-Ashbury neighborhood. The oldest neighborhood, the Mission District, remains a multicultural area with a large Latin American community, as reflected in the political and cutural murals that decorate the buildings.

Best for
Art and LGBTQ+ culture

Home to
Castro Street and Haight-Ashbury

Experience
A walk down Castro Street, the heart of the city's world-famous LGBTQ+ hub

PAGE 188

GOLDEN GATE PARK AND SUNSET

A masterpiece of 1890s landscaping, natural environments, and botanical gardens, Golden Gate Park sweeps to the Pacific. It encompasses three major museums, an outdoor concert plaza, biking and walking trails, and a lake where rowboats and pedal boats cruise. On the western edge of the Sunset district, Land's End offers miles of coastal foot-paths and the stunning Ocean Beach.

Best for

Nature and museums

Home to

California Academy of Sciences, de Young Museum, and Legion of Honor

Experience

Warming up with a sunset bonfire on Ocean Beach

PAGE 208

THE BAY AREA

North of San Francisco is Marin County, covered in beautiful parks and forests. The cities of Oakland and Berkeley take up much of the East Bay area, while farther south along the peninsula are beautiful beaches and the tech enclaves of Silicon Valley Stanford. Napa Valley and Sonoma County will be well known to wine lovers, while farther afield there are plenty of new places to discover, like the tiny town of Carmel-by-the-Sea and the delights of Old Town Sacramento.

Best for

Beaches and national parks

Home to

Santa Cruz Beach Boardwalk, Half Moon Bay, Napa Valley Wine Country, Healdsburg, and Monterey

Experience

A hike in the Marin Headlands to see the Golden Gate Bridge against the San Francisco skyline

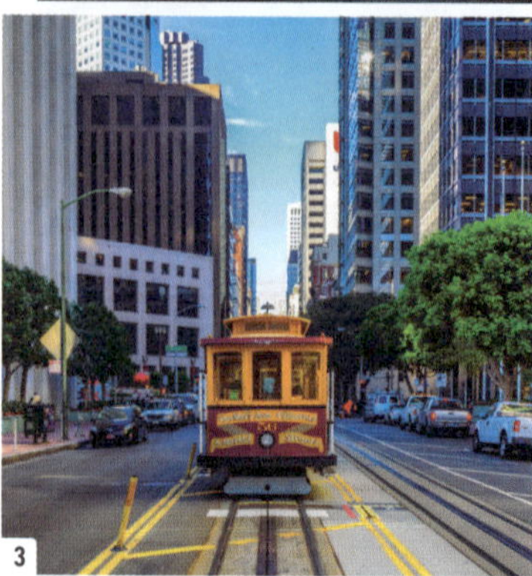

←

1 Bay Bridge and downtown skyline, lit up at dusk.

2 A solitary confinement cell in the infamous Alcatraz prison.

3 Vintage streetcar traveling through the city streets.

4 Fisherman's Wharf, one of the city's most popular destinations.

San Francisco is a treasure trove of things to see and do, and its compact size means that the city and its surrounding area can be easily explored. These itineraries will inspire you to make the most of your visit.

in San Francisco

Morning

Enjoy an all-American breakfast with a bay view at the Eagle Café *(PIER 39, Space A-201)*, before strolling through the famous pier's many stores and entertainments. Continue to Fisherman's Wharf, taking in steaming crab pots and fishers unloading their catches at Pier 45, where you can clamber aboard the historic ships at the Maritime National Historical Park. From Pier 33, ferries depart for tours of Alcatraz Island *(p94)*, and cruise under the Golden Gate Bridge *(p64)* and around the bay. If you aren't inclined to set sail, hop on the Powell-Hyde Cable Car for dizzying cityscape and ocean views.

Afternoon

In the historic Beacon Grand Hotel *(450 Powell St)*, where uniformed "Beefeaters" greet guests and regale passersby, you'll find The Post Room, an elegant all-day cocktail and afternoon tea lounge with a restaurant serving Mediterranean-Californian cuisine. It hosts live music, from classical piano to punk, in the afternoons and evenings. Afterward, walk off your meal en route to Yerba Buena Gardens *(p142)*. Here you can view outdoor art installations, and the Martin Luther King, Jr. Memorial Waterfall. Across the street is the Contemporary Jewish Museum *(p148)* and the stunning SFMOMA *(p138)*, home to one of the world's most important collections of contemporary art.

Evening

As the glittering "Bay Lights" blink on across the Bay Bridge *(p224)*, ride a vintage streetcar down Market Street to the Embarcadero *(p144)*, a palm-tree-lined, waterfront promenade. Drop into the Exploratorium *(p98)* at Pier 15, an interactive museum that is open to adults only on Thursday evenings. At the nearby cruise ship terminal, multi-storied passenger liners are lit up at night like Christmas trees against the backdrop of the glowing Golden Gate Bridge. Head to the various vendors inside the Ferry Building *(p136)* for a wonderful meal and amazing views of this sparkling nighttime display.

→

1 Sculpture garden of the de Young Museum.

2 Bowl of crab cioppino.

3 The pastel-colored Painted Ladies.

4 Seals basking at the Point Lobos State Natural Reserve.

3 DAYS

in San Francisco, Monterey, and Carmel

Day 1

Morning Breakfast at the Beach Chalet *(p204)* and stroll along Ocean Beach *(p202)* before heading off to explore the greenery of Golden Gate Park *(p206)*. On the same site, the de Young Museum *(p194)* is filled with treasures; you'll want to devote a couple of hours to browsing the exhibits here.

Afternoon Have lunch at the on-site Museum Café before making your way to PIER 39 to hop on a sightseeing cruise. Don't forget to bring your camera: out in the Bay you'll get spectacular close-up views of the Golden Gate Bridge and Alcatraz. Afterward, walk up Columbus Avenue towards Coit Tower *(p106)* to take in vibrant 1930s-era frescoes at the tower's base and dazzling views from the top.

Evening Nab a sidewalk table at Sotto Mare *(552 Green St)*, famous for its *cioppino* (seafood stew) and fresh oysters. As darkness falls, head to The Castro Theatre to watch a movie at the city's most iconic cinema house.

Day 2

Morning Breakfast at Peacock Pansy *(392 Fulton St)* before strolling to the upscale boutiques and galleries of Hayes Valley *(p166)*. After browsing, head to Patricia's Green, a small park nearby, and view one of the temporary art displays.

Afternoon Lunch and libations can be sought at the hip Absinthe Brasserie *(398 Hayes St)*, known for its French-Italian cuisine and a lively bar scene. Walk to Alamo Square *(p168)* to see the Victorian houses known as the Painted Ladies *(p168)*, then grab a cab to Mission Dolores *(p182)* in the Latin American district to tour the oldest structure in the city. A stroll through the neighborhood's side streets turns up striking murals and the Mission Cultural Center for Latino Arts *(p185)*.

Evening You'll probably need to queue up for dinner from La Taqueria *(2889 Mission St)*, but their tacos are well worth the wait. End your evening by heading down the street to Foreign Cinema, where you can relax with creative cocktails and a vintage movie.

Day 3

Morning Drive south past the surfers' city of Santa Cruz to Monterey *(p248)* for some oceanfront fun. Get here early for the small, well-curated art galleries, a walking and biking trail by the water's edge, and shopping along Cannery Row, where author John Steinbeck once roamed.

Afternoon Art lovers should head for the leafy lanes of Carmel-by-the-Sea *(p251)*, a century-old artist's colony of galleries and cottages. Don't miss the 16th-century Mission Carmel and the Point Lobos State Natural Reserve, called the "greatest meeting of land and water in the world."

Evening A favorite sunset destination is cypress-fringed Carmel Beach, where you can drink in spectacular views across the Pacific. For dinner, aim for a historic restaurant such as Mission Ranch *(26270 Dolores St)*, located in an old farmhouse owned by actor Clint Eastwood.

7 DAYS

in San Francisco and the Bay Area

Day 1

Grab a cup of coffee and a pastry at Bluestone Lane *(55 2nd St)* and ascend to the 61st-floor skydeck of the Salesforce Tower *(p149)* for jaw-dropping views. When back on the ground, wander through the downtown Financial District to Chinatown, where you can pick up lunch and do a bit of browsing. In the evening, go for a seafood dinner at Tadich Grill *(p147)* – the oldest continuously run restaurant in the state of California.

Day 2

From Pier 41, take a ferry across the Bay to Oakland *(p222)* for a waterfront breakfast on Jack London Square. Spend some time at the contemporary Oakland Museum of California, which showcases the state's art, history, and natural sciences. In the evening enjoy live music at the Greek Theatre on the Berkeley College campus *(p226)*. Afterward, head to the North Shattuck dining district for a wealth of excellent farm-to-table options.

Day 3

An early-morning drive one hour north of San Francisco is rewarded with breakfast at Model Bakery *(644 1st St)* in Napa *(p241)*, where food vendors, a brew pub, and oyster bar are all worth a lingering visit. Napa Valley Wine Country *(p238)* is the queen of California's wine regions and has over 400 wineries; call ahead to tour Castello di Amorosa, a massive, castle-like winery, or the Inglenook Winery. Dinner is French fare at Napa's Angèle *(540 Main St)*, an old boathouse on the Napa River. From here, walk through the Old Town to catch a comedy show at the Uptown Theater.

4

5

1 Views from the Salesforce Tower.

2 Paper lanterns in Chinatown.

3 Fresh oysters, served throughout the region.

4 Bodega Bay at sunset.

5 A forest path through Muir Woods.

Day 4

In Sonoma town *(p246)* grab breakfast at Sunflower Caffé *(421 1st St W)* on the historic Sonoma Plaza, then head straight to a tour of vine-covered Buena Vista, the state's oldest premium winery. Hop on the open-air tram through the vineyards at Benziger Family Winery and visit the Gloria Ferrer Caves & Vineyards *(p246)*. In the late afternoon, visit the Jack London State Historic Park *(p247)*, a nature park on the literary legend's ranch, before spending the night in a B&B on the Sonoma Coast.

Day 5

After breakfast at Willow Wood Café *(9020 Graton Rd)* in Graton, head to Bodega Bay *(p244)* for a spot of whale-watching. Warm up with a bowl of cracked Dungeness crab chowder at the tiny Spud Point Crab Company *(1910 Westshore Rd)*, then take a coastline drive along Highway 1 to the Armstrong Redwoods State Park *(p245)* to admire groves of ancient redwoods. End your day with dinner at Boon Eat + Drink *(16248 Main St)* in Santa Rosa, followed by a walk in the beautiful hotel grounds.

Day 6

Start your Marin County day trip with an organic breakfast at Café del Soul *(247 Shoreline Hwy)*. Then get an early start at Muir Woods and Beach *(p219)*, a wonderful hiking and cycling area and a haven for old-growth redwoods. Take a beach stroll or go waterfowl-watching, before heading to Sausalito's Cavallo Point Lodge *(601 Murray Cir)* – a former military base – for a comfortable dinner and cocktails.

Day 7

Houses cling to steep hillsides above the town of Sausalito on Richardson Bay *(p216)*, where kayaks, ferryboats, and sea lions share the choppy water. Breakfast at the Bayside Café *(1 Gate 6 Rd)*, then take the short ferry ride from Tiburon to Angel Island *(p217)* for dazzling Bay Area vistas and a seafood lunch. When you've had your fill of exploring the island on its excellent walking and cycling trails, take the ferry back to San Francisco for an evening of gallery viewing and good food at Fort Mason *(p76)*.

A CITY TOUR
49-MILE DRIVE

Length 49 miles (79 km) **Signs** Follow the blue signs for the "49Mile-Scenic Drive"

Linking the city's most intriguing neighborhoods, fascinating sights, and spectacular views, the 49-Mile Scenic Drive is an official route that provides a splendid overview of San Francisco. You could drive, but it is easier to take advantage of the city's excellent public transport system and bike-friendly infrastructure. Keeping to the well-marked route is simple enough – just follow the blue-and-white seagull signs. Some of these are hidden by overhanging vegetation or buildings, so you need to be alert. The trip can be done in a single day or split over several; there are plenty of places to stop to take photographs or admire the views, so it's worth taking your time.

The **Palace of Fine Arts** *Theatre (p68) stands near the wooded Presidio.*

It's worth getting out at **Golden Gate Park** *(p188) to explore some of the sights tucked away in the grounds.*

Lake Merced *is the largest inland waterbody in San Francisco. During the weekends it brims with locals and tourists enjoying activities such as hiking, running, and strolling around the lake.*

From both summits of **Twin Peaks** *(p184), the views over the city and bay are truly magnificent.*

INSIDER TIP
Know Before You Go

Avoid driving during rush hours: 7-10am and 4-7pm. Chinatown and Fisherman's Wharf are heavily pedestrianized, so take care in these areas. On weekends and holidays, a section of the Great Highway is pedestrian-only; check online in advance.

Marina Green *is an excellent vantage point from which to view the Golden Gate Bridge (p64).*

The **Maritime Museum** *(p102) has a fine collection of model ships. Real historic ships are moored nearby at Hyde Street Pier.*

Overlooking North Beach, Telegraph Hill is topped by the **Coit Tower** *(p106), which has stunning murals and a viewing terrace.*

The **Ferry Building** *(p136) is a great place to stop for lunch or dinner during your drive.*

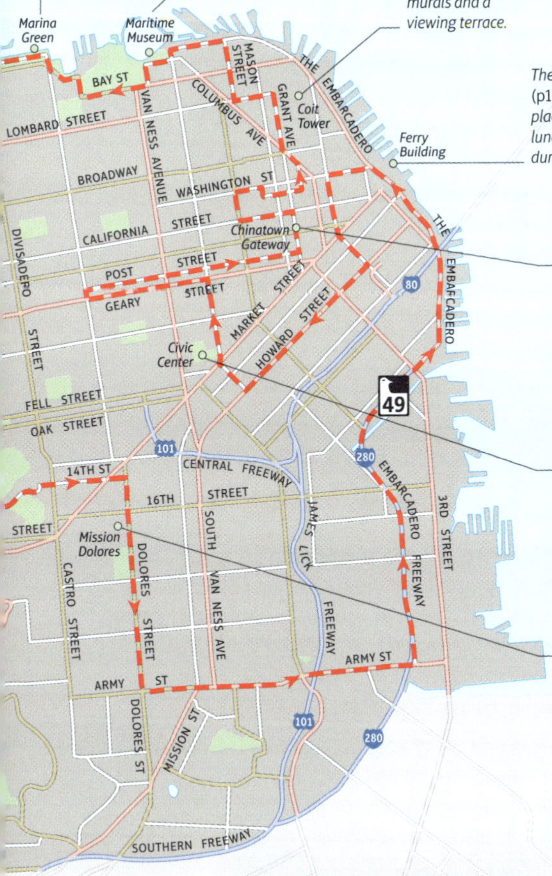

The triple-arched portal of the **Chinatown Gateway** *(p124) marks the southern entrance to San Francisco's famous Chinatown district.*

The **Civic Center** *(p158) is the stately heart of San Francisco, where imposing Beaux Arts buildings surround a central plaza.*

Mission Dolores *(p182) is one of the city's few remaining buildings from San Francisco's early Mission era (1776–1823).*

→ Stunning view of the downtown San Francisco skyline

Stroll Through Museums and Galleries

The San Francisco Museum of Modern Art (SFMOMA) on Third Street is a cultural hot spot *(p138)*. Discover modern art by the likes of Georgia O'Keeffe, Henri Matisse, and Glenn Ligon, or see one of the thought-provoking exhibitions. The Fine Arts Museums of San Francisco, meanwhile, comprise the de Young Museum *(p194)*, nestled in the leafy Golden Gate Park, and the Legion of Honor (p196), housed in a replica of a Parisian building of the same name.

→

Bracket (1989) by Joan Mitchell, an artwork on display at SFMOMA

THE BAY AREA FOR ART LOVERS

Famously creative, San Francisco and the surrounding Bay Area have plenty of art and culture to explore. From beautiful art collections to bright and expansive murals that speak to the area's communities and history, seek out the works that bring this part of California to life.

Experience Endless Street Art

San Francisco is famous for the thousands of works that adorn its walls. The Mission District neighborhood is the go-to area for mural-covered walls: its roads, including the famous Balmy Alley and Clarion Alley, are full of bright, photographable pieces. Take a stroll around and you might stumble upon San Franciscan artist Apexer's colorful, kaleidoscopic murals or fnnch's endearing, emblematic honey bears, among others.

→

A street in Mission District, home to many bright street art displays

TOP 3 PUBLIC ART PIECES

Lantern Stories
In Chinatown, this work by artist Yu-Wen Wu illustrate the history of the Chinese community in the US.

Yangge: Dance of the New Year
Paper cutting artist Yumei Hou's depiction of Chinese folk dance at Chinatown Metro station is excellent.

Silent Stream
This sculpture by Jim Campbell and Werner Klotz at the Union Square BART station mirrors the movement of the crowd.

→

Aileen Bar and Colette Crutcher's *16th Avenue Tiled Steps*; a detail *(inset)*

INSIDER TIP
Oakland Art Walks

Oakland Art Murmur's gallery trail is a great way to explore the art in the city *(oaklandartmurmur.org)*. There's an online self-guided tour map featuring around 50 venues. Informal art walks take place on Oakland First Fridays, the neighborhood's monthly street festival.

Climb Secret Staircases

Hilly San Francisco has some impressive hidden stairways that provide alternative, and sometimes more artistic, routes through town. Head to the Golden Gate Heights to scale Aileen Bar and Colette Crutcher's *16th Avenue Tiled Steps*, where the 163-steps are covered in colorful mosaic images of animals and sealife. Despite being undecorated, the Lyon Street Steps are also worth a visit - those who climb the heart-racing 288-step path are rewarded with beautiful views from the top.

Brightly colored vintage stores in Haight-Ashbury

SAN FRANCISCO FOR SHOPPING

Shopping in San Francisco is all about keeping it local: the city is sprinkled with small stores that stock everything from vinyl records to handcrafted pottery. Sustainability is key when it comes to fashion, and a thriving second-hand scene goes hand-in-hand with eco-friendly items made in the Bay Area.

Record Stores

Over the years, San Francisco has become one of the foremost destinations along the West Coast to go rifling through record store shelves. Vinyl still has a massive cachet here, and music stores carry records and cassettes catering to all tastes. Head to Rooky Ricardo's Records *(419 Haight St)* for funk and soul, Thrillhouse Records *(thrillhouserecords.com)* for Bay Area punk, and Vinyl Dreams *(vinyldreamssf.com)* for house, techno, disco, and electronica.

Listening to vinyl records at Rooky Ricardo's Records

Flea Markets and Vintage Stores

San Francisco is a treasure trove of second-hand gems. Antiques stores in Haight-Ashbury and the Castro are known for carrying all sorts of nostalgic goods, from mid-century light fixtures to decades-old used books. For unbeatable flea markets, look no further than the pop-ups that spill onto the streets on Sundays - the Alemany Flea Market *(100 Alemany Blvd)* and Inner Sunset Flea *(isflea.com)* are two of the best. Though most local vendors now accept cashless payments, it's a good idea to carry some cash as a back-up.

← Antique clock on display at the Alemany Flea Market

SHOP

Golden Gate Fortune Cookie Factory

Enjoy fortune cookies here *(p125)*.

56 Ross Alley **goldengatefortunecookies.com**

MAC

This shop offers clothing by local designers.

387 Grove St **macmodernappealingclothing.com**

Williams-Sonoma

Buy kitchen gadgets and great cookware here.

340 Post St

williams-sonoma.com

HIDDEN GEM

Bi-Rite

This family-run market *(biritemarket.com)* is loved by locals for its unique food products. There are multiple branches across town, at 18th St, Divisadero St, and Polk St, and an ice creamery at 18th St.

A showroom for Heath Ceramics, a world-class designer brand ↑

Local Makers

Small business owners in San Francisco take pride in bringing handcrafted wares to their customers, and will tell you the histories of these original items. Downtown's Financial District has long been the best place to check out high-quality, handmade products by designers and craftspeople - a local tradition that includes Levi's jeans. Now other areas of the city are making names for themselves in the word of top-class design, including the Mission District - home of Heath Ceramics *(2900 18th St)*.

Michelin-Starred Menus

In San Francisco's SoMa district, Benu (*benusf.com*) and Saison (*saisonsf.com*) are just two of the many Michelin-starred spots you can visit after a day exploring the area's fantastic art and entertainment venues. Farther afield in Oakland, chef James Syhabout's Commis (*p223*) showcases local ingredients with subtle flair, while shining brightly with three Michelin stars is The French Laundry (*p238*), Thomas Keller's seasonally focused restaurant, tucked away in the tiny Napa Valley village of Yountville.

→ An elegant torte served at Coi in the SoMa district

THE BAY AREA FOR FOODIES

From fun food trucks to some of the world's most celebrated restaurants, the city's vibrant food scene should be a key part of any visit to the Bay Area. All the ingredients are here: the heady mix of cultural influences and flavors, and an abundance of fresh, high-quality local produce.

Farmers' Markets

Pottering around markets is a favorite weekend pastime for many San Franciscans, who take pride in the Bay Area's quality produce, like the fruit and veg sold at Alemany Farmers' Market (*100 Alemany Blvd*). For local artisanal products, try the thrice-weekly Ferry Plaza Farmers' Market (*p136*), which has a beautiful harbor-side setting.

→ Fresh produce on sale at the farmers' market by the Ferry Building

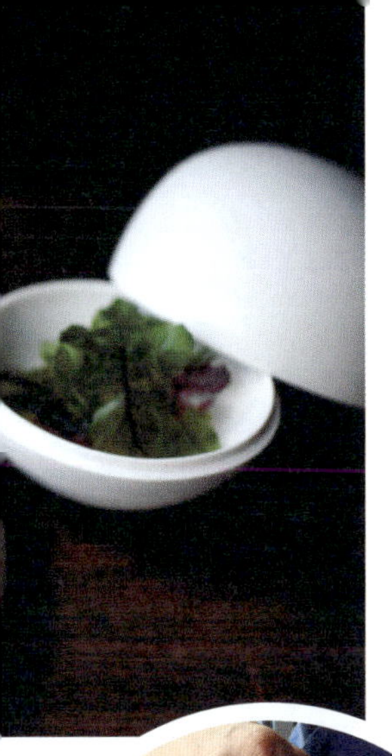

Global Grub

San Francisco is defined by its range of world cuisines. It's also the only region in California with so many three-starred Michelin restaurants. Home to the country's oldest Chinatown *(p115)*, the City by the Bay is a bastion for Asian cuisine – as evident by the fare at Empress by Boon *(838 Grant Ave)* and Delicious Dim Sum *(752 Jackson St)*. Nob Hill *(p115)* and North Beach *(p91)* are popular for their Italian restaurants and pizzerias. Try the pies from Gusto Pinsa Romana *(1000 Bush St)*, and the pasta dishes at Sotto Mare *(552 Green St)*.

← Tucking into a fully-laden, soft tortilla

TOP 3 FOOD HOTSPOTS

Haight-Ashbury
Peppered with fantastic cafés, Haight-Ashbury is perfect for grabbing a tea or coffee. It has an excellent burger scene.

Mission District
Tacos are the go-to here. Taquería El Farolito's *(2779 Mission St)* tacos are considered to be the city's best.

The Castro
Perfect for a night out, the Castro has a mix of rooftop bars and upscale restaurants. Visit the stylish and popular Frances *(3870 17th St)*.

↑ Fresh, locally sourced clams served at a San Francisco restaurant

Farm-to-Table Cuisine

Cooking with fresh, local, seasonal produce isn't just a trend in the Bay Area – it's a way of life. When the farms in question produce some of the most flavorsome and sought-after ingredients around, it's hard to think why it wouldn't end up on local tables first and foremost. Not just any table, mind you – many of the area's most beloved restaurants, from Sons & Daughters *(708 Bush St)* on Nob Hill to the venerable French Laundry *(p238)*, build their menus around ingredients sourced from local ranchers, farmers, and fishing crews.

Beautiful Beaux Arts

The Neo-Classical style of the Parisian École des Beaux Arts was favored for major buildings following the 1906 earthquake. Opulent colonnades, sculptures, and pediments are typical of this lavish style. The most perfect illustration is the Palace of Fine Arts Theatre *(p68)* in the Marina District of San Francisco.

↑ Palace of Fine Arts Theatre, built in 1915 for a world's fair

SAN FRANCISCO FOR ARCHITECTURE

San Francisco's hilly landscape means that this is one American city where its towering skyscrapers do not immediately capture the eye. Instead, the architectural highlights are woven throughout the fabric of the city streets.

Iconic Victorian

The city's most distinctive architecture is its array of Victorian houses, with their wooden frames and elaborate ornamentation. There are several different styles from this 55-year period *(p170)* and well-preserved Victorian buildings can be seen all over San Francisco, making a casual stroll along the city streets feel like walking through a colorful gallery. To see inside, head to the Haas-Lilienthal House *(p83)* and the Octagon House *(p83)*, which are open to the public.

Classic Stick style Victorian houses in the Haight-Ashbury district

Arts and Crafts

A more rustic, down-to-earth style was adopted after the turn of the 20th century, inspired by the English Arts and Crafts movement. Architects used materials such as redwood and uncut stone, and borrowed decorative Japanese motifs to achieve a natural look. In the East Bay city of Berkeley *(p226)*, the First Church of Christ, Scientist is a particularly fine example of the style, by architect Bernard Ralph Maybeck.

↑ First Church of Christ, Scientist in Berkeley, completed in 1910

The Evolving City

The Transbay redevelopment project downtown has changed the city's skyline. The project's centerpiece – the Salesforce Tower *(p149)* – is now the tallest skyscraper in San Francisco and the second tallest building in the western United States. As well as office and retail spaces in the tower, the project is gradually creating thousands of much-needed new homes in the city.

Salesforce Tower rising high over the San Francisco skyline

→ Mission San Francisco de Asís, or Mission Dolores, founded in 1776

RELIGIOUS ARCHITECTURE

The architectural diversity of the city is most apparent in its churches. Since the first simple missions, the city's churches have been built in an array of styles, from Gothic to Baroque, with numerous hybrids in between. Many prominent churches reflect the traditions and styles of the countries from which their original congregations came.

Spanish San Francisco

From 1776 to 1823, Spanish missionaries employed laborers to construct seven missions and three fortresses. Seen at places like Mission Dolores *(p182)*, the style is characterized by thick walls of rough adobe bricks, red tile roofs, and arcaded galleries surrounding courtyards. During the Gold Rush most buildings were only temporary but later fireproof brick was used; see the best survivors in the Jackson Square Historic District *(p144)*.

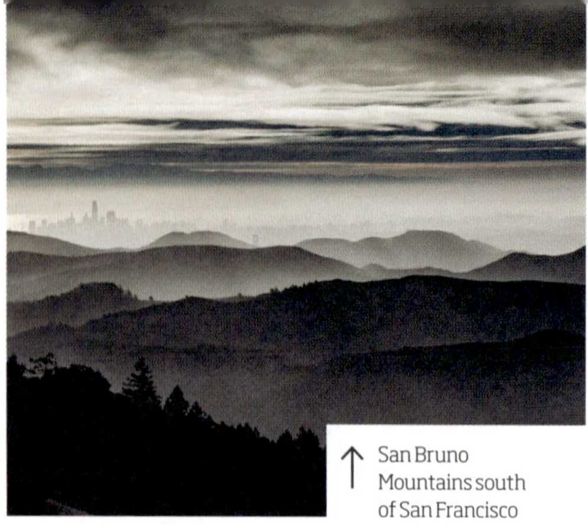

San Bruno Mountains south of San Francisco

Mountain Highs

Mountains dominate the Bay Area landscape, offering invigorating hikes and scenic views. The vistas from atop Mount Tamalpais are particularly stunning, especially at dusk. The San Bruno Mountains (south of San Francisco) and the East Bay Hills are laced with trails through the redwoods. At 3,849 ft (1,173 m), Mount Diablo is the highest mountain in the region; from its summit you can see the snow-capped Sierra Nevada.

TOP 3 RESPONSIBLE TRAVEL TIPS

Keep to the path
Stay on designated hiking trails to protect delicate ecological environments.

Respect the wildlife
Refrain from picking flowers and always observe local wildlife from a distance.

Leave no trace
Dispose of your rubbish properly. San Francisco is at risk of wildfires, so be careful when discarding cigarette butts and glass bottles.

THE BAY AREA FOR NATURAL BEAUTY

From gorgeous beaches framed by rugged cliffs to redwood forests abundant with wildlife, the Bay Area is full of breathtaking natural beauty. San Francisco's rolling hills offer stellar views of the bay, ocean, and mountains. Experience nature's delights by hiking, sailing, biking, or taking scenic drives.

Golden Sands

Beach lovers are spoilt for choice in the Bay Area, which has around 150 miles (250 km) of coastline. Large waves make for great surfing. San Francisco's Baker Beach has stellar views of the Golden Gate Bridge, while Ocean Beach has nighttime bonfires. Farther afield, Stinson Beach *(p216)* is popular for its heaps of activities. Half Moon Bay has tide pools, and Santa Cruz is revered by surfers.

Sunset at Ocean Beach on the shores of San Francisco Bay

Fabulous Forests

Surprisingly close to San Francisco you can find great swaths of ancient California coast redwood forests, with their cool, damp air and otherworldly serenity. The most famous is Muir Woods *(p219)*, which offers 6 miles (10 km) of easy trails. The glorious old-growth trees of Armstrong Redwoods State Park *(p245)* dwarf even those of Muir Woods, while Big Basin Redwoods State Park is an emerald gem in the Santa Cruz Mountains mere minutes from Silicon Valley.

→

Coast redwoods and a fallen tree *(inset)* in Big Basin Redwoods State Park

Wildlife Wonders

The Pacific waters and varied terrain of the Bay Area abound with wildlife. Migrating whales can be seen in winter from the cliffs of Point Reyes and from Santa Cruz pier, or year-round on trips to the Farallon Islands. Seals and sea lions sunbathe along the shore. Meadows and forests teem with mammals, from deer to Tule elk. Those in luck may even spot mountain lion.

→

Elephant seals on a beach, Año Nuevo State Park

Vibrant Santa Cruz Beach Boardwalk on a sunny day

THE BAY AREA FOR FAMILIES

The Bay Area is chock-full of kid-friendly activities and attractions, so you'll never be short of ways to keep the family entertained. Children of all ages will enjoy the gorgeous beaches, hands-on museums, fun educational experiences, and unique thrills like a ride on the clanging cable cars.

The Must Sees

No family vacation is complete without a visit to PIER 39 *(p100)*. Highlights include street entertainers, a carousel, and San Francisco's resident sea lions – just follow the sounds of barking and you'll find them lounging in a heap by the water. If you venture farther afield, The Walt Disney Family Museum *(p69)* puts the life and creations of Walt Disney on full display in a family-friendly setting. The museum's store offers souvenirs designed with iconic Disney characters that both the young and young-at-heart will find appealing.

The beautiful, old-fashioned carousel on PIER 39 in Fisherman's Wharf

Full-Day Fun

If you have the whole day to fill, you can't go wrong with the California Academy of Sciences *(p192)*. There's enough to keep kids fascinated for eons, including an aquarium, natural history museum, planetarium, and a domed, four-story rainforest with 40,000 live animals in three distinct ecosystems. For the ultimate day out at the seaside, head to Santa Cruz Beach Boardwalk *(p230)*, a classic seaside amusement park with rides, games, and entertainment galore, while the beach itself is the perfect place for a picnic.

← Arcade center at the Santa Cruz Beach Boardwalk

TOP 3 PLACES TO TAKE A BREAK

South Park
64 S Park St
This oval oasis has play areas, a hummingbird garden, plus climbing structures and a sandbox.

Alamo Square
While parents snap photos of the beautiful hilltop views and the Painted Ladies, kids can enjoy the playground *(p168)*.

Yerba Buena Gardens
A serene space in the heart of downtown, this garden makes a great stop to take a break between visits to the area's many museums *(p142)*.

INSIDER TIP
Reduced Prices

Nearly all of San Francisco's museums have regular "community days" when you can visit for free or at a discounted rate. Make sure to check the institutions' website for details.

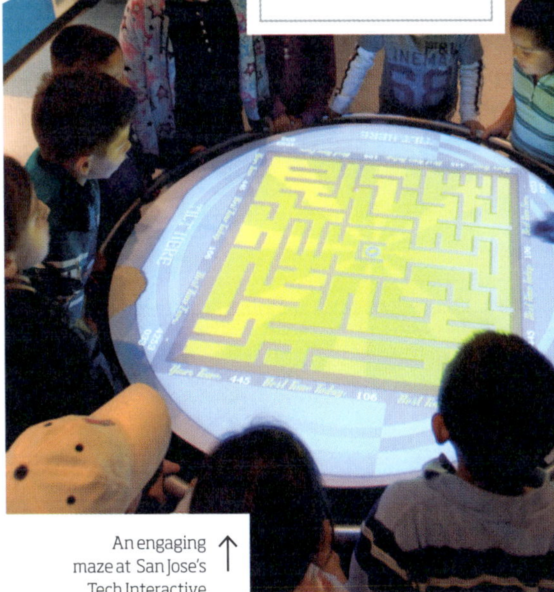

An engaging maze at San Jose's Tech Interactive ↑

Hands-On Museums

Whether your children's interests tend toward art or science, you'll find scores of fun-filled museums that may spark a lifelong interest. If you're in Marin County to walk over the Golden Gate Bridge, don't miss the Bay Area Discovery Museum *(p218)*, which has heaps of hands-on exhibits that are so fun your kids won't even realize they're learning. And if you venture out into San Jose *(p234)*, your child (or the child within) can even build a robot at The Tech Interactive.

Club Scene

Like almost everything else in San Francisco, the city's nightlife is fairly casual, friendly, and low key, and even trendy venues like August Hall *(augusthallsf.com)* may only be open a few nights a week. If you want to sample an aspect of nightlife that is typically San Franciscan, try the stand-up comedy clubs or a cozy piano bar.

A DJ plays to a crowd of dancers letting off steam in a nightclub

THE BAY AREA LIVE!

San Francisco has prided itself on being the cultural capital of the West Coast since the city first began to prosper in the 1850s. With a huge variety of entertainment options, it's one of the most exciting cities in the world, with big names in every branch of the arts performing here.

Popular Music Paradise

The Bay Area has the West Coast's best opera, ballet, and symphony orchestra, but popular music is where it really excels. Some of the city's quintessential sounds and venues are jazz at SFJazz *(sfjazz.org)*, blues at Biscuits and Blues *(biscuitsandblues.com)*, and rock at The Fillmore *(thefillmore.com)*, the birthplace of psychedelic rock in the 1960s.

Twin Peaks stage at the Outside Lands Music Festival in Golden Gate Park

Fantastic Festivals

There are so many festivals across the whole spectrum of performing arts that it's definitely worth checking a Bay Area calendar of events while planning your trip. You may find that your visit coincides with the annual Comedy Day celebrations *(comedyday.org)* in Golden Gate Park, or a literary festival dedicated to Steinbeck or Shakesepeare. Naturally, there are plenty of cool music festivals throughout the Bay Area, as well.

Did You Know?

The Beatles played their final official concert in San Francisco, at Candlestick Park in August 1966.

On Stage in San Francisco

The main Theater District *(p151)* hosts major Broadway shows on tour, but it's really the alternative scene visitors should check out. The Mission District has venues such as The Marsh *(themarsh.org)* and Project Artaud *(project artaud.org)*. In Berkeley, the Shotgun Players *(shotgun players.org)* and Berkeley Repertory Theatre *(berkeley rep.org)* present cutting-edge productions.

Gary Clark Jr. performing in San Francisco, and *(inset)* The Fox in Oakland

Geary Theater, longtime home of the American Conservatory Theater

Sail the Bay

Blustery San Francisco Bay has the perfect sailing conditions. On any sunny weekend, the waters are mottled with billowing sails. Cruising across the bay is a breathtaking sensation and offers stunning views of the City skyline and Golden Gate Bridge. The bay is one of the most challenging sailing environments in the world, due to lots of other vessels, strong currents, and the shifting winds that howl through the Golden Gate strait. Experienced sailors can charter yachts. Novices can take lessons with sailing schools and clubs, or you can choose a sailing excursion if you'd prefer to sit back and let someone else hoist the sails.

→

Sailboats navigating the choppy waters of San Francisco Bay

THE BAY AREA FOR THRILL-SEEKERS

Bay Area inhabitants are famously active for good reason. Blessed with soaring mountains, a rugged coast, and a vast bay to choose from, there's no shortage of adventures to enjoy. The hills are laced with biking and hiking trails, and wind-whipped San Francisco Bay is nirvana for kite-surfing and yachting.

Mountain bike "Mount Tam"

Marin County is considered the most ideal for mountain biking, which was born in the 1970s on Mount Tamalpais *(p219)*. The mountain summit is easily accessed via the Railroad Grade Fire Road (once the route of a scenic railroad), which begins in Mill Valley and snakes 4.5 miles (7 km) to the top, where you're rewarded with superlative views.

The beautiful Railroad Grade Fire Road on Mount Tamalpais

ESCAPE FROM ALCATRAZ TRIATHLON

As punishing as a spell in the famous prison, this grueling triathlon draws 2,000 Olympic champions, seasoned pros, and hardened amateur triathletes from around the globe each June. The main event is a 1.5-mile (2.4-km) swim from Alcatraz to San Francisco's Aquatic Park in biting-cold waters renowned for their ferocious currents. Next comes a brutal 18-mile (29-km) bike ride to Golden Gate Park and 8-mile (13-km) run to Baker Beach over varied terrain.

Motorbiking California's Coastal Highway

Few motorbike rides are as thrilling as that to Point Reyes Lighthouse *(p218)*. The undulating, sinuous, and spectacularly scenic road along the coastal promontory combines everything that's fun about two-wheel touring. You'll sweep through lush rolling meadows and wind-scoured moorland and, finally, along a cliff-hugging ribbon snaking above crashing surf.

→

Motorcyclist on the stunning Coastal Highway

Surf Mavericks

The Mavericks surf break, at Pillar Point off Half Moon Bay *(p232)*, is world-renowned for ferocious waves that can top 66 ft (20 m). Big, scary and barreling ashore at 50 mph (80 km/h), these are for true experts only. Nearby Santa Cruz *(p230)* is the capital of Bay Area surfing, with waves for every level, including Cowell's Beach for starters and Steamer Lane for savvy surfers. Wetsuits are de rigueur in the Bay.

←

Courageous surfers riding monster waves at Pillar Point

Did You Know?

The original rainbow flag was created by Gilbert Baker for the 1978 San Francisco Pride parade.

SAN FRANCISCO FOR LGBTQ+ CULTURE

Dubbed "the gay capital of the world," San Francisco has a vibrant LGBTQ+ culture, which started in the 1920s, albeit underground. Castro was the original center of the LGBTQ+ community, but today other areas of the city such as SoMa, The Mission, and Haight-Ashbury have thriving scenes too.

Community History

The city is steeped in LGBTQ+ history. The first Gay Liberation organization in the US emerged here in 1965, and with the first Pride march in 1970, the LGBTQ+ community stood proud across the city. Learn about San Francisco's LGBTQ+ history at the GLBT Historical Society Museum *(p182)*. Then head to Castro's main drag, which has rainbow "Walk of Fame" bronze plaques honoring the neighborhood's long history of queer activism. Nearby, Pink Triangle Park is home to the USA's only memorial to the thousands of LGBTQ+ community members who were persecuted in Nazi Germany in World War II.

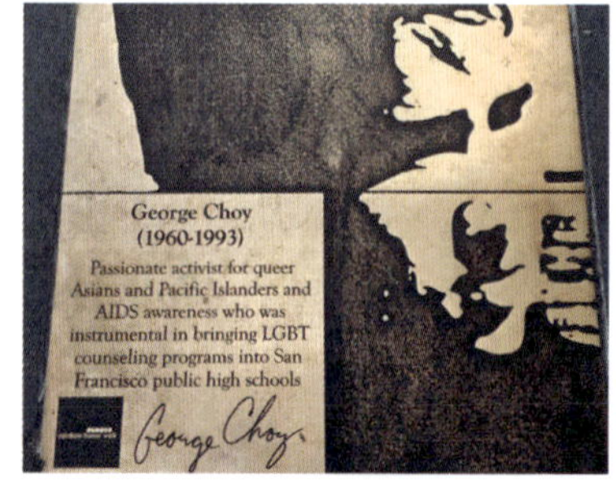

↑ Bronze plaque of activist George Choy at the Rainbow Honor Walk

Iconic Festivals

San Francisco's Pride festival at the end of June is world-famous. While the focus is on fun, the event also aims to commemorate the highs and lows of LGBTQ+ history and to educate. Held to coincide with Pride are Frameline, an LGBTQ+ film festival with screenings at venues all over the city, and Fresh Meat Festival, which hosts live music and dance performances, from opera to pop and voguing to hip hop.

← Performers in costumes at the San Francisco Pride parade

HARVEY MILK

In 1977, local business-owner Harvey Milk was elected to the San Francisco Board of Supervisors, becoming one of the first gay elected officials in the US. His tenure was cut short in 1978 when he and Mayor George Moscone were shot and killed by Dan White, a conservative supervisor. White was found guilty only of manslaughter and was given a light sentence - sparking riots. Milk was posthumously awarded the Presidential Medal of Freedom in 2009.

↑ City Hall illuminated in rainbow colors to celebrate San Francisco Pride

Stores, Cafés, and Bars of The Castro

The Castro *(p176)* is San Francisco's most famous LGBTQ+ neighborhood. The welcoming stores, clubs, and cafés are a huge draw for visitors. For an introduction to the area, join a walking tour *(sfcityguides.org)* to learn about local history and sights. Check out the Castro Street Fair during the first weekend in October when dance parties, performances, crafts stalls, and much more take place.

↑ A rainbow crosswalk heralding gay pride in the Castro district

Napa and Sonoma Valleys

Although often said in one breath, these adjacent wine regions have two distinctive personalities. Napa *(napavalley.com)* oozes glamour: Sterling Vineyards, for example, are accessible via an aerial gondola with breathtaking views. Sprawling Sonoma *(sonoma.com)* is known as the birthplace of Californian wine; many varieties can be enjoyed throughout its 19 viti-cultural areas. Get close to the action on a tractor tram tour at biodynamic Benziger *(benziger.com)*. Can't make it to the vineyards? Enjoy wine from either valley at the cozy bars Bodega *(bodegasf.com)* or Press club *(pressclubsf.com)*.

→ Verdant, rolling hills covering the landscape in the Napa Valley area

SAN FRANCISCO
RAISE A GLASS

Whether enjoying a cocktail at a retro bar, a warm cup of joe from a trendy coffee shop, a locally brewed ale from a craft brewery, or a glass of something special from a nearby winery, sociable San Francisco is always ready to toast the day.

Coffee Culture

Forget diner brew: San Franciscan institutions like Caffe Trieste *(caffetrieste.com)* champion artisan coffees. Try a Salvadoran *café con leche* – a Central American staple – at Abanico *(abanicocoffee.com)*, or sip an expertly roasted espresso at Four Barrel *(fourbarrelcoffee.com)*, a socially responsible independent outfit in the Mission District.

→ Inside Caffe Trieste, once a favorite meeting point of the Beat writers and poets

Did You Know?

San Francisco is home to Folgers, the first roast ground coffee brand available in California.

Craft Beer

San Francisco's laid-back West-Coast style and love of the artisanal and home-grown unite in the great craft beer culture found in the city. At 21st Amendment's Brewpub *(21st-amendment.com)*, try a juicy watermelon wheat or a blood orange IPA while taking part in one of the weekly trivia nights. Standard Deviant *(standarddeviantbrewing.com)* serves super-fresh brews on tap, in a former garage in the trendy Dogpatch neighborhood; come for a cold one and stay for the shuffle-board. Enterprise Brewing *(enterprisebeer.com)* in SoMa has a warm, welcoming atmosphere, with vinyl records spinning in the background.

← Thirst-quenching IPAs from 21st Amendment Brewery

DRINK

Trick Dog

Enjoy imaginative cocktails and small plates in a converted Mission District warehouse.

N8 · 3010 20th St · trickdogbar.com

Palm House

The signature frozen slushy with rum and lime is a must-try at this local favorite.

K3 · 2032 Union St · Mon · palmhousesf.com

Historic Watering Holes

The city is home to many historic drinking spots. Head to Buena Vista for its Irish coffee, concocted in 1952 to imitate the original, as served at Ireland's Shannon Airport, *(the buenavista.com)*. The Fairmont Hotel's Tonga Room *(fairmont-san-francisco.com)* shakes up San Francisco's 1930s tiki bar tradition with a dramatic flair - drinks are served among sporadic (and artificial) indoor hurricanes. The Old Ship *(oldship saloonsf.com)*, open since 1851, is the place to go for a Two Sheets - a pint and a shot.

↑ Irish coffee drinks being prepared at the beloved Buena Vista

A YEAR IN SAN FRANCISCO AND THE BAY AREA

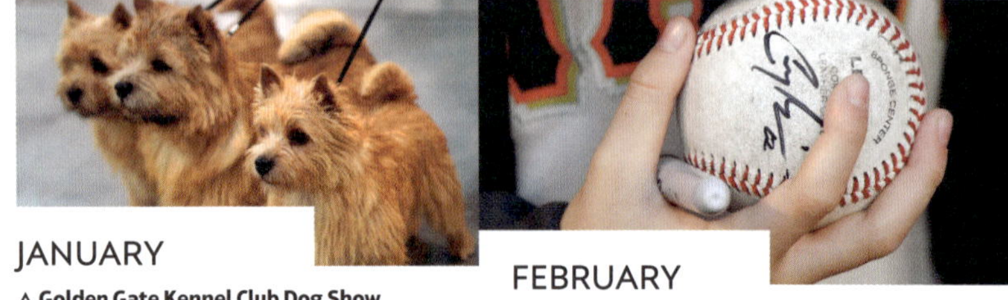

JANUARY

△ **Golden Gate Kennel Club Dog Show** *(mid-Jan).* 2,000+ dogs and 175+ breeds vie for "Best in Show" at the Cow Palace.

SF Art Week *(Jan).* The city's many art museums and galleries host special shows and happenings during this lively event.

FEBRUARY

Chinese New Year Celebration *(late Jan or early–mid-Feb).* A parade in Chinatown.

△ **Giants Winter Fanfest** *(Feb/Mar).* At Oracle Park, team members and alumni thrill fans with autographs and selfies.

MAY

Cinco de Mayo *(May 5).* A big block party on Valencia Street in the Mission District, with plenty of music, food, and dance.

△ **Bay to Breakers** *(late May).* Tens of thousands of costumed walkers and serious runners join in one of the world's largest foot races, from Embarcadero to Ocean Beach.

JUNE

San Francisco Jazz Festival *(mid-Jun).* For three decades, more than 30 live shows with famous headliners at the SFJazz Center.

△ **San Francisco Pride** *(mid–late Jun).* The biggest event in the LGBTQ+ calendar. A colorful celebration and parade on Market Street with huge crowds of spectators.

SEPTEMBER

Opera in the Park *(early Sep).* World-famous opera stars perform in free concerts in Golden Gate Park.

△ **Folsom Street Fair** *(late Sep).* Music, comedy, crafts, drink, and dancing at the largest leather, alternative, and fetish street fair in the world.

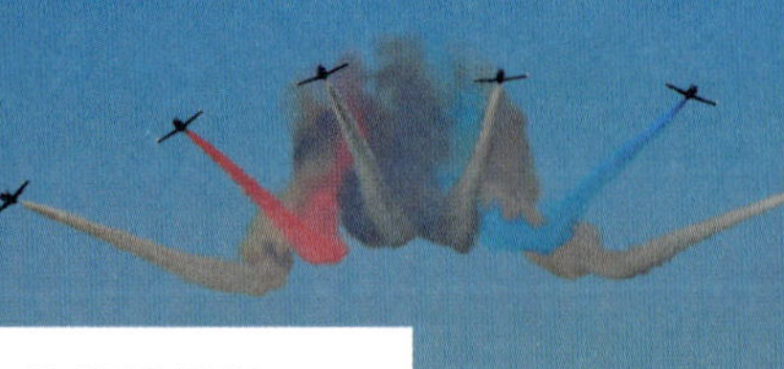

OCTOBER

△ **Fleet Week** *(early Oct).* Honoring the US Navy and Marines, a breathtaking Blue Angels air show and ship tours on the Bay.

Castro Street Fair *(first Sun).* Arts, crafts, music, and dancing at this ever-popular, LGBTQ+ street festival.

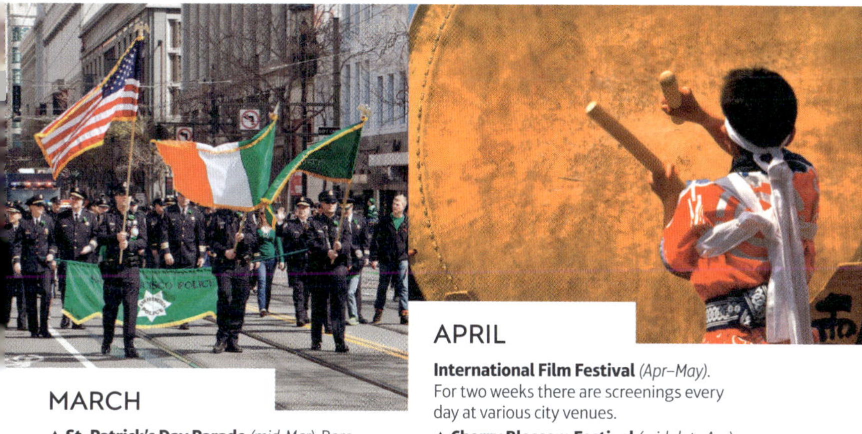

MARCH

▵ **St. Patrick's Day Parade** *(mid-Mar).* Bars filled with green-clad patrons watch one of America's oldest parades down Market Street.

San Francisco International Ocean Film Festival *(mid-Mar).* Dozens of ocean-themed films are shown at Fort Mason.

APRIL

International Film Festival *(Apr–May).* For two weeks there are screenings every day at various city venues.

▵ **Cherry Blossom Festival** *(mid–late Apr).* Japantown hosts a celebration of Japanese arts, crafts, food, and performers, and a colorful parade.

JULY

▵ **Fourth of July** *(Jul 4).* Dazzling fireworks, local bands, food, arts, and crafts on PIER 39. The main fireworks extravaganza can be seen along the entire waterfront.

San Francisco Playwrights Festival *(late Jul).* Readings, workshops, lectures, and performances of new works at the bay-side Fort Mason center.

AUGUST

Nihonmachi Street Fair *(early Aug).* A celebration of the Asian and Pacific communities held in Japantown.

▵ **Stern Grove Festival** *(mid-Aug).* The Golden Gate Park comes alive every summer with free music concerts each Sunday.

NOVEMBER

▵ **Dia de los Muertos** *(Nov 2).* A Mexican celebration marked by a nighttime procession through the Mission District, and the Festival of Altars, honoring deceased family members.

Illuminate SF *(late Nov).* Eco-friendly light-art installations throughout the city.

DECEMBER

▵ **Union Square Holiday Windows** *(Nov–Dec).* Glittering, animated store windows around Union Square.

The Nutcracker *(mid–late Dec).* Each year, the San Francisco Ballet presents Tchaikovsky's beloved classic at the War Memorial Opera House.

A BRIEF HISTORY

Today famous as a metropolis and a bastion of social inclusivity, San Francisco has a complex history. It was inhabited by Indigenous peoples for thousands of years before the 1776 Spanish arrival. On their heels came settlers and gold seekers, giving the area its enduring boomtown spirit.

Early Settlers

The first inhabitants of the area now known as San Francisco were the Ohlone people, who are believed to have arrived in the region in around 3000 BCE. Organized into over 50 societal tribes, they thrived in the Bay Area for centuries, thanks to the fertile lands and abundant fishing opportunities on the coast.

European Colonization

Although European explorers sailed along the California coast in the 16th century, it was not until 1776 that the Bay Area was colonized and the city founded. A group of Spanish settlers

1 A depiction of San Francisco in the mid-19th century.

2 The Spanish Mission San Francisco de Asís a la Laguna de los Dolores.

3 Gold Rush miners gambling in a city saloon.

4 California Street, rebuilt following damage in the 1906 earthquake.

Timeline of events

1769

Spanish explorer Gaspar de Portola leads the first European expedition into San Francisco Bay.

3000 BCE

Indigenous tribes set up fishing communities along the San Francisco Bay.

1847

Formerly called "Yerba Buena," San Francisco is renamed after the Mission San Francisco de Asís a la Laguna de los Dolores.

1848

Carpenter James Wilson Marshall discovers gold near Coma, California, starting the Gold Rush.

1850

San Francisco is adopted as part of the State of California and John W. Geary becomes the city's first mayor.

2

3

4

established missions and military forts, transforming the landscape with the introduction of agriculture and livestock. Their arrival had a devastating impact on the Ohlone people, and communities shrunk drastically as a result of practices such as enslavement and the introduction of diseases like smallpox, to which there was little immunity.

A Growing City

Having temporarily become part of Mexico following a break away from Spain in 1821, the city (then called Yerba Buena) was taken over by the US in 1846 and renamed San Francisco a year later. Gold was discovered in the foothills of the nearby Sierras the following year, which led to a stampede of prospectors descending on the city during the famous Gold Rush from 1848 to 1855 and the expansion of the city. Although a massive earthquake and fire in 1906 destroyed much of the prosperous Victorian-era city, the ambitious residents rebuilt San Francisco; invented cable cars to conquer the steep hills; hosted the Panama-Pacific International Exposition; and constructed bridges to connect the growing towns of the bay.

AMERICAN TAKEOVER

Impending war with Mexico in the 1840s inspired US leaders to arouse the interest of Bay Area settlers in joining the Union. In 1846, a party of Yankees in Sonoma declared California's independence from Mexico, christening it the Bear Flag Republic. Shortly after, California was claimed as a US territory. It officially became a state in 1850.

1853

The California Academy of Sciences is established and becomes a fixture of global innovation.

1870

Golden Gate Park is created and becomes one of the largest urban parks in the country.

1877

Anti-Chinese sentiment leads to civil unrest in Chinatown, with violent riots and vandalism impacting the neighborhood.

1906

A strong 7.9 magnitude earthquake strikes the city, destroying an estimated 80 per cent of San Francisco.

1

Early 20th Century and World War II

Neither World War I, Prohibition, nor the Great Depression could dampen the city's energy in the early 20th century, and the 1920s saw the creation of major arts venues and civic buildings. In the 1930s, two major bridges connected the city to the growing towns around the bay. The San Francisco-Oakland Bay Bridge opened in 1936 and the following year the Golden Gate Bridge was unveiled. It had the longest bridge-width in the world at the time and spanned the strait between the Pacific Ocean and the Bay of San Francisco. World War II brought industrial investment in the form of shipyards and military bases, as San Francisco became a major port for the ongoing war in the Pacific.

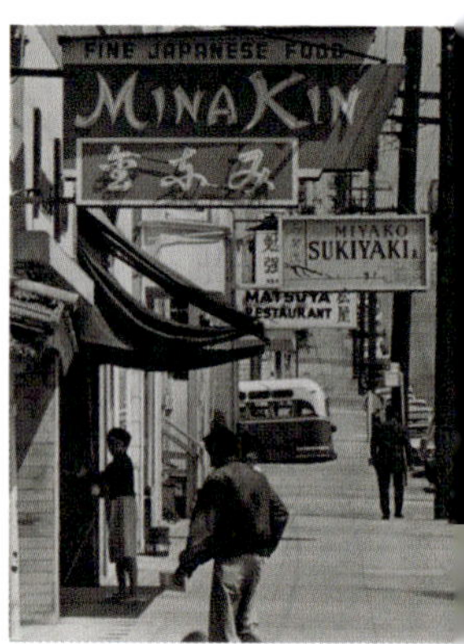

↑ Street view of the Oakland Bay Bridge today from a Spear St intersection.

A Multicultural Metropolis

A rise in anti-Japanese sentiment following the attack on Pearl Harbor had a big impact on San Francisco. In February 1942, President Roosevelt authorized the relocation of those of Japanese descent; residents of the city's Japantown were taken to internment camps as a result. Japantown was later revived in the 1960s and, today, it remains the largest and oldest of its

Timeline of events

1924

The Immigration Act of 1924 bans immigration from Asia and limits immigration from eastern and southern Europe.

1936

The Golden Gate Bridge opens, connecting San Francisco with Marin County to the north.

1942

Residents of Japanese descent are forcibly relocated to internment camps.

1945

The United Nations is founded at the San Francisco Conference.

kind in the US. Nearby to Japantown was Fillmore, then one of the most integrated communities on the West Coast. It was home to a large African American population, as well as people of Japanese, Filipino, Russian, and Mexican descent. In the 1940s and '50s, the jazz scene flourished here; Billie Holiday performed at the New Orleans Swing Club, while Duke Ellington and Miles Davis among others played at Bop City. From the 1960s, redevelopment of the area meant that the "Harlem of the West" was effectively erased, taking the jazz scene with it.

1 Making the cables for the Golden Gate Bridge. ↑

2 A ship at Hunters Point Naval Shipyard in 1947.

3 A gathering during the famous Summer of Love.

4 Activists at the 1969 occupation of Alcatraz.

Flower Power and Civil Rights

Postwar, the Beat Generation kicked off an era of experimental art, recreational drugs, and sexual freedom that peaked with the 1967 Summer of Love. This enabled progressive ideas to flourish in the city, with protests against wars, the foundation of the Black Panthers in Oakland, and the occupation of Alcatraz by Indians of All Tribes contributing to a growing call for greater civil rights. San Francisco became a key center for gay rights activism, with Castro resident Harvey Milk *(p47)* becoming the first openly gay elected official in California in 1977.

Did You Know?

In 1961, city resident José Julio Sarria became the nation's first openly gay candidate for public office.

1955

Allen Ginsberg's reading of "Howl" at the Six Gallery places the Beat poets and writers on the literary map.

1967

During the Summer of Love, 100,000 people flock to San Francisco to celebrate peace and free love.

1969

Indians of All Tribes occupy Alcatraz to protest for the return of lands taken from Indigenous communities.

1978

Harvey Milk, the first openly gay elected official, and Mayor George Moscone are assassinated.

1

Urban Regeneration and Modern Parity

The 1970s ushered in yet another era of major development that began with the 48-story Transamerica Pyramid and paved the way for further gentrification of the downtown area. The 1989 Loma Prieta earthquake occurred against this backdrop of continuing urban renewal, destorying the Victorian center of Santa Cruz and part of the Bay Bridge. The 1980s and '90s saw the height of the AIDS crisis in San Francisco, where the highest number of cases in the US was recorded in 1992. The city continued its progressive history during this period and, in the same year, the city's former mayor Dianne Feinstein was one of two female Senators elected to the US Congress by the state. As of 2019, boards of corporations based in California were also required to have at least one woman at the table.

↑ The Transamerica Pyramid rising above Columbus Avenue

The Rise of the Dot-Com, the Tech Boom, and Gentrification

The dot-com boom at the turn of the millennium cemented San Francisco's reputation as an international center of innovation and technology, although later downsizing of businesses as

Timeline of events

1980s

The AIDS epidemic reaches overwhelming proportions in the city, taking the lives of many.

1989

The Loma Pieta earthquake hits during a World Series game, killing dozens in Oakland, the Bay Area, and Santa Cruz.

2003

The Asian Art Museum moves into the former Main Library building in the Civic Center, becoming one of the most important centers of Asian culture outside of Asia.

well as rising homelessness impacted the downtown area. Ongoing gentrification, meanwhile, continues to displace residents and compromise the identities of neighborhoods like the once predominantly Latino Mission District.

San Francisco Today

While the redevelopment of historic areas remains a contentious talking point and the housing crisis continues to be a long-standing problem in the city, San Francisco today is pulled in two directions, trying both to conserve its historic past while also building the society of the future. In the face of these challenges, San Franciscans are committed to preserving their identity as a multicultural, inclusive, and diverse society. The city's well-documented heritage of social and intellectual countercultures and a history of activism as well as social engagement remain powerful forces. Each district of the city continues to retain a unique character, while community-led initiatives work to make an impact on their locals. While the city grapples with questions about the future, it remains a vibrant, progressive place to live and visit.

1 The impact of the 1989 Loma Pieta earthquake. ↑

2 Dianne Feinstein, the first female Mayor of San Francisco addresses the Democratic National Convention in July 1992.

3 Del Martin and Phyllis Lyon after their wedding in June 2008.

4 The modern skyline of San Francisco.

2008

Del Martin, 87, and Phyllis Lyon, 84, together for over 50 years, are the first gay couple to legally wed in the city.

2010

San Francisco Giants win their first World Series title since moving out of New York City in 1958.

2016

The greatly expanded San Francisco Museum of Modern Art reopens, covering nearly 45,000 sq ft (4,200 sq m).

2020

History-making wildfires ravage much of the Bay Area, turning the sky above the city orange.

EXPERIENCE

Golden Gate Bridge towering above the Bay

The central rotunda at the Palace of Fine Arts Theatre

PRESIDIO AND RICHMOND

Despite being neighbors, the Presidio area and the Richmond district have very different histories. The Presidio, a large park, was home to an 18th-century Spanish fort, which fell under Mexican rule when the nation became independent from Spain in 1821. It was taken over again by the US military during the Mexican–American War (1846–48), and continued to play a role in American military endeavors in the Pacific until 1994. Since then, it has been developed by the National Park Service and is now a mix of parkland, with 24 miles (39 km) of trails, homes, museums, and private businesses.

The Richmond district, meanwhile, has been a green, tranquil, and sophisticated neighborhood since the mid-19th century, with much development taking place in the aftermath of the 1906 earthquake. It has long had a highly multicultural population of Irish, Russian, and particularly Chinese Americans; its busy Clement Street is also sometimes referred to as the city's second Chinatown.

PRESIDIO AND RICHMOND
Must See
1 Golden Gate Bridge
Experience More
2 Fort Point and Crissy Field
3 Palace of Fine Arts Theatre
4 Presidio Officers' Club
5 Baker Beach
6 Holy Virgin Cathedral
7 The Walt Disney Family Museum
8 Clement Street
9 Presidio
10 Temple Emanu-El
11 Lyon Street Steps
12 Presidio Tunnel Tops
13 Letterman Digital Arts Center
Golden Gate Bridge
Fort Point
Golden Gate Bridge Welcome Center
Pacific Ocean
Baker Beach
PRESIDIO
James D Phelan Beach State Park
Mountain Lake
Mountain Lake Park
RICHMOND
Clement Street
Holy Virgin Cathedral
GOLDEN GATE PARK AND SUNSET
p188

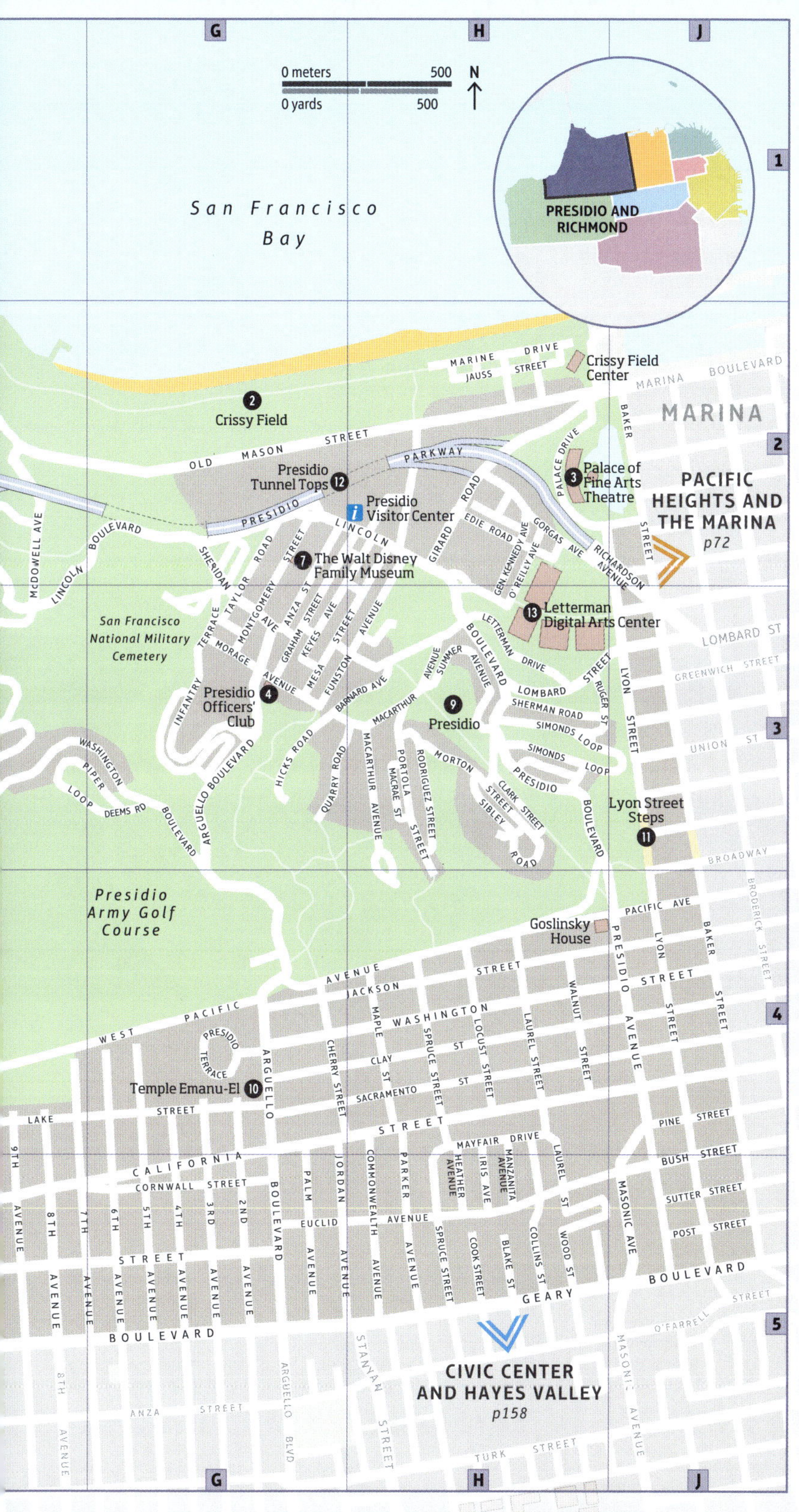
San Francisco Bay
PRESIDIO AND RICHMOND
MARINA
PACIFIC HEIGHTS AND THE MARINA
p72
CIVIC CENTER AND HAYES VALLEY
p158
Crissy Field
Crissy Field Center
Palace of Fine Arts Theatre
Presidio Tunnel Tops
Presidio Visitor Center
The Walt Disney Family Museum
Letterman Digital Arts Center
San Francisco National Military Cemetery
Presidio Officers' Club
Presidio
Lyon Street Steps
Presidio Army Golf Course
Goslinsky House
Temple Emanu-El
0 meters 500
0 yards 500

1

GOLDEN GATE BRIDGE

E1 2, 28, 76 Hours vary, check website goldengate.org

This famous landmark is an ever-present symbol of both the West Coast and the city it calls home. Its immense scale and impressive construction are breathtaking, whether it's the first or hundredth time you see it. Journey across to experience the bridge first-hand, or get a fresh perspective on it from the shore or one of the nearby viewpoints.

Named for the entrance to the Strait of San Francisco Bay called "Golden Gate" by John Fremont in 1846, the bridge that most people said could never be built opened in 1937, connecting San Francisco with Marin County *(p216)*.

On May 27, 1937, it was opened for pedestrians only, and an estimated 200,000 people were the first to walk across. The roadway opened the next day, when an official convoy of Cadillacs and Packards became the first vehicles to cross the bridge. Despite being built during the Great Depression, it was completed on time and below budget under chief engineer, Joseph Strauss. It was both the tallest and the longest suspension bridge in the world when it was built, a title it held for nearly 30 years.

→ The first pedestrians on the Golden Gate Bridge, May 27, 1937

Timeline of events

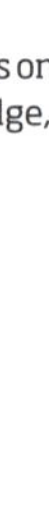

Aug 11, 1930

▲ After decades of debate and deliberation a construction permit is finally issued for a suspension bridge over the Golden Gate strait.

Jan 5, 1933

Construction officially begins.

Feb 26, 1933

▲ The official ground-breaking ceremony takes places - a festive event with over 100,000 attendees eager to celebrate the long-awaited bridge project.

Jun 1934

▲ The north tower (near the Marin County end of the Bridge) is finished, although some records claim it was completed in November.

The Golden Gate Bridge against the San Francisco skyline

Jun 1935

The south tower (closest to San Francisco) is completed.

Jun 1936

▲ Work begins on the roadway that will connect San Francisco and Marin County.

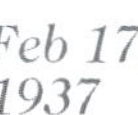

Feb 17, 1937

10 workers are killed when a safety net fails.

Apr 27, 1937

▼ With a ceremonious insertion of a final gold rivet, work on the bridge is completed.

May 27, 1937

▲ Opening day. Every siren and church bell in San Francisco and Marin sounds in unison as part of a huge celebration. The following day, President Roosevelt holds a dedication ceremony via telegraph.

The Bridge Today

The bridge remains a world-famous landmark and symbol of 20th-century engineering. The two great 7,650-ft (2,332-m) main cables are more than 3 ft (1 m) thick, and contain 80,000 miles (128,744 km) of steel wire – enough to encircle the Earth at the equator three times. It was designed to withstand 100 mph (160 km/h) winds, while each pier has to resist a tidal flow of more than 60 mph (97 km/h) as well as supporting a 22,000-ton steel tower.

Today, the bright red structure draws visitors and locals alike. San Franciscans use it regularly: the Golden Gate has six lanes for vehicles, as well as pedestrian and bicycle paths spanning its length. Cycling across is a unique experience – check online for top tips and rules of the road *(goldengate.org/bridge/visiting-the-bridge/bikes-pedestrians)*.

THE BRIDGE IN FIGURES

Crossing the Bridge
Every year, approximately 41 million vehicles (about 112,000 a day) cross the Bay via the expansive bridge - but only southbound drivers heading into the city have to pay a toll.

The Concrete
The volume of concrete poured into the piers and anchorages during the bridge's construction would be enough to lay a 5-ft- (1.5-m-) wide sidewalk from New York to San Francisco.

On the Silver Screen
The iconic bridge has featured in over 40 movies since its opening; in *X-Men: The Last Stand* (2006), it's ripped up and moved by a mutant.

↑ Looking through the towers of the Golden Gate Bridge

Photographers setting up to capture the Golden Gate Bridge from Baker Beach ↑

TOP 3 VIEWS OF THE BRIDGE

Baker Beach
The city's biggest and most popular beach isn't ideal for swimming, but it makes up for this with stunning views *(p68)*.

Fort Point
The northernmost point of San Francisco offers angles that really highlight the incredible scale of the bridge *(p68)*.

Vista Point
Head to this popular spot on Marin County side to get a photo of the Golden Gate Bridge with a San Francisco backdrop *(p218)*.

EXPERIENCE MORE

Fort Point and Crissy Field

E1 & G2 Marine Dr 561-4959 Fort Point: 10am-5pm Thu-Mon; Crissy Field: open daily

Completed by the US Army in 1861, Fort Point was built partly to protect San Francisco Bay from any attack, and partly to defend ships carrying gold from California mines. It is the most prominent of the many fortifications constructed on the coast, and is a classic example of a pre-Civil War brick fortress. The building soon became obsolete, as its 10-ft- (3-m-) thick brick walls could not stand up to powerful modern weaponry. It was closed in 1900, never having come under attack.

The brickwork vaulting is unusual for San Francisco, where the ready availability of good timber encouraged wood-frame constructions. This may have saved the fort from collapse in the 1906 earthquake. It was nearly demolished in the 1930s to make way for the Golden Gate Bridge, but it survived and is now a good place from which to view the bridge. National Park Service rangers in Civil War costume conduct guided tours. A tidal marsh once covered the area called Crissy Field. After two centuries of military use, the Field was transformed into a waterfront park for recreation and education. Crissy Field offers a rich array of programs, including many geared toward kids, from wildlife treks to kite-flying.

Did You Know?

Crissy Field was named after Major Dana H. Crissy, the base commander of Mather Air Force Base.

Palace of Fine Arts Theatre

H2 3301 Lyon St, Marina District 22, 28, 29, 30, 41, 43, 45 For events only palaceoffinearts.com

One of San Francisco's most prominent pieces of architecture, the Palace of Fine Arts Theatre is the sole survivor of the many grandiose monuments built as part of the 1915 Panama-Pacific International Exposition, a world fair celebrating San Francisco's recovery after the 1906 earthquake. The building has been restored and is now a space for theater, music, and dance.

Presidio Officers' Club

G3 50 Moraga Ave 29, 43 11am-4pm Fri-Sun presidio.gov

The Officers' Club overlooks the parade grounds of the Presidio and the 19th-century barracks. Built in the Spanish Mission style *(p36)* in the 1930s, it incorporates the adobe (sun-dried brick) remains of the original 18th-century Spanish fort and hosts events and exhibits on California history.

Baker Beach

D3 Dawn-dusk daily

Baker Beach is the largest and most popular stretch of sand in the city and is often

The grandiose Palace of Fine Arts Theatre, an events and performance space ↑

crowded with sunbathers. The chilly water and strong currents make it a dangerous spot to swim, but it is a fine place to go for a walk. Fishing is also good here. There are forests of pine and cypress on the bluffs above the beach, where visitors can explore Battery Chamberlin, a gun emplacement from 1904. On the first weekend of each month rangers show the "disappearing gun," a heavy rifle that can be lowered behind a thick wall to protect it from enemy fire and then raised again to be fired.

Mickey Mouse memorabilia and exhibits at The Walt Disney Family Museum

Holy Virgin Cathedral

D5 6210 Geary Blvd 29, 38, 38L 7:30am-7:30pm daily sfsobor.com

Shining, gold, onion-shaped domes crown the Russian Orthodox Holy Virgin Cathedral of the Russian Church in Exile, a startling landmark in the suburban Richmond District. It was designed by Oleg N. Ivanitsky and built in the early 1960s. In contrast to those of many other Christian denominations, the services here are conducted with the congregation standing, so there are no pews or seats.

The cathedral and the many Russian-owned businesses nearby, such as the lively, long-established Russian Renaissance restaurant, are situated at the heart of San Francisco's extensive Russian community. This has flourished since the 1820s, but expanded greatly when more immigrants arrived after the Russian Revolution of 1917, and especially in the late 1950s and late 1980s.

The Walt Disney Family Museum

G2 104 Montgomery St 28, 43 10am-5:30pm Thu-Sun waltdisney.org

Opened in 2009, this superb museum documents the life and amazing career of Walt Disney (1901–66). A must for Disney fans, the museum has ten interactive galleries with film clips, storyboards, photographs, movies, and original artwork, such as early drawings of Mickey Mouse.

Did You Know?

Presidio is the Spanish word for a fortified military base, built to protect against pirates and other enemies.

Clement Street

F5 2, 29, 44

This is the bustling main thoroughfare of the otherwise rather quiet Richmond District. Bookstores and small boutiques flourish here, and the inhabitants of the neighborhood meet together in a lively mix of bars, fast-food cafés, and restaurants. Most of these are patronized more by locals than by tourists. Clement Street is surrounded by a district known as New Chinatown, home to more than one-third of the Chinese population of San Francisco. As a result, some of the city's best Chinese restaurants can be found here, and the emphasis in general is on East Asian cuisine. However, the area is known for the diversity of its restaurants, and Peruvian, Russian, and French establishments, among many others, also flourish here. The street stretches from Arguello Boulevard to the north–south cross-streets which are known as "The Avenues."

Presidio

H3 210 Lincoln Blvd, on the Main Post; open 10am–5pm daily; presidio.gov

The Presidio is a national park and former military fort. The site has a long military history. It has played a key role in San Francisco's growth, and has been occupied longer than any other part of the city. Remnants of its military past, including barracks, can be seen everywhere. There are 24 miles (39 km) of hiking trails, cycle paths, and beaches. A free shuttle, the PresidiGo bus, operates within the park, stopping at over 40 destinations. Golden Gate Bridge crosses the bay from the northwest corner of the Presidio. The visitor center is a good place to get your bearings and find out what events are on; there are regular ranger walks, live music, and family activities.

→ The steeply descending Lyon Street Steps, with their beautiful views over the bay

Temple Emanu-El

G4 Lake St & Arguello Blvd 1, 2, 33, 38 By appointment emanuelsf.org

After World War I hundreds of Jews from Russia and Eastern Europe moved into the Richmond District and built religious centers, many of which are still major landmarks. Among these is the Temple Emanu-El, its dome inspired by that of the 6th-century Santa Sophia in Istanbul. The temple is a majestic piece of architecture. It was built in 1925 for the city's longest-established Jewish congregation (which was founded in 1850). The architect was Arthur Brown, who also designed San Francisco's City Hall *(p166)*. With its red-tiled dome, Emanu-El is a Californian architectural hybrid, combining the local Mission style *(p37)* with Byzantine ornament and Romanesque arcades. Its interior, which holds nearly 2,000 worshippers,

Former military housing in the Presidio, with the Golden Gate Bridge in the background ↑

is especially fine when bright sunlight shines through the earth-toned stained glass.

Lyon Street Steps

J3 Lyon St & Broadway 3, 41, 43, 45

A real gem hiding in plain sight, the Lyon Street Steps consist of 332 steps and offer jaw-dropping views of the city and the bay for those who brave the climb. Given their location within the Richmond neighborhood, they can easily be worked into walks extending from the Presidio to Pacific Heights, or from the Panhandle to the Marina. As you climb (or even better, descend) the steep steps, you'll see the Presidio forests to the west and Billionaires Row to the east. Because of the area's beauty, the homes in this area tend to be owned by the seriously wealthy. Residents include United State Senator Dianne Feinstein, oil heir Gordon Getty, and Oracle founder Larry Ellison.

Presidio Tunnel Tops

G2 210 Lincoln Blvd 30, 43 9:30am-6pm daily presidio.gov/explore/attractions/presidio-tunnel-tops

Opened in 2022, this ingenious public park, designed by James Corner Field Operations, was built over the Presidio Parkway highway tunnels. It reclaims an unused swathe of urban space, creating a park-within-a-park. The tunnels offer magnificent views of the Golden Gate Bridge and have added a new dimension to the corner of San Francisco between the Pacific and San Francisco Bay.

The park connects two of the Presidio's main areas, Main Post and Crissy Field, and features pathways, benches, children's play areas, meadow planting and lawns. Locals come here for exercise, picnics, and to buy light bites from the park's varied food trucks. The selection of vendors changes daily, with regular offerings including coffee and donuts, Mexican birria tacos and bacon Cuban sandwiches.

Letterman Digital Arts Center

H3 Chestnut St & Lyon St 28, 43 7am-7pm Mon-Fri presidio.gov/places/letterman-digital-arts-center

A pilgrimage spot for *Star Wars* fans, the Letterman Digital Arts Center was founded by filmmaker George Lucas and the Presidio Trust in 2005 to house Industrial Light and Magic, Lucasfilm Ltd, and other companies. The sprawling campus includes landscaped grounds, a natural lagoon, and photo-worthy views of the Golden Gate Bridge and the Palace of Fine Arts Theatre. Aside from the beautiful views, the other draw is the life-size statue of Yoda, the wise *Star Wars* character. Take a peek in the lobby to see more life-size figures and other movie memorabilia.

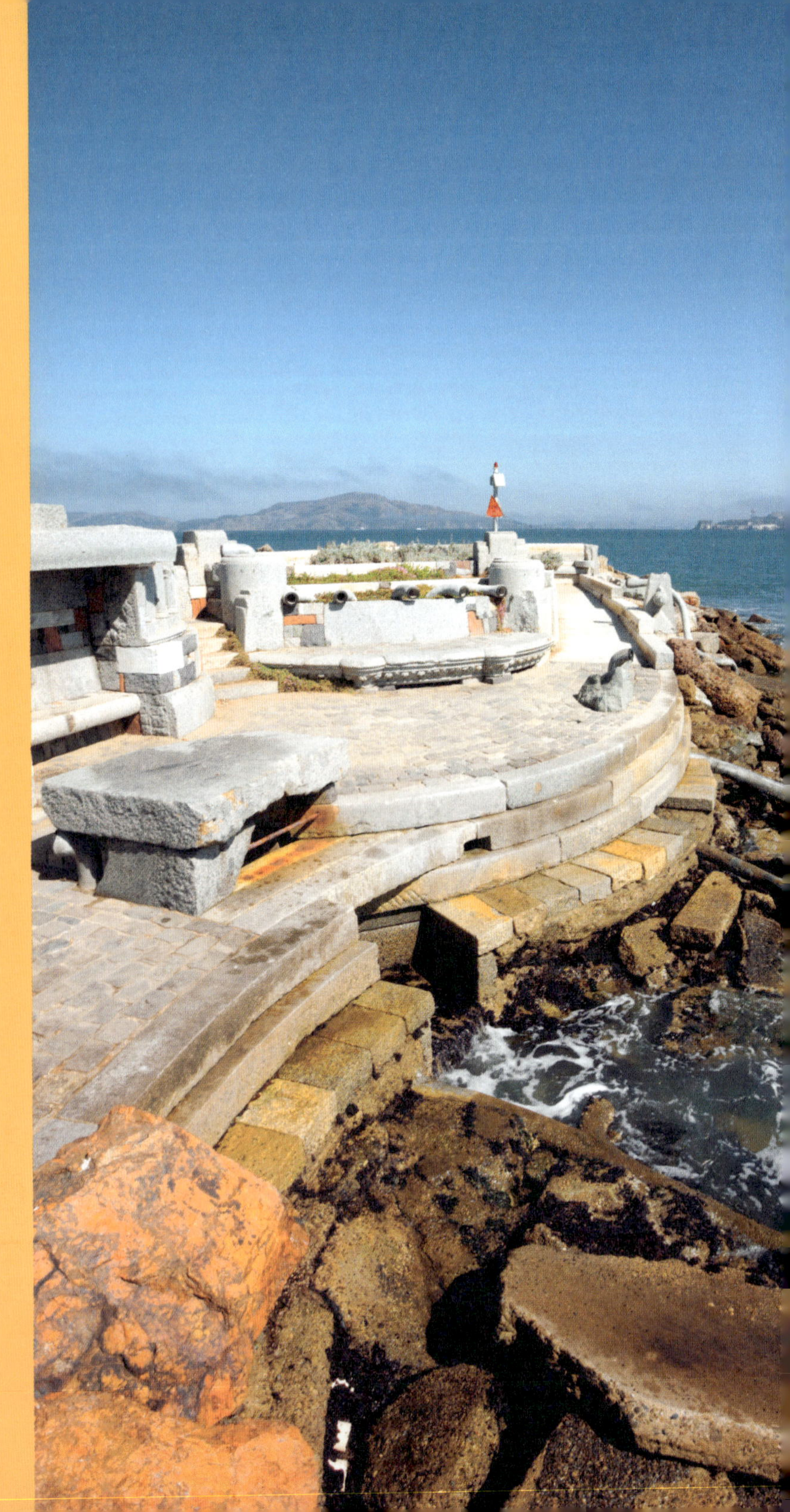

The Wave Organ, designed by Peter Richards and George Gonzalez

PACIFIC HEIGHTS AND THE MARINA

Pacific Heights is an exclusive neighborhood that clings to a hillside rising 300 ft (100 m) above the city. The area was developed in the 1880s after cable cars linked it with the city center. With its magnificent views and elegant Victorian houses lining its tree-shaded streets, it quickly became a desirable place to live. To the north of Broadway, the once-marshy site descending all the way to San Francisco Bay was cleared and drained for the 1915 Panama-Pacific International Exposition, of which the Palace of Fine Arts Theatre is the sole survivor. Anchored by the boutiques and restaurants on Fillmore Street, Pacific Heights today is one of the most expensive neighborhoods in the US.

To the north of Broadway, the streets drop steeply to the Marina District, ending at San Francisco Bay. The houses here were built on a once-marshy site which was also cleared and drained for the Panama-Pacific Exposition Today, the area feels like a wealthy seaside resort, with boutiques, lively cafés, and two prestigious yacht clubs.

PACIFIC HEIGHTS AND THE MARINA

Must Sees

1. Fort Mason
2. Japantown

Experience More

3. Spreckels Mansion
4. Fillmore Street
5. Alta Plaza Park
6. Lafayette Park
7. Trinity + St. Peter's Episcopal Church
8. Church of St. Mary the Virgin
9. Vedanta Temple
10. Haas-Lilienthal House
11. Cow Hollow
12. Octagon House
13. Chestnut Street
14. Marina Green
15. Cottage Row
16. Wave Organ
17. Arion Press

Eat

① The Coffee Berry SF
② Café Boho

Drink

③ The Snug
④ The Tipsy Pig

Shop

⑤ Anomie
⑥ Gio Gelati

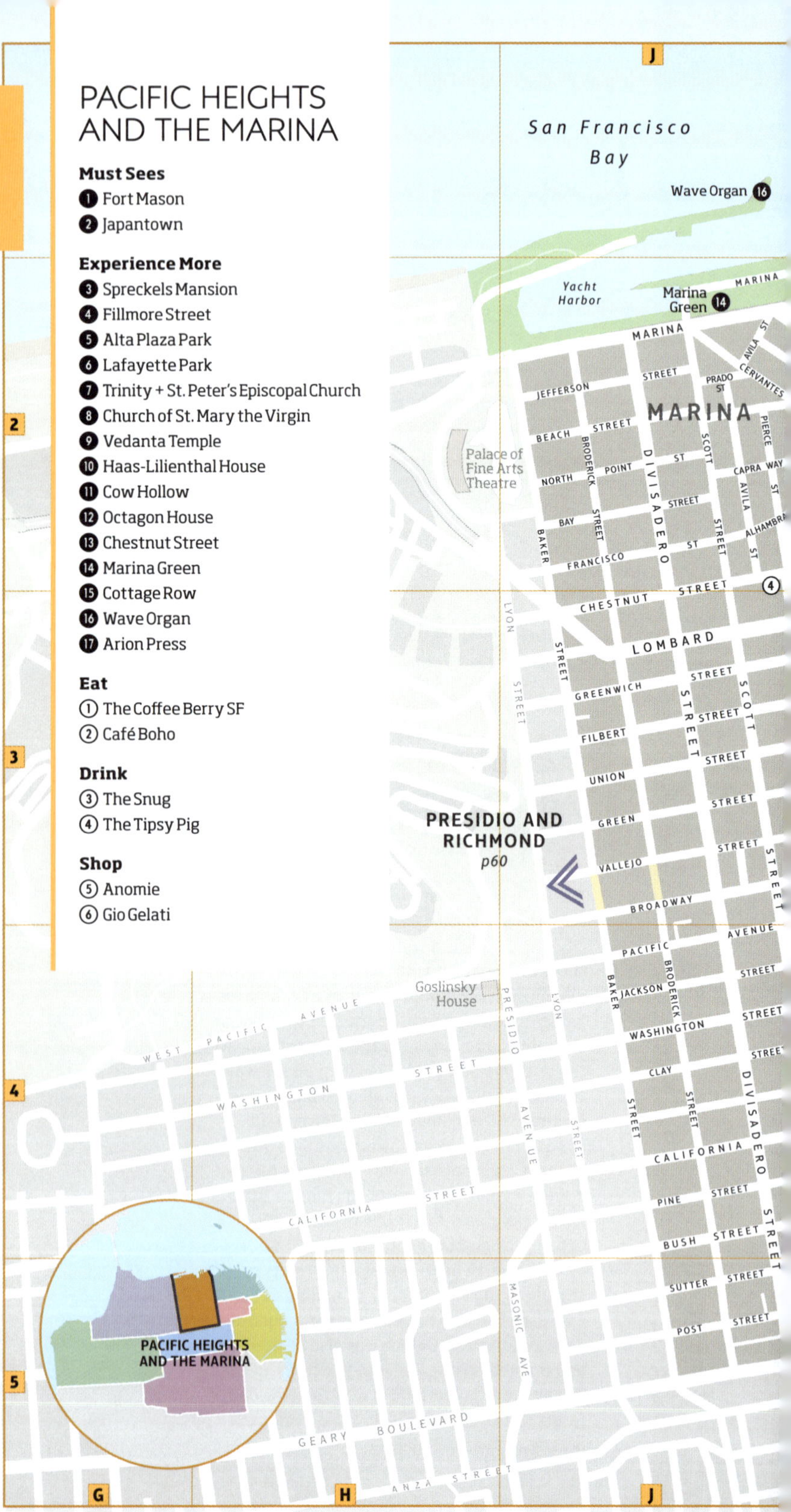

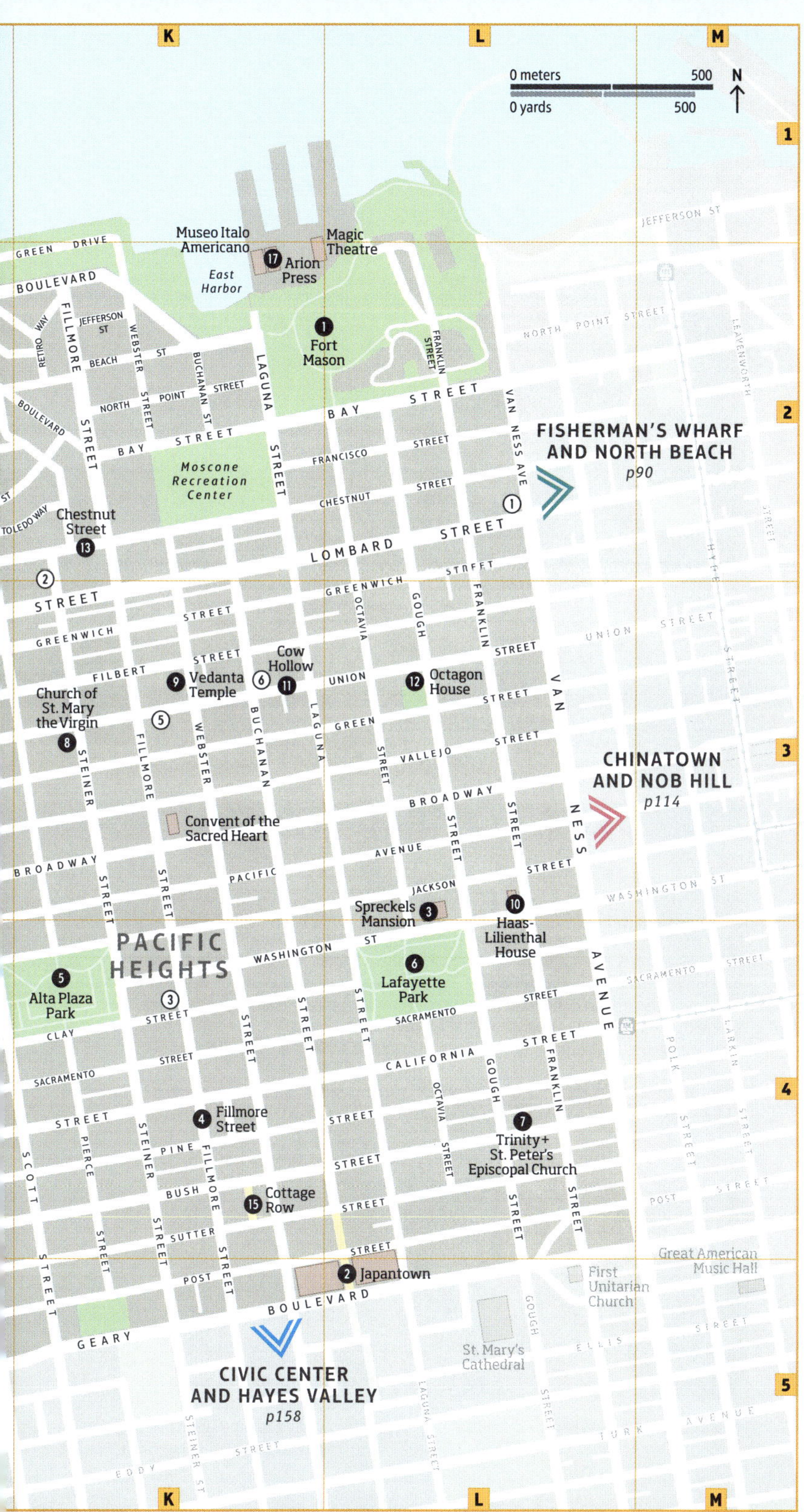

FISHERMAN'S WHARF AND NORTH BEACH
p90
CHINATOWN AND NOB HILL
p114
CIVIC CENTER AND HAYES VALLEY
p158
PACIFIC HEIGHTS
Museo Italo Americano
Magic Theatre
Arion Press
East Harbor
Fort Mason
Moscone Recreation Center
Chestnut Street
Cow Hollow
Vedanta Temple
Octagon House
Church of St. Mary the Virgin
Convent of the Sacred Heart
Spreckels Mansion
Haas-Lilienthal House
Alta Plaza Park
Lafayette Park
Fillmore Street
Trinity+ St. Peter's Episcopal Church
Cottage Row
Japantown
First Unitarian Church
Great American Music Hall
St. Mary's Cathedral
0 meters 500
0 yards 500

1

FORT MASON

K/L2 2 Marina Blvd 22, 28, 30, 30X, 43, 49
9am-5pm Mon-Fri fortmason.org

Once a military base, Fort Mason is now a cool and vibrant arts and culture center, and a definite hotspot for foodies. Some of the city's finest views across the bay can be enjoyed from here.

Fort Mason reflects the military history of San Francisco. The original buildings were private houses, erected in the late 1850s, which were confiscated by the US Government when the site was taken over by the US army during the American Civil War (1861–5). The fort remained an army command post until the 1890s, and later housed refugees left homeless by the 1906 earthquake. During World War II, Fort Mason Army Base was the point of embarkation for around 1.6 million soldiers. Fort Mason was converted to peaceful use in 1972. The original barracks and the old hospital – which serves as a Visitor Center and headquarters of the Golden Gate National Recreation Area (GGNRA) – are both open to the public. Fort Mason has some of the city's finest views, looking across the bay toward Golden Gate Bridge and Alcatraz.

↑ Fine art exhibition in the Fort Mason Center for Arts and Culture

Fort Mason Center for Arts and Culture

Part of the fort is now occupied by one of San Francisco's prime art complexes. Fort Mason Center for Arts and Culture is home to over 25 cultural organizations, art galleries, museums, and theaters. Particular highlights include the the Museo Italo Americano, with works by Italian and Italian-American artists. Prestigious publisher Arion Press *(p85)* has a free gallery in the center, showcasing the art and craft of traditional book-making. It's home to the largest collection of metal typefaces in the US, outside the Smithsonian. Among the many places to eat at Fort Mason Center is Greens, one of the city's best vegetarian restaurants. Hours vary for each venue, so check the website in advance. Fort Mason Center also hosts thousands of events every year.

↑ The buildings of the Fort Mason complex on the piers in the Marina District

Fort Mason with its many art galleries ↓

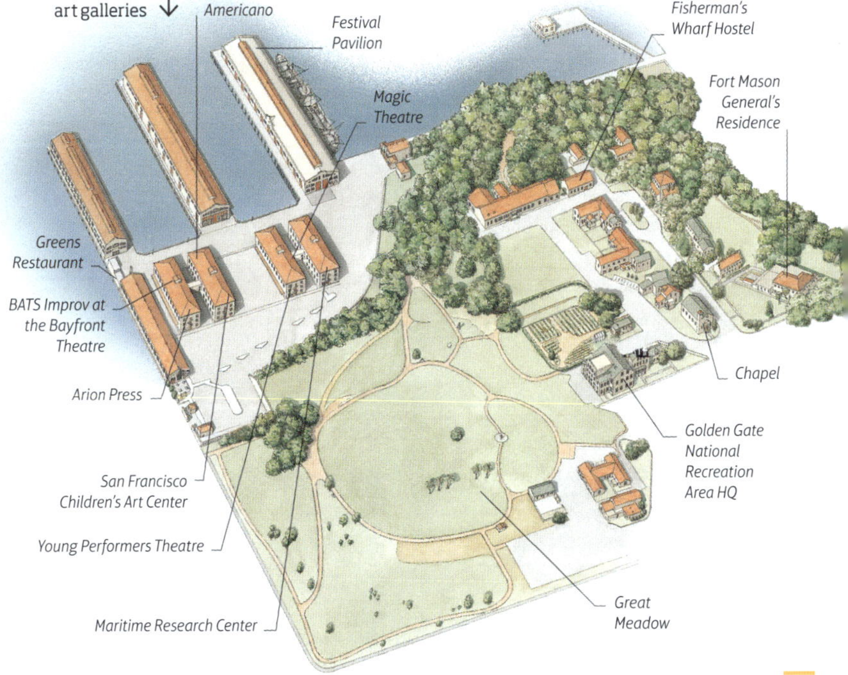

Museo Italo Americano

Festival Pavilion

Magic Theatre

HI San Francisco Fisherman's Wharf Hostel

Fort Mason General's Residence

Greens Restaurant

BATS Improv at the Bayfront Theatre

Arion Press

Chapel

Golden Gate National Recreation Area HQ

San Francisco Children's Art Center

Young Performers Theatre

Maritime Research Center

Great Meadow

2

JAPANTOWN

L5 2, 3, 22, 31, 38 sfjapantown.org

It may be smaller than San Francisco's famous Chinatown, but visitors should make sure not to overlook the city's Japantown district. Full of fun stores, great food, and cultural experiences, the buildings of the Peace Plaza make you feek like you've stepped off the streets of San Francisco and right into urban Japan.

Japantown has a full calendar of cultural events from spring to fall, and even without any traditional festivals in winter it's an unmissable place for foodies, shoppers, and Japanophiles at any time of year. Many of the restaurants come complete with plastic food displays in the window, just like you'd find in Tokyo. And stores selling traditional clothing and homeware are interspersed with modern stores selling anime merchandise, beauty products, and all things *kawaii* (cute).

Historic Japantown

At one time in the early 20th century, this area had one of the largest populations of Japanese people in the western world. Also known as *Nihonmachi* (the Japanese translation for "Japantown"), the area was the heart of the local Japanese-American community, and had the look and feel of downtown Tokyo. That changed when those of Japanese birth or descent were tragically interned during World War II. It wasn't until the 1960s when the area regained some of its historic character, that the original Japan Center shopping complex was built as part of a scheme to revitalize the Fillmore District. At the heart of the complex, and centered upon a five-tiered, 75-ft (22-m) concrete pagoda, is the Peace Pagoda Garden.

Did You Know?

This is one of only three Japantowns in the US, all of which are in California.

↑ Ceramic bowls decorated with traditional designs, on sale in Japantown

Festival Seasons Calendar

Spring

▼ The Anime Festival and Cosplay takes place in March, when fans of Japanese animation dress up like their favorite characters.

Summer

▲ Japan Week, held in June, features *taiko* drumming and *awa odori* dance performances, calligraphy workshops, and other cultural events.

Fall

▲ In September the Sumo Champions Exhibit takes place outside in the Peace Plaza.

Winter

The Japantown Center Mall is busy in December with shoppers looking for holiday gifts.

← The Peace Pagoda at the heart of Japantown, a gift from San Francisco's sister city, Osaka.

↑ A cyclist rides past the boutiques and restaurants on Fillmore Street

EXPERIENCE MORE

Spreckels Mansion

L3 2080 Washington St 1, 3, 10, 47, 49 To the public

Dominating the north side of Lafayette Park, this imposing Beaux Arts mansion *(p36)* is sometimes known as the "Parthenon of the West" on account of its Classical-style columned facade. It was built in 1912 for the flamboyant Alma de Bretteville Spreckels and her husband Adolph, who was heir to the sugar fortune of Claus Spreckels. Alma filled the house with antiques bought on trips to Europe and was renowned for her lavish parties. The house is now owned by novelist Danielle Steel. It occupies a block on Octavia Street, which is landscaped in the style of Lombard Street *(p103)*. The mansion's architect was George Applegarth, who in 1916 designed the Legion of Honor *(p196)* to house Alma Spreckels' burgeoning collection of fine art.

Fillmore Street

K4 1, 2, 3, 10, 22, 24

Fillmore Street survived the devastating 1906 earthquake virtually intact, and for several years afterward served as the civic heart of the city. Government departments, as well as private businesses, were housed in the district's stores, homes, and even churches. Today the main commercial district of Pacific Heights is located here, from Jackson Street to Japantown around Bush Street. This area has an abundance of bookstores, restaurants, and boutiques.

Alta Plaza Park

K4 1, 3, 10, 22, 24

Situated in the center of Pacific Heights, Alta Plaza is a beautifully landscaped urban park, where San Francisco's elite come to relax. There are stone steps (offering great city views) rising up from Clay Street on the south side of the park. These steps may be familiar from the movies – Barbra Streisand drove down them in *What's Up, Doc?* From the north side you can see several splendid mansions, including Gibbs House at 2622 Jackson Street, built by Willis Polk in 1894. Covering nearly 12 acres (4.8 ha), Alta Plaza was the site of a quarry when it was purchased by the city of San Francisco in 1877. It was another 20 years, however, before landscaping works began. The area served as a campsite for victims of the 1906 earthquake and fire.

Did You Know?

Trinity + St. Peter's Episcopal Church is the second oldest congregation in the city of San Francisco.

6

Lafayette Park

L4 1, 10, 47, 49

One of San Francisco's prettiest hilltop gardens, this is a leafy green haven of pine and eucalyptus trees, although its present tranquility belies its turbulent history. Along with Alta Plaza Park and Alamo Square, the land was set aside in 1855 as city-owned open space, but squatters and others, including a former City Attorney, laid claim to the land and built houses on it. The largest of the houses stood at the center of the hilltop park until 1936, as the squatter who had built it refused to move. It was finally torn down after the city authorities agreed to swap it for land on Gough Street. Steep stairways now lead to the park's summit and its delightful views. In the surrounding streets are scores of palatial buildings, with particularly ornate examples along Broadway, Jackson Street, and Pacific Avenue going east–west, and on Gough and Octavia streets north–south.

7

Trinity + St. Peter's Episcopal Church

L4 1620 Gough St 1, 2, 3, 10, 19, 22, 38, 47, 49 trinity-stpeters.org

Designed in the Norman style by American architect A. Page Brown and constructed of Colusa sandstone, the Trinity + St. Peter's Episcopal Church dates back to 1849. It survived an earthquake in 1906 and the ensuing fires without damage. Sunday services are still held in the main sanctuary. Its colorful stained-glass windows were designed by a pupil of John La Farge, a leading figure in the New York art scene during the late 19th century. The high altar displays the 1894 jewel-encrusted Trinity Cross, presented as a gift on Trinity Sunday by the women of the parish. The church also has a rich musical and artistic tradition; featuring a fine pipe organ and an art gallery. It regularly hosts concerts and theatrical performances.

DRINK

The Snug

Classic cocktails are given a fresh update in this bright, stylish spot. The hip clientele lounge on comfy leather sofas to sip raspberry negronis or bourbon sours with Chinese plum.

K4 2301 Fillmore St
thesnugsf.com

The Tipsy Pig

Low lighting and polished wood surfaces give this bar a warm, old-fashioned feel, but the cocktails - shaken and muddled with fresh fruit, herbs, and house-made syrups - are thoroughly modern.

J2 2231 Chestnut St
thetipsypigsf.com

The grand and historic Trinity + St. Peter's Episcopal Church ↑

Did You Know?

Frank Pixley, editor of the *Argonaut*, donated the lot on which the Church of St. Mary the Virgin was built.

8

Church of St. Mary the Virgin

K3 2325 Union St 22, 41, 45 9:30am-4:30pm Mon-Fri, 8am-noon Sun smvsf.org

Evoking the more rural early 19th-century years of Cow Hollow, this rustic, wooden-shingled Episcopal church stands at the west end of what is now the busy Union Street shopping area.

One of the natural springs that provided water for the Cow Hollow dairy herds still bubbles up in the grounds, now largely hidden from the view of passersby on the street by the church's original lych-gate and hedge.

The small, plain building is an early example of the Arts and Crafts style *(p37)* later used in more prominent Bay Area churches. Below the steeply sloping roof, the walls are faced with "shingles," which are strips of redwood nailed in overlapping rows onto the building's wooden frame. Part of the building was remodeled in the 1950s, when the main entrance was moved from Steiner Street to the opposite end of the building; however, the fabric has been well preserved.

Vedanta Temple

K3 2963 Webster St 22, 41, 45 To the public sfvedanta.org

One of the Bay Area's most unusual structures, the Vedanta Temple is an eclectic combination of a host of divergent decorative traditions. The roof is crowned by a rusty red, onion-shaped dome similar to those seen on Russian Orthodox churches. It also has a tower resembling a crenellated European castle, and an octagonal Hindu temple cupola. Other architectural features include highly decorated Moorish arches, medieval parapets, and elements of Queen Anne *(p171)* and Colonial styles.

SHOP

Anomie

Stand-out fashion, handcrafted jewelry, and quirky homeware line the shelves of this boutique, with a focus on items designed and made in the city.

K3 2149 Union St
11am-7pm daily
shopanomie.com

GIO Gelati

This small shop prides itself on offering the healthiest and freshest gelato in San Francisco. It expertly combines local Californian flavors to create deliciously creamy ice cream.

K3 1998 Union St
8am-9:30pm daily
giogelati.com

One of the rooms in the Haas-Lilienthal, with its original decor and furniture

It was built in 1905 by the architect Joseph A. Leonard, working closely with the Northern California Vedanta Society minister, Swami Trigunatitananda.

Vedanta is the highest of the six schools of Hinduism, and the building symbolizes the Vedanta concept that every religion is just a different way of reaching one god. The Temple is now a monastery, but it is worth a visit just to marvel at this remarkable building from the outside.

The striking Vedanta Temple, built in an unusual mix of architectural styles

Haas-Lilienthal House

L3 2007 Franklin St 1, 12, 19, 27, 47, 49 For guided tours only: noon-3pm Wed & Sat haas-lilienthalhouse.org

This exuberant mansion in Queen Anne style *(p171)* was built for the rich merchant William Haas in 1886. Alice Lilienthal, his daughter, lived there until 1972, when it was given to the Foundation for San Francisco's Architectural Heritage. It is the only intact private home of the period open as a museum, and is complete with original furniture. A fine example of an upper-middle-class Victorian dwelling, the house has very decorative gables, a circular corner tower, and elaborate ornamentation.

A display of photographs describes the history of the building and reveals that this grandiose house was modest in comparison with some of those destroyed in the earthquake and fire of 1906.

Cow Hollow

K3 22, 28, 30, 30X, 41, 43, 45, 49

Cow Hollow, an attractive, upmarket shopping district along Union Street, is so called because it was used as grazing land for the city's dairy cows up until the 1860s. It was then taken over for development as a residential neighborhood. In the 1950s the area became fashionable, and chic boutiques, antiques stores, and art galleries took over the old neighborhood stores. Many of these are housed in restored 19th-century buildings, lending an old-fashioned air to the district, in stark contrast to the sophistication of the merchandise on display. It's a popular place for brunch and has some fine coffee shops.

Octagon House

L3 2645 Gough St 28, 45, 47, 49 Noon-3pm on second & fourth Sun of the month Jan nscda-ca.org/octagon-house

Built in 1861, the Octagon House is an eight-sided wooden building. It houses a small, but engaging, collection of decorative arts and historic documents of the Colonial and Federal periods. Included are furniture, paintings, Revolutionary playing cards, and the signatures of 54 of the 56 signatories of the Declaration of Independence. Entry to the house is free, though a donation is suggested.

The angular Octagon House, now a fine decorative arts museum

Relaxed alfresco dining on Chestnut Street, the Marina District's main hub

13 Chestnut Street

K2 22, 28, 30, 30X, 43

The main shopping and nightlife center of the Marina District, Chestnut Street has a varied mix of movie theaters, markets, cafés, coffee houses, and restaurants. It's a great place to stop for a meal and people-watch, having a much more low-key and local feel than you'll find in the busier tourist areas. The commercial strip stretches just a few blocks from Fillmore Street west to Divisadero Street, after which the neighborhood becomes predominantly residential in character.

INSIDER TIP
Flicks on Chestnut Street

After shopping or as a prelude to a night out, head to one of the old-school movie theaters a block apart on Chestnut Street. The Presidio and the Marina theaters both screen new releases and offer an intimate movie-watching experience.

14 Marina Green

J2 22, 28, 30, 30X, 43

A long, thin strip of lawn running the length of the Marina District, Marina Green is popular with kite-flyers and for picnics, especially on July 4, when the city's largest firework show can be seen from here. Paths along the waterfront are the city's prime spots for cyclists, joggers, and roller-skaters. Golden Gate Promenade leads from the west end of the green to Fort Point, or you can turn east to the Wave Organ at the harbor jetty.

15 Cottage Row

K4 2, 3, 8AX, 8BX, 22, 38

One of the few surviving remnants of working-class Victorian San Francisco, this short stretch of flat-fronted cottages was built in 1882, at the end of the Pacific Heights building boom. Unusual for San Francisco, the cottages share dividing walls, like terraced houses in Europe. Their utter lack of ornament, and their location on what was a dark and crowded back alley, emphasize their lower-class status. The Cottage Row houses were saved from destruction during the process of slum clearance in the 1960s. A program organized by Justin Herman awarded grants to

help people restore their existing houses, rather than replace them. All but one have now been restored; they face a small attractive park.

Wave Organ

J1 30, 30X

Sitting at the tip of the breakwater that protects the Marina is what has to be the world's most peculiar musical instrument. Built by scientists from the Exploratorium *(p98)*, the Wave Organ consists of a number of underwater pipes that echo and hum with the changing tides. Listening tubes are embedded in a mini-amphitheater that has views of Pacific Heights and the Presidio. "Organ" is a little misleading: the sounds you hear are more like gurgling plumbing than organ music.

↓ Peter Richards and George Gonzalez's Wave Organ sculpture

17 

Arion Press

K2 2 Marina Blvd
22, 28, 30, 30X, 43, 49
Noon-5pm Tue-Sat
arionpress.com

Considered a leading national publisher of fine press books, Arion Press is highly sought after by collectors for their quality and rarity. With titles ranging from classic literature to new works, the texts from the Press are famous for their erudition and diversity. Its impressive roster of authors includes Ovid, Shakespeare, Laurence Sterne, Herman Melville, Emily Dickinson, Gertrude Stein, Sigmund Freud, Allen Ginsberg, and David Mamet. Visitors can explore San Francisco's rich literary history and its tradition of producing high-quality handmade items at the free gallery located in Fort Mason. Guided tours are available in the afternoons, taking place on the second Thursday and third Saturday of every month.

EAT

The Coffee Berry SF

A cozy café serving organic coffee, soft serve ice cream and luscious pastries such as strawberry guava pastelitos and Swedish-style cinnamon buns.

L2 1410 Lombard St thecoffeeberrysf.com

Café Boho

Fresh, local seafood takes center stage here, particularly with the signature "seacuterie board": a sharing platter with tuna pastrami and octopus dip.

K2/3 3321 Steiner St (415) 374-7518

$$

EXPERIENCE **Pacific Heights and the Marina**

A SHORT WALK PACIFIC HEIGHTS

Distance 1 mile (1.5 km) **Time** 20 minutes
Nearest buses 3, 10, 24

The blocks between Alta Plaza and Lafayette Park are at the heart of Pacific Heights. The streets in this upscale neighborhood are quiet and tidy, lined with smart apartment blocks and palatial houses. Some date from the late 19th century, while others were built after the earthquake and fire of 1906 *(p53)*. To the north of the area, the streets drop steeply toward the Marina District, affording outstanding views of the bay. Wander through the large Alta Plaza and Lafayette parks and past the luxuriant gardens of the mansions in between, then visit lively Fillmore Street, with its numerous fashionable bars, cafés, restaurants, and stores.

↑ Colorful Victorian houses on Washington Street

Did You Know?

A little north of this map, 2640 Steiner Street is the house where *Mrs Doubtfire* was filmed.

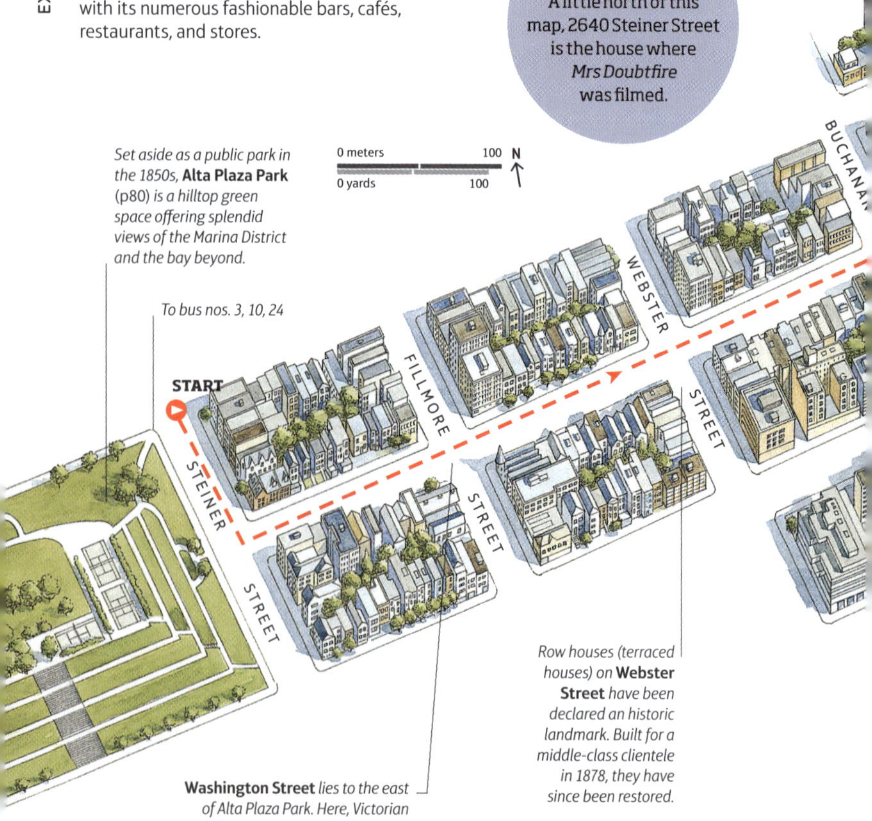

Set aside as a public park in the 1850s, **Alta Plaza Park** (p80) *is a hilltop green space offering splendid views of the Marina District and the bay beyond.*

0 meters 100
0 yards 100
N

To bus nos. 3, 10, 24

START

STEINER STREET

FILLMORE STREET

WEBSTER STREET

BUCHANAN

Row houses (terraced houses) on **Webster Street** *have been declared an historic landmark. Built for a middle-class clientele in 1878, they have since been restored.*

Washington Street *lies to the east of Alta Plaza Park. Here, Victorian houses in various architectural styles, fill an entire block.*

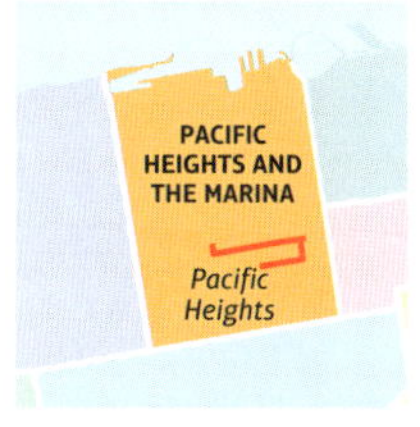

Locator Map
For more detail see p74

Furnished in Victorian style, **Haas-Lilienthal House** *(p83) evokes the elegance of affluent families in the late 19th century.*

The impressive limestone **Spreckels Mansion** *(p80), constructed on the lines of a Baroque palace, has been home to the family of best-selling novelist Danielle Steel since 1990.*

JACKSON STREET
LAGUNA
WASHINGTON STREET
STREET
GOUGH STREET
CLAY STREET
SACRAMENTO STREET
FINISH

No. 2004 Gough Street*, one of the more elaborate Victorian houses in Pacific Heights, was built in 1889.*

The quiet **Lafayette Park** *(p81) offers good views of the Victorian houses that surround it.*

No. 2151 Sacramento Street *is an ornate, French-style mansion. A plaque commemorates a visit by the author Sir Arthur Conan Doyle in 1923.*

↑ The hilltop Lafayette Park, a leafy green haven

A SHORT WALK
AQUATIC PARK

Distance 1.5 miles (2.5 km) **Time** 35 minutes
Nearest public transportation Powell-Hyde cable car to Hyde Street Pier; bus 19, 28, 49 to Van Ness Avenue-Beach Street

Side by side on San Francisco's northern waterfront, Aquatic Park and Fort Mason offer some fascinating glimpses into the city's past, especially its colorful history as a seaport. There are no cars here, just walkers, cyclists, and skaters sharing lushly overgrown paths. The route winds past historic ships moored in the bay at Hyde Street Pier, Depression-era swim clubs, Gold Rush cottages, and military installations dating from Spanish colonial times to World War II. You can swim if you don't mind the chilly bay water, fish for crabs, paddle off a small beach, or just stop to admire the view and picnic in one of the many grassy spots.

The Golden Gate Promenade *climbs upward, rounding Black Point and giving superb views of Alcatraz and Angel Island.*

At the top of the slope, the **Youth Hostel** *is one of the few ornate houses open to the public.*

Narrow steps lead down the hill to **Fort Mason** *(p76). Visit the Mexican Museum or view the Outdoor Exploratorium, which illustrates the history of the shoreline and the area's natural environment.*

The grassy knolls of **Great Meadow** *were where refugees from the 1906 earthquake camped until they could be rehoused.*

Magic Theater
Youth Hostel
FINISH
Fort Mason
Golden Gate National Recreation Area
Great Meadow
WEBSTER STREET
NORTH POINT STREET
BAY STREET
OCTAVIA ST
GOUGH ST
LAGUNA ST
FRANCISCO ST
Moscone Recreation Center
CHESTNUT STREET

Near the Fort Mason General's residence is the headquarters of the **Golden Gate National Recreation Area (GGNRA).**

←
The historic Hyde Street Pier on San Francisco's northern waterfront

0 meters 300
0 yards 300
N

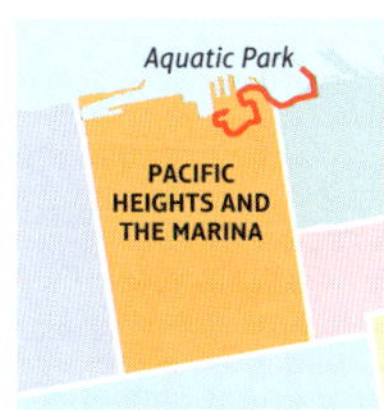

Locator Map
For more detail see p74

This curving concrete pier marks the western end of Aquatic Park. People fish here at all hours, mostly for crabs. The Mission-style building at the foot of the pier is an emergency pumping station.

Begin at the seaward end of ***Hyde Street Pier****. Until 1938, this pier was the center of activity on the city's northern waterfront. It is now part of the Maritime Museum (p102).*

Among the ships moored here is a handsome steam-powered ferry boat, the ***Eureka****, built in 1890.*

The two whitewashed clapboard buildings on the sandy beach house the ***South End*** *and* ***Dolphin*** *swimming and rowing clubs.*

In flower-filled ***Victorian Park*** *street musicians perform.*

The large Casino was built in 1939 as a public bathing club. Since 1951 it has been the West Coast home of the ***Maritime Museum*** *(p102).*

The sun-soaked ***Francisco Park*** *offers gorgeous views of the Aquatic Park Cove.*

A topiary sign spells out "Aquatic Park." Behind this are red-and-white, plastic-roofed ***bocce ball courts****.*

→ Skyline of San Francisco with Aquatic Park in the foreground

HYDE ST. PIER

A hazy Alcatraz Island, as seen from atop Hyde Street

FISHERMAN'S WHARF AND NORTH BEACH

Chinese and Italian immigrants made a living catching fish at San Francisco's northern waterfront during the days of the Gold Rush in the mid-19th century, thus founding the San Franciscan fishing industry. In 1893, Genoese chocolatier Domenico Ghirardelli established the headquarters of his chocolate company in San Francisco at what would come to be known as Ghirardelli Square. Fishing has slowly given way to tourism since the 1950s – San Francisco Maritime National Historical Park got its start in 1951 and PIER 39 was developed in 1978 – but brightly painted boats still set out from the harbor on fishing trips early each morning.

To the south of Fisherman's Wharf lies North Beach, also known as "Little Italy." Italian immigration to the city was ignited by the Gold Rush, but it gained momentum after the 1906 earthquake, when *focaccia* (type of Italian bread) bakeries, salami grocers, and Italian cafés sprung up on empty lots. Italian-American baseball icon Joe DiMaggio grew up in the area in the 1920s and the late Lawrence Ferlinghetti, another famous Italian-American resident, opened the City Lights Bookstore on Columbus Avenue in 1953. Still operational, this store was a leading light in the Beat Movement and North Beach was home to beatniks Allen Ginsberg and Gregory Corso. Today the neighborhood still attracts tourists and young professionals, but few Italian Americans live here.

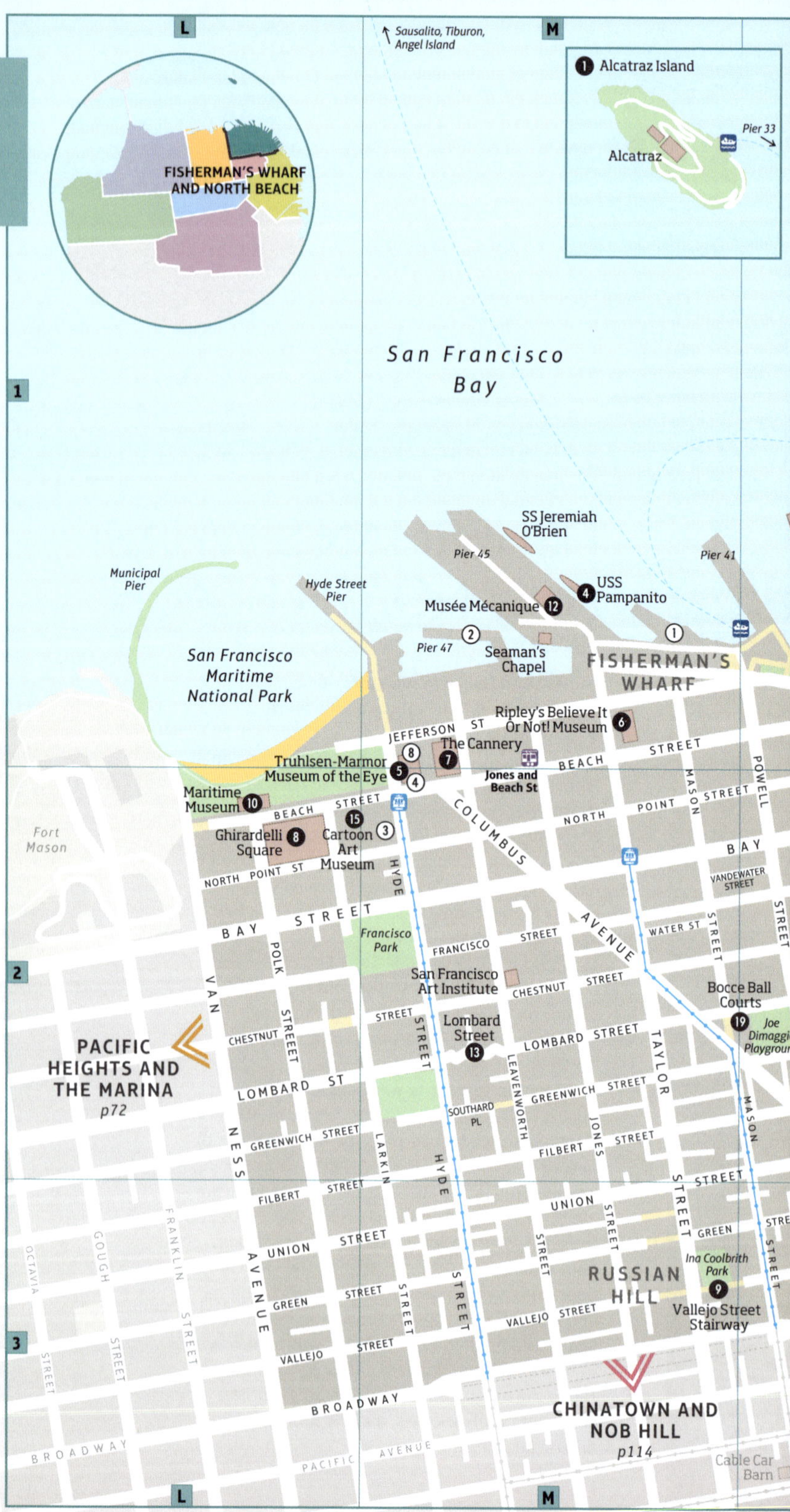

L
M
Sausalito, Tiburon, Angel Island
Alcatraz Island
Alcatraz
Pier 33
FISHERMAN'S WHARF AND NORTH BEACH
San Francisco Bay
SS Jeremiah O'Brien
Pier 45
Pier 41
USS Pampanito
Municipal Pier
Hyde Street Pier
Musée Mécanique
Pier 47
Seaman's Chapel
FISHERMAN'S WHARF
San Francisco Maritime National Park
Ripley's Believe It Or Not! Museum
JEFFERSON ST
The Cannery
Truhlsen-Marmor Museum of the Eye
Jones and Beach St
Maritime Museum
Ghirardelli Square
Cartoon Art Museum
Fort Mason
COLUMBUS AVENUE
Francisco Park
San Francisco Art Institute
Lombard Street
Bocce Ball Courts
Joe Dimaggio Playground
PACIFIC HEIGHTS AND THE MARINA p72
SOUTHARD PL
RUSSIAN HILL
Ina Coolbrith Park
Vallejo Street Stairway
CHINATOWN AND NOB HILL p114
Cable Car Barn

FISHERMAN'S WHARF AND NORTH BEACH

Must Sees

1. Alcatraz Island
2. Exploratorium

Experience More

3. PIER 39
4. USS Pampanito
5. Truhlsen-Marmor Museum of the Eye
6. Ripley's Believe It Or Not! Museum
7. The Cannery
8. Ghirardelli Square
9. Vallejo Street Stairway
10. Maritime Museum
11. Washington Square
12. Musée Mécanique
13. Lombard Street
14. The Beat Museum
15. Cartoon Art Museum
16. Saints Peter and Paul Church
17. City Lights Bookstore
18. Coit Tower
19. Bocce Ball Courts
20. Filbert Steps
21. Greenwich Steps

Eat

(1) Franciscan Crab Restaurant
(2) Scoma's Restaurant
(3) Gary Danko
(4) Café de Casa

Drink

(5) Player Sports Grill & Arcade
(6) Red Jack Saloon
(7) Wipeout Bar & Grill

Stay

(8) Argonaut Hotel

N
1
2
3
P
Q

PIER 39
Beach and Stockton St
Pier 33
Alcatraz
Pier 31
Embarcadero and Bay St
Pier 29
San Francisco Bay
Pier 27
Pier 23
Pier 19
Pier 17
Pier 15
Pier 9
Pier 7
Pier 5
Pier 1
Ferry Building
Embarcadero and Greenwich St
Exploratorium
Embarcadero and Broadway
THE EMBARCADERO
STOCKTON STREET
FRANCISCO STREET
PFEIFFER ST
CHESTNUT ST
LOMBARD STREET
MONTGOMERY ST
WINTHROP ST
TELEGRAPH HILL
Telegraph Hill Park
Greenwich Steps
Coit Tower
Filbert Steps
LEVI'S PLAZA
SANSOME STREET
BATTERY STREET
FRONT STREET
DAVIS STREET
Saints Peter and Paul Church
FILBERT STREET
Washington Square
UNION STREET
GREEN STREET
GRANT AVENUE
KEARNY STREET
COLUMBUS AVENUE
POWELL STREET
VALLEJO STREET
BROADWAY
PACIFIC AVENUE
NORTH BEACH
The Beat Museum
City Lights Bookstore
WASHINGTON ST
PORTSMOUTH SQUARE
DOWNTOWN AND SOMA
p132
0 meters 400
0 yards 400

ALCATRAZ ISLAND

M1 Pier 33 Hours vary, check website
nps.gov/alcatraz; alcatrazcruises.com

Visible from the crowded shores of San Francisco, this compelling rocky island and abandoned prison is the city's most notorious attraction.

Alcatraz means "pelican" in Spanish, a reference to the first inhabitants of this rocky, steep-sided island. Lying 3 miles (5 km) east of the Golden Gate Bridge *(p64)*, its location is both strategic and exposed to harsh ocean winds that elicit a chilling atmosphere. In 1859, the US military established a fort here that guarded San Francisco Bay until 1907, when the fort became a military prison. From 1934 to 1963, it served as a maximum-security Federal Penitentiary. Abandoned until 1969, the island was occupied by Indians of All Tribes who wanted to reclaim the island, which Europeans had taken from the Indigenous peoples in the 18th century. The group was expelled in 1971, and Alcatraz is now part of the Golden Gate National Recreation Area.

↑ The former prison and its lighthouse standing atop Alcatraz Island

Did You Know?

There were 14 escape attempts during the 29 years Alcatraz Federal Penitentiary was in operation.

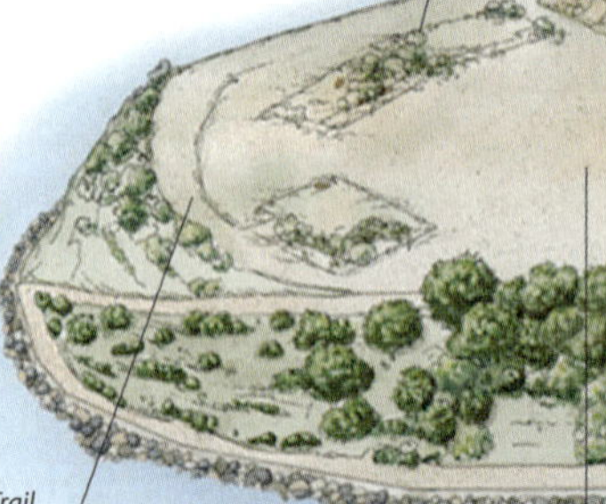

Timeline of events

1775

▲ Spanish explorer Juan Manuel de Ayala names Alcatraz after the "strange birds" that inhabit it.

1848

▲ Governor of California, John Frémont, buys Alcatraz from Francis Temple.

1850

Alcatraz is declared a military reservation by President Fillmore.

1854

▼ First Pacific Coast lighthouse activated on Alcatraz.

1859

▲ Fort Alcatraz completed; equipped with 100 cannon and 300 troops.

Must See

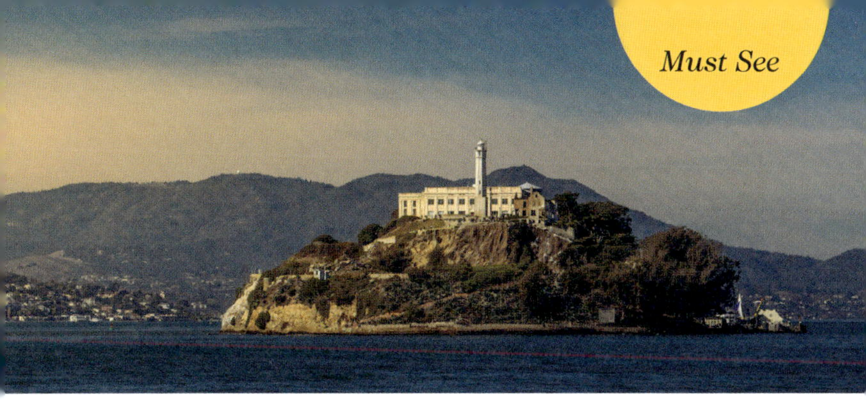

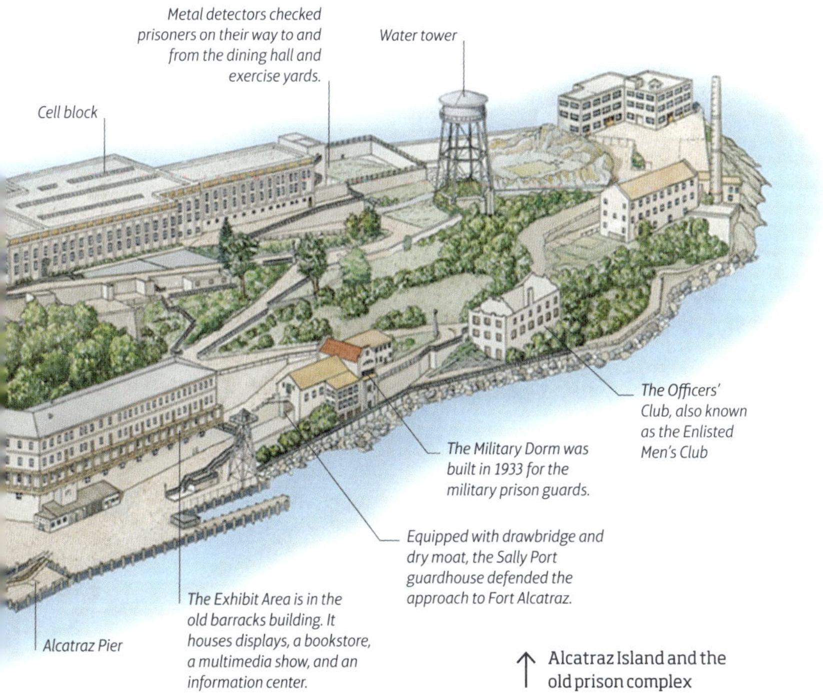
Metal detectors checked prisoners on their way to and from the dining hall and exercise yards.
Water tower
Cell block
The Officers' Club, also known as the Enlisted Men's Club
The Military Dorm was built in 1933 for the military prison guards.
Equipped with drawbridge and dry moat, the Sally Port guardhouse defended the approach to Fort Alcatraz.
The Exhibit Area is in the old barracks building. It houses displays, a bookstore, a multimedia show, and an information center.
Alcatraz Pier

↑ Alcatraz Island and the old prison complex

1909

▼ Army prisoners begin construction of the cell house.

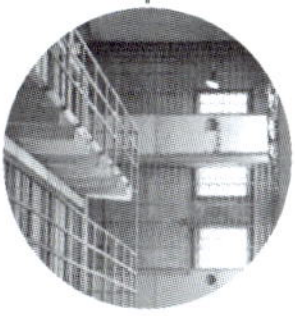

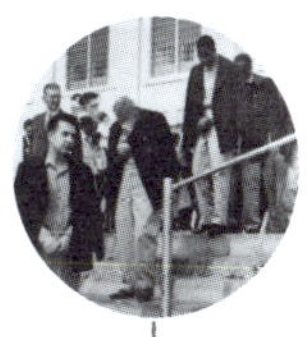

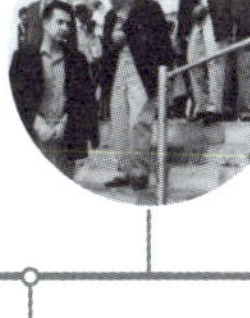

1934

▲ Federal Bureau of Prisons turns Alcatraz into a civilian prison.

1962

▼ Famed criminal Frank Morris escapes *(p97)*.

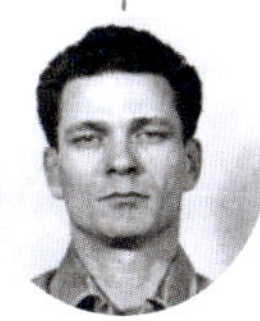

1963

Prison closed.

INDIANS WELCOME
UNITED STATES PENITENTIARY

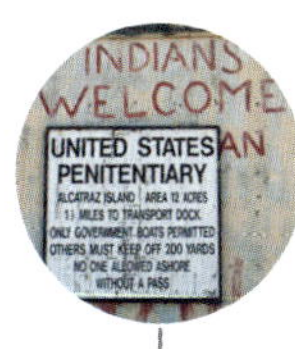

1972

▲ Alcatraz becomes a national park.

Inside Alcatraz

The maximum-security prison on Alcatraz, dubbed "The Rock" by the US Army, housed an average of 264 of the country's most hardened criminals, who were transferred here for disobedience while serving time in prisons elsewhere in the US. The strict discipline at Alcatraz was enforced by the threat of a stint in the isolation cells and by loss of privileges, including the chance at special jobs, time for recreation, use of the prison library, and visitation rights.

INSIDER TIP
Plan Ahead

Tickets for Alcatraz go on sale 90 days in advance and tours last two and a half to four hours, including the return ferry trip. Bring a jacket or sweater, as the weather can be far wilder and colder out here than it is in the city.

↑ The corridor that separates C and B blocks, nicknamed Broadway by the prisoners

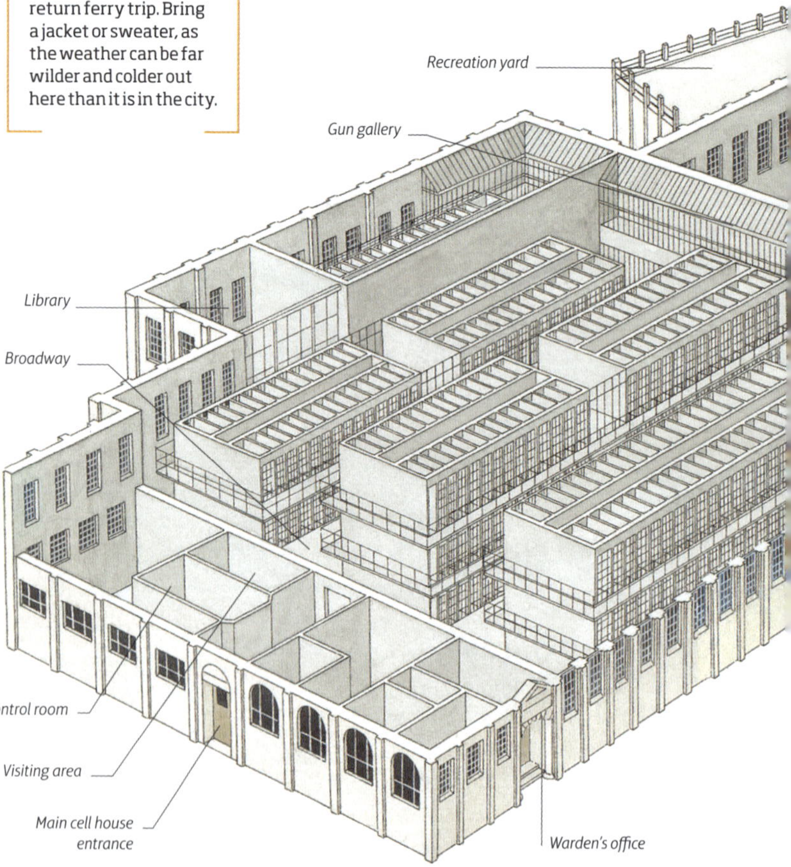

Recreation yard
Gun gallery
Library
Broadway
Control room
Visiting area
Main cell house entrance
Warden's office

↑ Cross-section of the interior of Alcatraz Federal Penitentiary

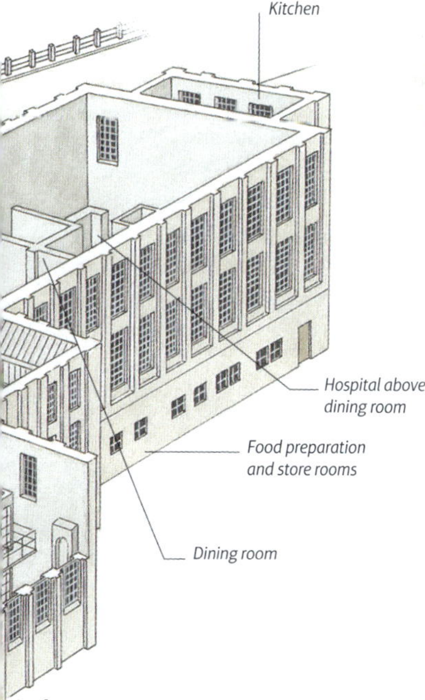

↑ The prison kitchen, off the dining room, where inmates were well fed to help quell rebellion

Infamous Inmates

Al Capone

▶ The notorious Prohibition-era gangster "Scarface" Capone was convicted, in 1934, for income tax evasion. He spent much of his 10-year sentence in a hospital isolation cell, and finally left Alcatraz mentally unwell after contracting syphilis years before his conviction.

Robert Stroud

◀ Convicted murderer Stroud spent all of his 17 years on The Rock in solitary confinement. Despite assertions to the contrary in the movie *The Birdman of Alcatraz* (1962), Stroud was in fact prohibited from keeping birds in his prison cell.

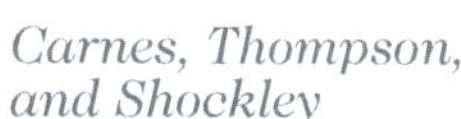

Carnes, Thompson, and Shockley

In May 1946, a group of prisoners led by Clarence Carnes, Marion Thompson, and Sam Shockley overpowered guards and captured their guns. The prisoners failed to break out of the cell house, but three inmates and two officers were killed in the "Battle of Alcatraz." Carnes received an additional life sentence, and Shockley and Thompson were executed at San Quentin prison, for their part as ringleaders of the insurrection.

Anglin Brothers

▶ John and Clarence Anglin, along with Frank Morris, chipped through the back walls of their cells, hiding the holes with cardboard grates. They left dummy heads in their beds and made a raft to enable their escape. They were never caught. Their story was dramatized in the movie *Escape from Alcatraz* (1979).

George Kelly

▶ "Machine Gun Kelly" served 17 years on The Rock for kidnapping and extortion. He was then sent to a Kansas jail, where he later died.

2

EXPLORATORIUM

P2 Pier 15 1, 2, 6, 10, 12, 14, 21, 31, 38, 41 E, F Embarcadero
10am–5pm Mon–Sat, noon–5pm Sun exploratorium.edu

One of the world's foremost hands-on science museums, the popular Exploratorium is an interactive playground of exhibits that ignite the senses. Covering everything from vast topics such as the science of human behavior right down to local geography, there's a subject to inspire everyone's curiosity – from kids to adults alike.

Since 1969 this renowned museum and global learning center has been influencing people of all ages with its creative and interactive exhibits. The museum uses unique hands-on displays that promote playful learning, and with so many topics to explore there's endless fun to be had. Learn how reflections work, understand how certain genes are passed on from parent to child, and examine local micro-organisms and their Bay Area habitats. The top draw is the Tactile Dome, a pitch-dark network of chambers and mazes that you find your way out of using only the sense of touch. When you need a break from all the excitement, the all-glass Fisher Bay Observatory Gallery and Terrace offers excellent views of the Bay.

There are also a variety of events to look out for on the museum's calendar, including a guided walk during the highest tides of the year (known as the "King Tides"), and Community Days when patrons can pay whatever they wish (though admission is first-come-first-served and can't be guaranteed). After Dark Thursdays also give adults a chance to explore the exhibits in their own time (18+ only: 6–10pm Thursdays).

Colored light bathing visitors to the Central Gallery, and *(inset)* a child blowing bubbles

MUSEUM GUIDE

The long building is laid out into five galleries. The Bernard and Barbro Osher Gallery 1 contains the Human Phenomena exhibit on topics such as emotions and human behavior. Gallery 2's tinkering exhibits and the Bechtel Gallery 3 on seeing and listening take up a large part of the museum, followed by Gallery 4 on living systems. Covering both the natural sciences and local history and geography are the outdoor Gallery 5, and the Fisher Bay Observatory Gallery on the upper level of the museum.

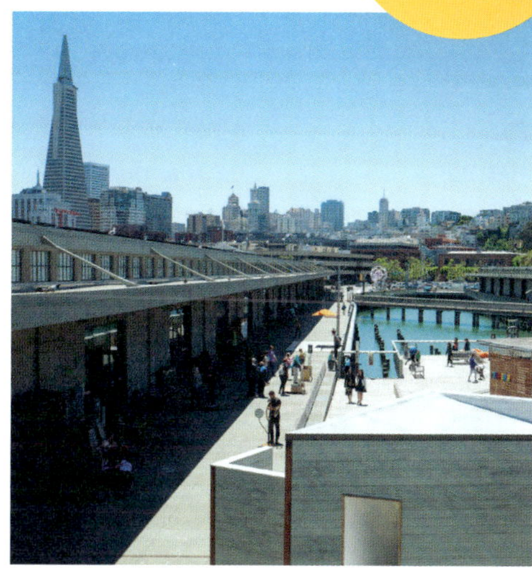

↑ The skyline of downtown San Francisco behind the Exploratorium

EXPERIENCE MORE

PIER 39

N1 4, 8, 8BX, 39, 47 E, F Powell-Hyde SF Bay Ferry

Refurbished in 1978 to resemble a quaint wooden fishing village, this 1905 cargo pier now houses many tourist and specialty stores spread through two levels.

The pier's street performers and amusements are popular with families, as is the giant sculpture of a crab at its entrance. Visitors can enjoy a ride on the two-story carousel, or take home a new hat from Krazy Kaps.

You can take a closer look at the pier's most famous residents at the Sea Lion Center; exhibits include a sea lion skeleton and interactive videos. Step outside afterward to view wild sea lions at close range.

USS Pampanito

M1 Pier 45 4, 8, 8BX, 39, 47 E, F Powell-Hyde SF Bay Ferry Check website for seasonal variations maritime.org/uss-pampanito

This World War II submarine fought in, and survived, several bloody battles in the Pacific, sinking six enemy ships and severely damaging others. Tragically for the allies, two of its fatal targets were carrying British and Australian POWs. The *Pampanito* managed to rescue 73 men and carry them to safety in the US. A tour of the ship takes visitors from stern to bow to see the torpedo room, the claustrophobic kitchen, and officers' quarters.

When the *Pampanito* was in service, it had a full crew of 10 officers and 70 seamen.

Truhlsen-Marmor Museum of the Eye

M2 645 Beach St 4, 8, 8BX, 30, 39, 47 E, F Powell-Hyde 11am-4:30pm Wed-Sun aao.org/museum-of-the-eye

Opened in 2021 by the American Academy of Ophthalmology, this museum is dedicated to the science of sight. It showcases nearly 4,000 items from the academy's vast collection, including spectacles, sunglasses, monoculars, binoculars, and telescopes, as well as rare books and other specialized items designed to enhance vision. As well as demonstrating how our eyes work, the exhibits explore the significance of eyes and the sense of sight across various cultures. Visitors

→ Ghirardelli Square shopping center, site of the original famous chocolate factory

can also experience a 3D tour of a human eye using virtual reality headsets.

Ripley's Believe It Or Not! Museum

M1 175 Jefferson St 4, 8, 8BX, 30, 39, 47 E, F Powell-Hyde 11am-6pm Mon-Thu & Sun, 10am-8pm Fri & Sat ripleys.com/sanfrancisco

California native Robert L. Ripley was an illustrator with a penchant for collecting peculiar facts and artifacts. He earned his fame and fortune by syndicating his newspaper cartoon strip, called *Ripley's Believe It Or Not!* Among the 350 oddities on display are a cable car built of 275,000 matchsticks, a two-headed calf, and an image of a man who had two pupils in each eyeball. Get lost in the Marvelous Mirror Maze and sample some candy from the factory. Some of Ripley's famous cartoon strips are on display, too.

1,701

The highest number of sea lions recorded on PIER 39, in November 2009.

The Cannery

M1 2801 Leavenworth St 4, 8, 8BX, 30, 39, 47 E, F Powell-Hyde

This 1909 fruit-canning plant was refurbished in the 1960s to incorporate footbridges, sunny courtyards, and rambling passages, with restaurants and specialty stores selling clothes, collector dolls, Indigenous arts and crafts, and much else.

The Cannery also used to house the Museum of the City of San Francisco, but a fire forced the premises to close. However, the collection has moved to the City Hall *(p166)*, where all the exhibits are now on display. Among these is the massive head of the statue that capped City Hall before the 1906 earthquake *(p53)*. The glowing crown on the head is an example of early electric illumination.

← The huge crab sculpture at the entrance of PIER 39

Ghirardelli Square

L2 900 North Point St 4, 18, 19, 24, 27, 28, 30, 38, 47, 49 E, F Powell-Hyde ghirardellisq.com

Once a chocolate factory and woollen mill, this is the most attractive of San Francisco's refurbished factories, a mix of old red-brick buildings and modern stores and restaurants. The shopping center retains the famous Ghirardelli trademark clock tower and the original electric roof sign. The Ghirardelli Chocolate Manufactory on the plaza beneath the tower still houses vintage chocolate-making machinery and sells the confection, although these days the chocolate bars are made in San Leandro, across the Bay.

The square's centerpiece and a popular gathering point for shoppers day and evening is Andrea's Fountain, decorated with bronze sculptures of mermaids and turtles.

HIDDEN GEM
Willis Polk

The work of architect Willis Polk can be seen at several points while climbing Vallejo Street. Look out for the stylish Williams-Polk House at 1013-1019 Vallejo and the terraced stairway near Taylor Street.

9

Vallejo Street Stairway

M3 Vallejo St, between Mason St and Jones St 10, 12, 41, 45 Powell-Mason

The steep climb from Little Italy to the southernmost summit of Russian Hill reveals some of the city's best views of Telegraph Hill, North Beach, and the encompassing bay. The street gives way to steps at Mason Street, which climb up through the quiet and pretty Ina Coolbirth Park. Higher still, above Taylor Street, there is a warren of lanes, with several elegant Victorian-style wooden houses *(p36)*. At the crest of the hill is one of the few pockets of the city that was not destroyed in the earthquake and fire of 1906.

Argonaut Hotel

This grand, red-brick building has a nautically inspired interior. The most sought-after rooms have windows gazing over the San Francisco Bay.

M1 495 Jefferson St argonauthotel.com

$$$

↑ The *CA Thayer*, an 1895 lumber schooner on Hyde Street Pier, part of the Maritime Museum

10 

Maritime Museum

L2 900 Beach St 4, 8, 19, 39, 47 E, F Powell-Hyde 10am-4pm Wed-Sun maritime.org

Constructed in 1939, the Aquatic Park Bathhouse Building has housed the Maritime Museum from 1951. Visitors can still admire the renovated Streamline Moderne building with its clean lines, rather like that of an ocean liner.

Moored at nearby Hyde Street Pier is one of the world's largest collections of old ships. Among the most spectacular is the *CA Thayer*, a three-masted schooner built in 1895 and retired in 1950. The *Thayer* carried lumber along the North California coast, and was later used in Alaskan fishing.

Also at the pier are the steam tug, *Hercules* (1907), and the side-wheel ferry boat, *Eureka*, built in 1890 to ferry trains between the Hyde Street Pier and the counties north of San Francisco Bay. It carried 2,300 passengers and 120 cars, and was the largest passenger ferry of its day.

Washington Square

N2 Filbert and Stockton St 30, 45 Powell-Hyde, Powell-Mason sfrecpark.org/902/Washington-Square

Established in 1847, this park is famous for its expansive green meadows, and is perfect for a picnic. Located right next to San Francisco's "Little Italy" (in the North Beach area), it was used as a place of refuge for those who were impacted by the fires on the nearby Telegraph Hill in the late 1800s and early 1900s. This was also where hundreds of people were forced to temporarily take shelter in the aftermath of the devastating earthquake of 1906. Nowadays, the 3-acre (1.25-ha) park is popular among tourists and locals alike for its spectacular views and overall quiet nature. Look out for the stunning Saints Peter and Paul Church on the park's northern border.

Musée Mécanique

M1 Pier 45, at the end of Taylor St 1 E, F 10am-8pm daily museemecaniquesf.com

Kids and adults alike will love the experience of combing through and playing at this museum of penny-arcade games from the early 20th century. The privately owned collection is one of the largest of its kind in the world and consists of over 300 items, including automatons, early examples of pinball, coin-operated pianos, antique slot machines, orchestrions, laughing fortune tellers, and more. It was an insiders-only local spot for many years, and is still popular with young San Franciscans looking for a unique and fun evening out. Located close to PIER 39 and Fisherman's Wharf, Musée Mécanique can be part of a whimsical, memorable day. General admission is free, but the cost to play games ranges from a penny (true to their name!) up to a dollar.

Did You Know?

The speed limit down the twisted, one-way route of Lombard Street is 5 mph (8 km/h).

Lombard Street

M2 19, 41, 45 Powell-Hyde

Banked at a natural incline of 27°, this hill proved too steep for vehicles to climb. In the 1920s the section of Lombard Street close to the summit of Russian Hill was revamped, and the severity of its gradient lessened by the addition of eight curves.

Today it is known as "the crookedest street in the world." Cars can travel downhill only, while people take the steps or the cable car.

A car driving down the winding ribbon of Lombard Street

14 The Beat Museum

N3 540 Broadway 8, 8AX, 10, 12, 30, 39, 41, 45, 91 10am-7pm Thu-Sun kerouac.com

This quirky museum displays memorabilia related to the artists of the Beat Generation, associated with San Francisco in the 1950s. Photographs, books, album covers, and letters line the walls and floors of the building, offering an absorbing insight into this non-conformist literary movement, including the works and lives of Beat icons such as Jack Kerouac, William S. Burroughs, and Allen Ginsberg. The museum hosts events related to Beat culture, while the store sells a fascinating range of books, videos, T-shirts, and posters.

15 Cartoon Art Museum

L2 781 Beach St 11am-5pm Thu-Tue cartoonart.org

The world of cartoons can be explored at this museum, housed in a 1912 building overlooking the bay. Among the 7,000 items on display are political caricatures, anime, graphic novels, and iconic cartoons from Warner Bros. and Walt Disney.

Workshops held at the museum encourage guests to try their hand at visual storytelling. On the first Tuesday of every month, the admission fee is flexible and visitors can decide what to pay.

16 Saints Peter and Paul Church

N2 666 Filbert St 8BX, 8X, 30, 39, 41, 45, 91 Powell-Mason 7am-3pm Mon-Fri, 7am-6pm Sat, 8am-6pm Sun salesiansspp.org

Known by many as the Italian Cathedral, this large church is situated at the heart of North Beach, and serves the area's Italian-American community. The building, designed by Charles Fantoni, has an Italianesque facade, with a complex interior notable for its many columns and ornate altar. The concrete and steel structure of the church, with its elegant twin spires, was completed in 1924.

Cecil B. DeMille filmed the workers laying the foundations of Saints Peter and Paul, and used the scene to show

→ The historic City Lights Bookstore, a literary meeting place since 1953

HIDDEN GEM

Beat Generation

Although prominent Beat figure Jack Kerouac never lived in San Francisco, his life and work are intrinsically linked to the city. An alley to the south of City Lights Bookstore was named after him in 2007, and contains plaques dedicated to the Beat Generation.

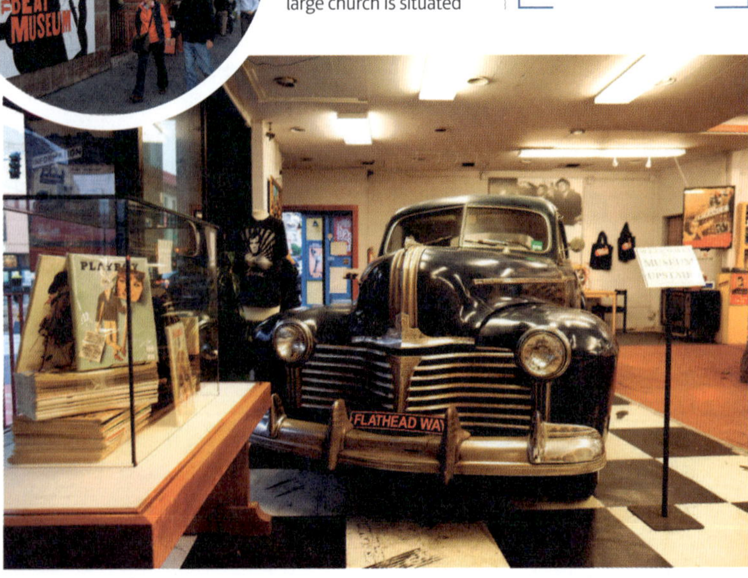

A favorite of the Beat poets and still a relevant and wonderful independent bookstore for browsing today, City Lights Bookstore is an intriguing stop.

the building of the Temple of Jerusalem in his movie *The Ten Commandments*.

The church is also known as the Fishermen's Church, and there is a Mass to celebrate the Blessing of the Fleet every October. Masses are held in Italian, Chinese, and English.

17

City Lights Bookstore

N3 261 Columbus Ave 8, 8AX, 8BX 10am-10pm daily citylights.com

A favorite of the Beat poets and still a wonderful independent store, City Lights Bookstore and publishing press was founded in 1953 by the poet Lawrence Ferlinghetti and sociology professor Peter D. Martin. Soon after opening, Ferlinghetti and Martin were arrested for disseminating obscene literature – Allen Ginsberg's *Howl and Other Poems* (1956). However, after a lengthy, highly publicized court trial the jury ruled against the charges, and the event only worked to increase the spotlight on the Beat poets and cement City Lights Bookstore as a cornerstone of the Beat movement.

Browsing the shelves and exploring the unique titles, it's easy to feel transported back to the 1960s. The upstairs aisles focus on poetry and offer plenty of cozy nooks to settle down with a new title. Be sure also to check out the used books on the more expansive lower level.

A 1940's Pontiac exhibited inside and *(inset)* the facade of the Beat Museum

EAT

Franciscan Crab Restaurant

Huge windows frame impressive views of the Golden Gate Bridge and Alcatraz at this seafood institution, whose crab-centric menu also includes fresh oysters and steamed mussels.

M1 Pier 43 1/2, Fisherman's Wharf franciscan crabrestaurant.com

$$$

Scoma's Restaurant

Jutting out onto the bay, this Italian spot oozes old-school charm. Ingredients for the seafood dishes are pulled straight from local fishing boats.

M1 1965 Al Scoma Way scomas.com

$$$

Gary Danko

A refined chef-owned spot with a seasonal five-course tasting menu showcasing classic French cooking with Californian wine pairings.

M2 800 North Point St gary danko.com

$$$

Café de Casa

Great value Brazilian breakfasts, crêpes, and traditional pastries are on the menu at this tiny café with a pretty, plant-filled patio.

M2 685 Beach St cafedecasa.com

$$$

Coit Tower

N2 1 Telegraph Hill Blvd 249-0995 8, 8BX, 8X, 30, 39, 41, 45, 91 10am-6pm daily (winter: to 5pm)

Coit Tower was built in 1933 at the top of 284-ft- (87-m-) high Telegraph Hill, with funds left to the city by Lillie Hitchcock Coit, an eccentric San Franciscan pioneer and philanthropist. The 210-ft- (63-m-) reinforced concrete tower was designed as a fluted column by the architect Arthur Brown. When floodlit at night it is an eerie white and can be seen from most parts of the eastern half of the city. The view around the North Bay from the observation platform (reached by elevator) is spectacular.

Many of the faces in the paintings are those of the artists and their friends, along with local figures such as Colonel William Brady, caretaker of Coit Tower.

In the lobby of the tower are murals that are even more absorbing. These were sponsored in 1934 by a government-funded program designed to keep artists employed during the Great Depression. Twenty-five artists joined efforts to paint a vivid portrait of life in modern California. Scenes range from the teeming streets of the city's Financial District (with a robbery in progress) to factories, dockyards, and Central Valley wheat fields.

There are many fascinating details, including a real light switch cleverly incorporated into a painting and a poor family of migrants encamped by a river, plus newspaper headlines, magazine covers, and book titles. The murals are effective social commentary and yet also whimsical in spirit. Various political themes depicting labor problems and social injustice run through them. Many of the faces in the paintings are those of the artists and their friends, along with local figures such as Colonel William Brady, caretaker of Coit Tower. The works' political content initially caused public controversy.

Bocce Ball Courts

M/N2 Lombard St & Mason St, Joe DiMaggio Playground 831-5500 8BX, 8X, 30, 39, 41, 45, 91 Powell-Mason 6am-10pm daily

Italian culture has been influential in North Beach since the main wave of immigration from Italy in the late 19th and early 20th centuries. Along with their food, customs, and religion, they also brought games to their new home. Among these was

←

Coit Tower and the lobby's fascinating 1930s murals *(inset)* depicting everyday Californian life

→ The pretty Filbert Steps with breathtaking views of the bay below

bocce, an Italian version of lawn bowling, played on a narrower and shorter court than the English version. In North Beach it is played most afternoons on the public court in a corner of the Joe DiMaggio Playground. There are four participants (or four teams), who roll a wooden ball at a smaller target ball, at the opposite end of an earth court. The aim is for the balls to lightly "kiss" *(bocce)*, and the highest score goes to the player whose ball gets closest to this target.

Filbert Steps

P2 8, 8BX, 39, 82X E, F

Telegraph Hill falls away sharply on its eastern side, and the streets here become steep steps. Descending from Telegraph Hill Boulevard, Filbert Street is a rambling, picturesque stairway, made of wood, brick, and concrete, where fuchsia, rhododendron, bougainvillea, fennel, and blackberries thrive, and offering panoramic views.

Greenwich Steps

N2 8, 8BX, 39, 82X Powell-Mason

Descending roughly parallel to Filbert Steps, the steps of Greenwich Street have splendid views, with luxuriant foliage from adjoining gardens overflowing onto them. Going up one set of steps and down the other makes a delightful walk around the eastern side of Telegraph Hill.

DRINK

Player Sports Grill & Arcade

This lively waterside spot combines a sports-bar vibe with an arcade and a fun tiki bar serving classic beach cocktails. Families and groups of friends gather here for live music and happy hour.

N1 2 Beach St playerssf.com

Red Jack Saloon

Red Jack Saloon is old-school San Francisco through and through. Patrons of the two-storied watering hole can play darts and pinball, all while sipping a well-priced drink and watching a sporting event on any one of the bar's elevated TVs.

N2 131 Bay St (415) 989-0700

Wipeout Bar & Grill

This Fisherman's Wharf bar is filled with nautical knickknacks and surfboards that make it unmistakably Californian. Enjoy global eats in this bar's friendly atmosphere, along with an on-tap craft beer of choice.

N1 Pier 39 wipeoutbarandgrill.com

A SHORT WALK
FISHERMAN'S WHARF

Distance 1 mile (1.5 km) **Time** 20 minutes **Nearest streetcars** E, F

World-class dining, shopping, and entertainment are the focus of this vibrant neighborhood – the center of San Francisco's fishing industry. Try the city's celebrated Dungeness crab, served from November to June, at one of the many seafood restaurants or outdoor crab stands. See the fishing boats along Jefferson Street, watch fishers at work on Fish Alley, then visit the museums and browse the many fun stores. The Wharf is also the launching point for bay cruises. Tickets for Alcatraz can be purchased from Pier 33.

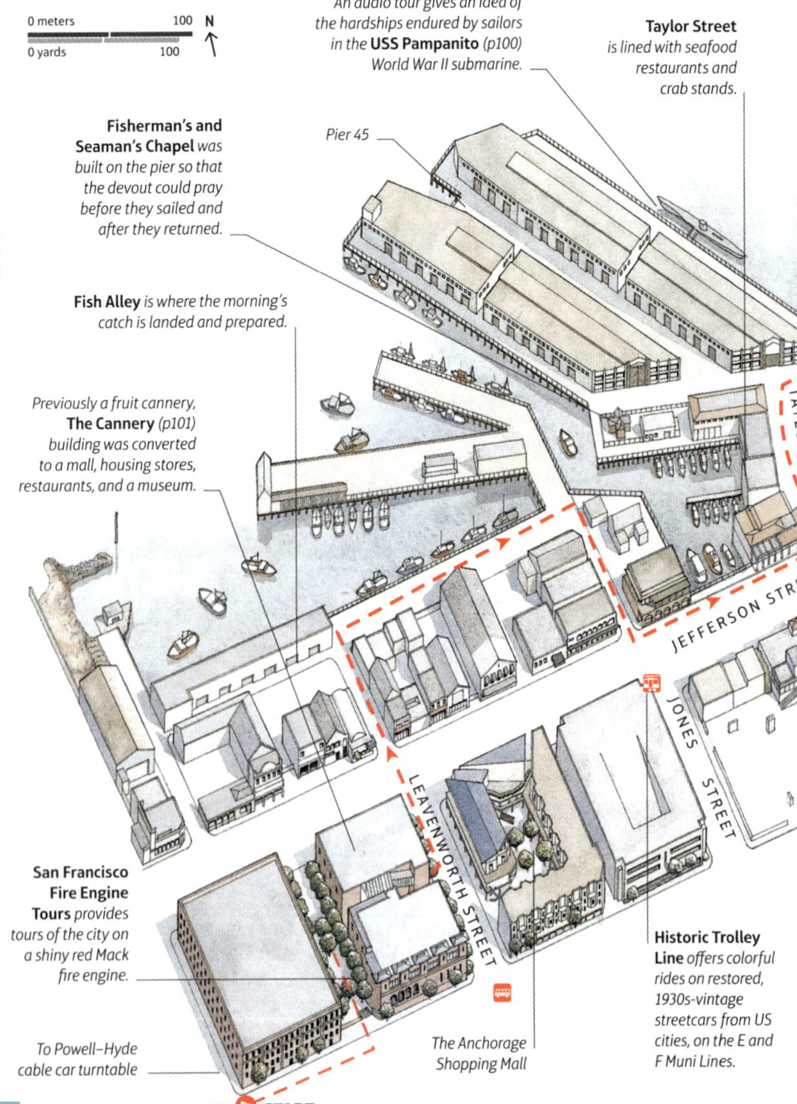

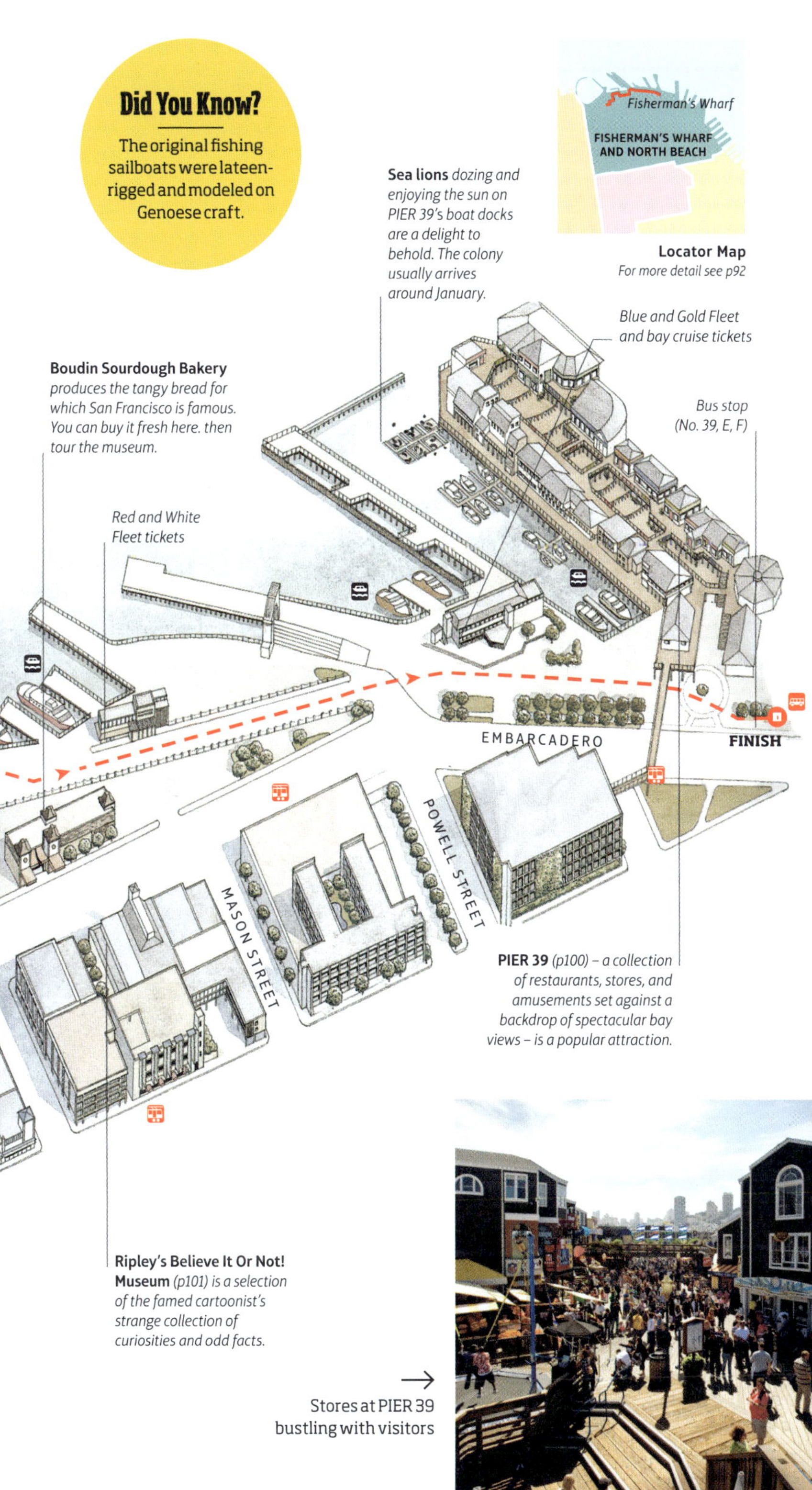

Stores at PIER 39 bustling with visitors

A SHORT WALK
TELEGRAPH HILL

Distance half a mile (1 km) **Time** 15 minutes
Nearest bus 39

Telegraph Hill was named for the semaphore installed on its crest in 1850 to alert merchants of the arrival of ships. Today's hill falls away abruptly on its eastern side, where it was dynamited to provide rocks for landfill and paving. There are steep paths on this side of the hill, bordered by gardens. The western side slopes more gradually into "Little Italy," the area around Washington Square. In the 1920s the hill attracted artists who appreciated the panoramic views. These days the quaint pastel clapboard homes are much sought after and this is one of the city's prime residential areas. Stroll through its quiet streets, finishing at the Art Deco Coit Tower, which houses interesting fresco murals in the American Social Realism style and a panoramic viewing platform at its summit.

↑ Beautiful interior of Saints Peter and Paul Church

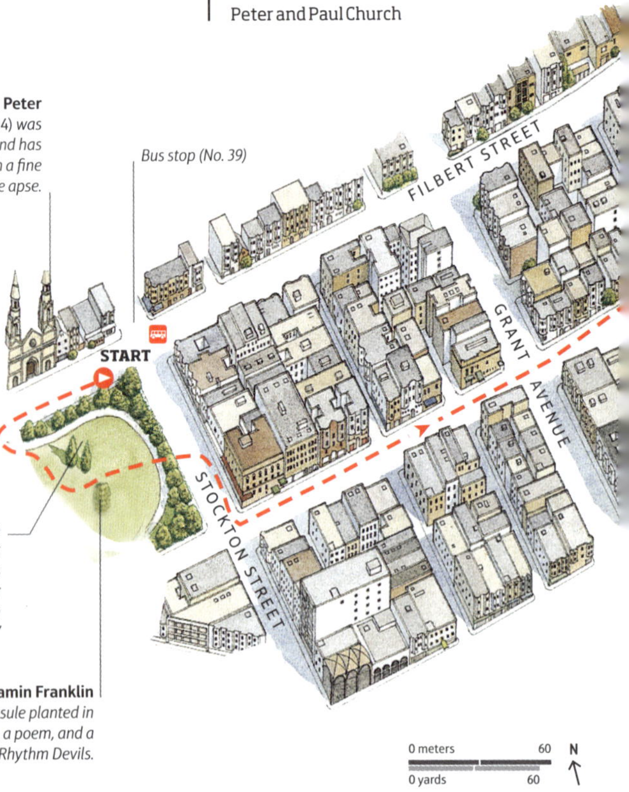

The Neo-Gothic **Saints Peter and Paul Church** (p104) *was consecrated in 1924 and has an ornate interior with a fine image of Christ in the apse.*

Bus stop (No. 39)

START

FILBERT STREET

GRANT AVENUE

STOCKTON STREET

Washington Square (p102), *a small park at the heart of Little Italy, is dominated by Saints Peter and Paul Church, known as the "Italian Cathedral."*

The Statue of Benjamin Franklin *stands above a time capsule planted in 1979, containing Levi's, a poem, and a recording of the Hoodoo Rhythm Devils.*

0 meters 60
0 yards 60
N

Locator Map
For more detail see p92

The Christopher Columbus Statue *was erected in 1957.*

The frescoes inside **Coit Tower** (p106) *were painted by local artists in 1933, as part of the Federal Art Project set up by President Roosevelt.*

Bus stop (No. 39)

The formally landscaped **Greenwich Steps** (p107) *contrast with the charmingly rustic Filbert Steps.*

The small **Napier Lane** *is lined with 19th-century cottages. It is the last of San Francisco's wooden plank streets and a tranquil retreat from the city.*

The ascent through flower gardens up the **Filbert Steps** (p107) *gives fine views over the harbor to the East Bay.*

No. 1360 Montgomery Street *is decorated with an Art Deco figure of a modern Atlas.*

→ The top of Coit Tower, rising above houses on Telegraph Hill

A SHORT WALK RUSSIAN HILL

Distance 1.5 miles (2.5km) **Time** 35 minutes **Nearest public transportation** Powell-Hyde cable car to Hyde St & Vallejo St; bus 10 or 12 to Pacific Ave & Jones St

The rewards for scrambling up the steep stairways and leafy alleys of Russian Hill are a lovely hilltop warren of parks and rare examples of architecture that survived the 1906 earthquake. Here you will encounter few cars and fewer people as you wander among carefully preserved buildings, and enjoy the dazzling views and luxuriant hill-side gardens that are the pride of the neighborhood. At the end of your walk, descend to indulge in European-style cafés and boutiques at the foot of the hill.

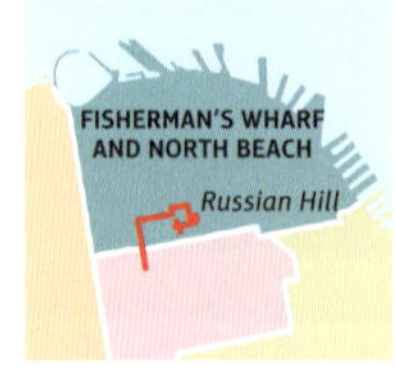

Locator Map
For more detail see p92

*The block between Hyde and Leavenworth streets is also called "**the Paris Block**," and is lined with a number of buildings on the National Register of Historic Places.*

*Continue to **Hyde Street** where cafés and boutiques cluster between Jackson and Union streets. The charming Cocotte at No. 1521 is a great place to pause and soak up views of the city.*

A cable car heading up the Hyde Street hill

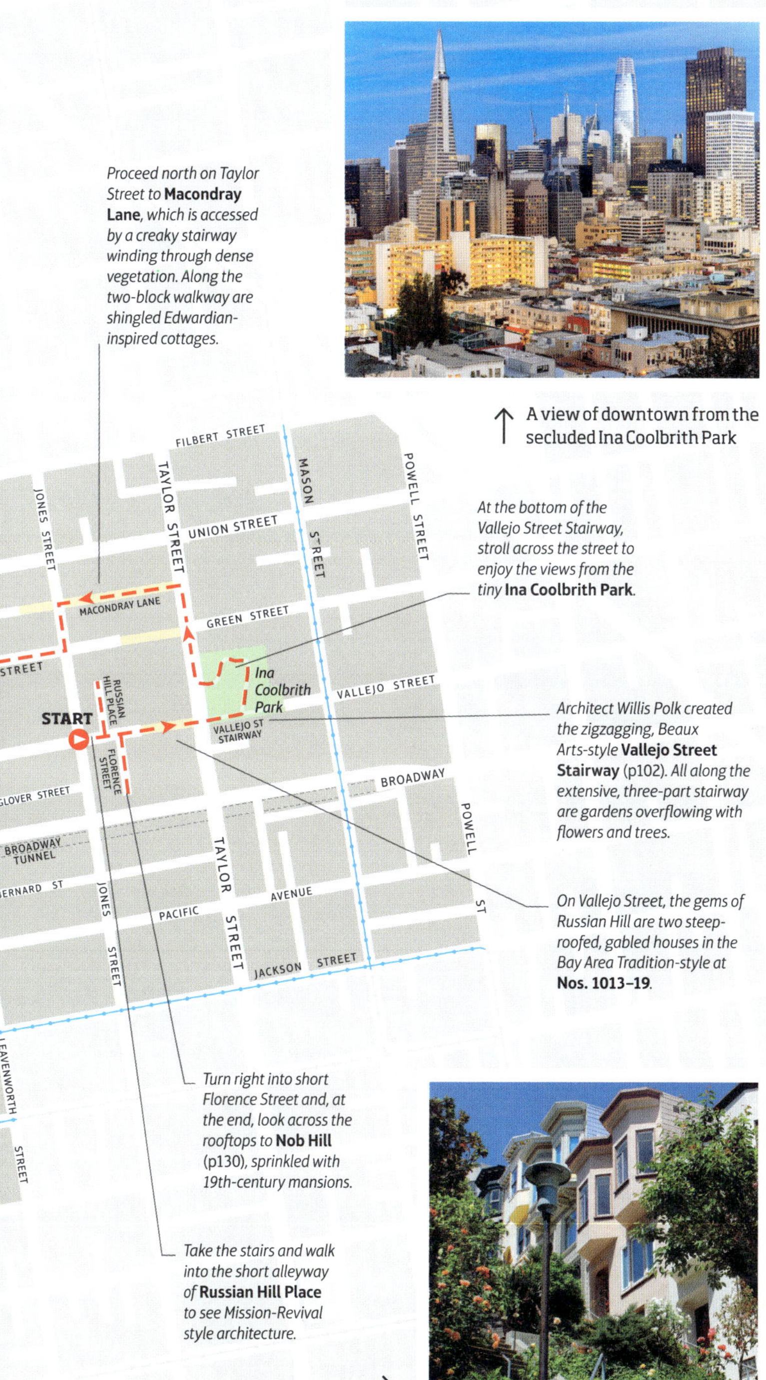

Proceed north on Taylor Street to **Macondray Lane***, which is accessed by a creaky stairway winding through dense vegetation. Along the two-block walkway are shingled Edwardian-inspired cottages.*

↑ A view of downtown from the secluded Ina Coolbrith Park

At the bottom of the Vallejo Street Stairway, stroll across the street to enjoy the views from the tiny **Ina Coolbrith Park***.*

Architect Willis Polk created the zigzagging, Beaux Arts-style **Vallejo Street Stairway** (p102)*. All along the extensive, three-part stairway are gardens overflowing with flowers and trees.*

On Vallejo Street, the gems of Russian Hill are two steep-roofed, gabled houses in the Bay Area Tradition-style at **Nos. 1013–19***.*

Turn right into short Florence Street and, at the end, look across the rooftops to **Nob Hill** (p130)*, sprinkled with 19th-century mansions.*

Take the stairs and walk into the short alleyway of **Russian Hill Place** *to see Mission-Revival style architecture.*

→ Vallejo Street Stairway leading to a row of pastel-colored houses

Far East
CHASE

Chinese-inspired architecture and street decor on Grant Avenue

CHINATOWN AND NOB HILL

Chinese immigrants who were keen to benefit from the Gold Rush and the transcontinental railroad settled on Stockton Street in the 1850s, rapidly creating one of the largest Chinese communities in the world outside Asia. San Francisco is still known in China as *Jiùjīnshān* (Old Gold Mountain). Nevertheless, times were often hard in the late 19th century; the city became the epicenter of anti-Chinese racism, with the two-day riot of 1877 destroying swaths of Chinatown. Although the Chinese Exclusion Act of 1882 effectively ended Chinese immigration to the US, Chinatown survived and prospered in the 20th century. Today, its stores and markets recreate the atmosphere of a typical southern Chinese town (albeit with distinctly American variations on a Cantonese theme), attracting visitors and locals alike.

Looming above Chinatown, Nob Hill is San Francisco's most celebrated hilltop, famous for its cable cars, plush hotels, and breathtaking views. "Nobs" was a name for the entrepreneurs who amassed huge fortunes during the development of the American West. In the late 19th century, the cable cars made Nob Hill more accessible to Gold Rush millionaires, and later the "Big Four" – Central Pacific Railroad barons Leland Stanford, Collis P. Huntington, Mark Hopkins, and Charles Crocker – built their mansions here. The earthquake and fire of 1906 leveled all but one of these houses, but the area's contemporary hotels still recall the opulence of Victorian times.

CHINATOWN AND NOB HILL

Must Sees

1. Cable Car Museum
2. Grace Cathedral

Experience More

3. Chinatown Gateway
4. Old St. Mary's Cathedral
5. Tin How Temple
6. Grant Avenue and Stockton Street
7. Golden Gate Fortune Cookie Factory
8. Portsmouth Square
9. Chinese Historical Society of America
10. Pacific Heritage Museum
11. InterContinental Mark Hopkins Hotel
12. Fairmont Hotel
13. The Pacific-Union Club

Eat

① China Live
② Mister Jiu's
③ Far East Café
④ Mee Mee Bakery

Shop

⑤ Chinatown Kite Shop

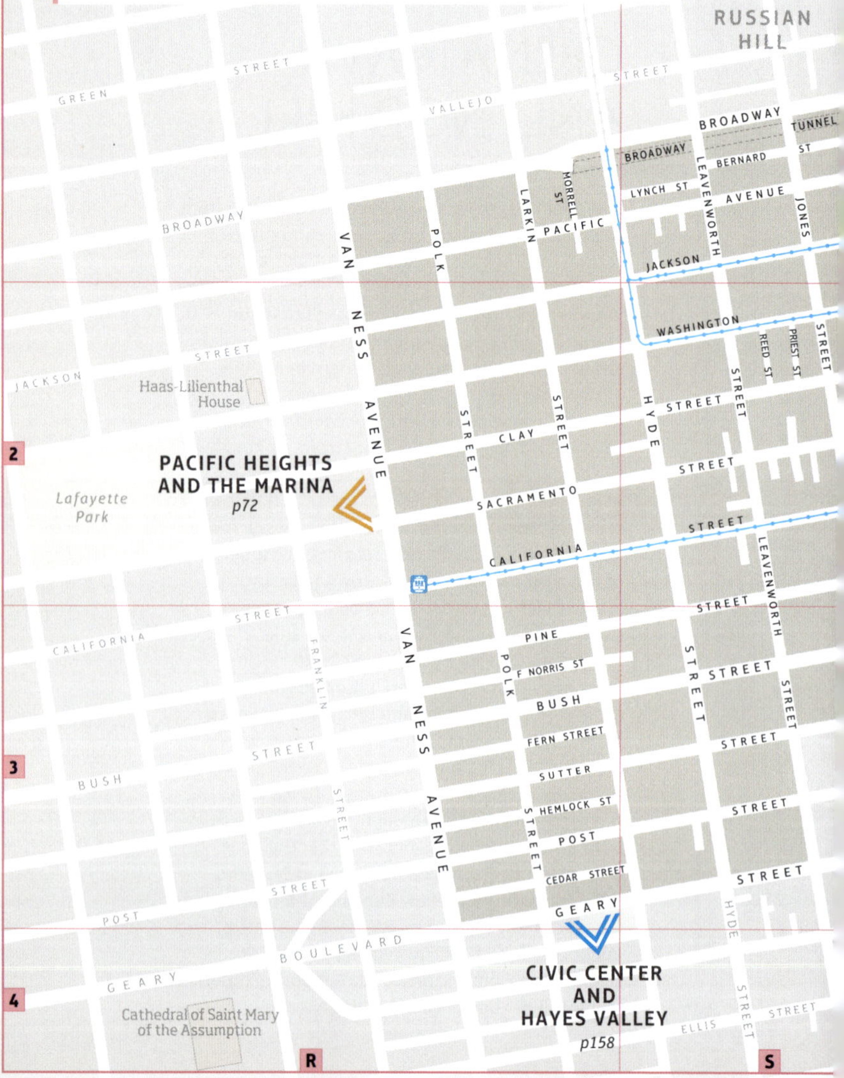

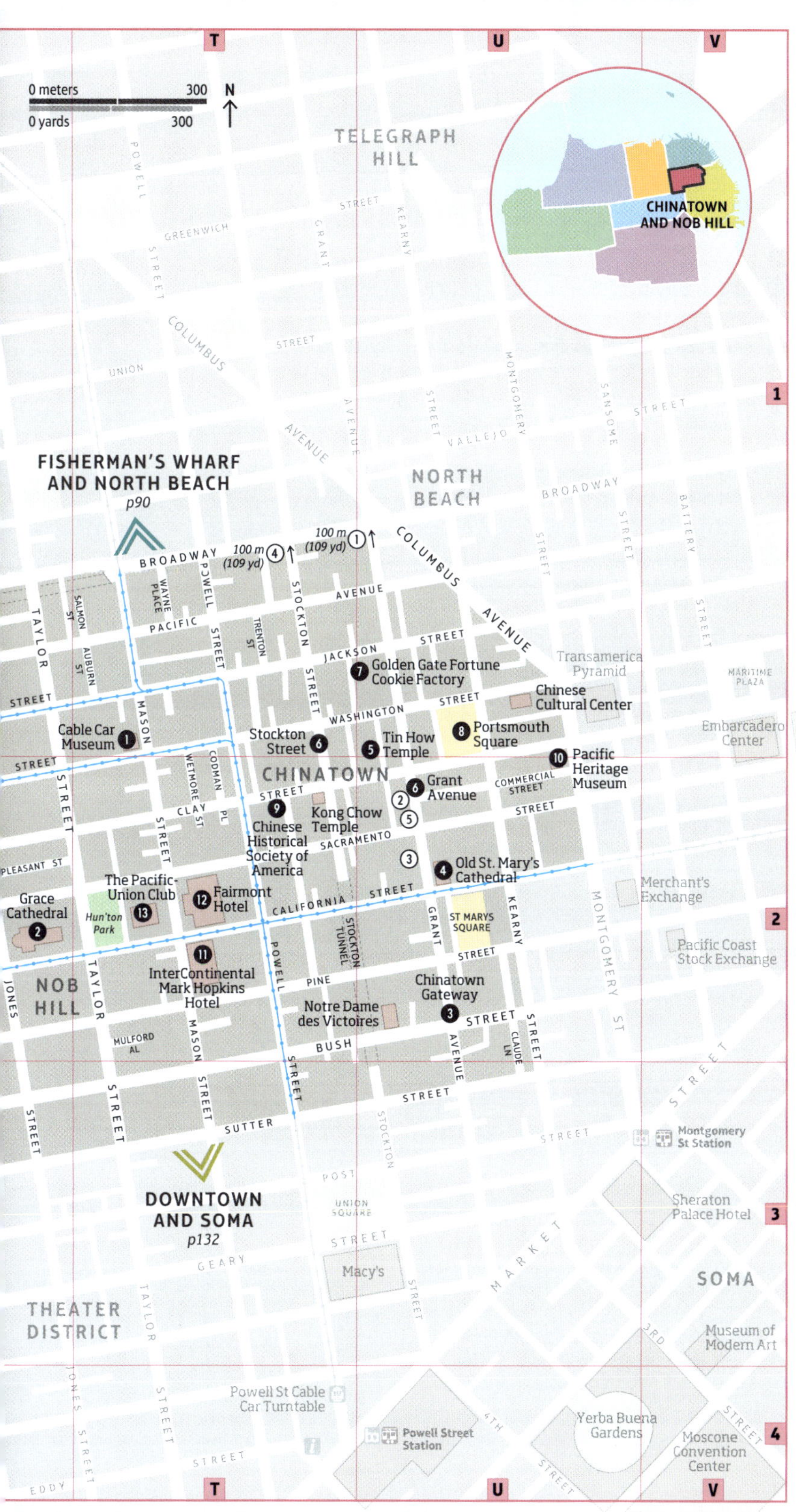

0 meters 300
0 yards 300
N
TELEGRAPH HILL
CHINATOWN AND NOB HILL
FISHERMAN'S WHARF AND NORTH BEACH
p90
NORTH BEACH
100 m (109 yd)
100 m (109 yd)
Transamerica Pyramid
Golden Gate Fortune Cookie Factory
Chinese Cultural Center
Cable Car Museum
Stockton Street
Tin How Temple
Portsmouth Square
Embarcadero Center
Pacific Heritage Museum
CHINATOWN
Grant Avenue
Kong Chow Temple
Chinese Historical Society of America
Old St. Mary's Cathedral
Merchant's Exchange
Grace Cathedral
The Pacific-Union Club
Fairmont Hotel
Hun'ton Park
ST MARYS SQUARE
Pacific Coast Stock Exchange
InterContinental Mark Hopkins Hotel
NOB HILL
Chinatown Gateway
Notre Dame des Victoires
Montgomery St Station
DOWNTOWN AND SOMA
p132
Sheraton Palace Hotel
Macy's
SOMA
THEATER DISTRICT
Museum of Modern Art
Powell St Cable Car Turntable
Powell Street Station
Yerba Buena Gardens
Moscone Convention Center
MARITIME PLAZA
UNION SQUARE

1

CABLE CAR MUSEUM

T3 1201 Mason St 1, 10, 12 Powell-Mason, Powell-Hyde 10am-4pm Tue-Thu (Fri-Sun: to 5pm) cablecarmuseum.org

Get up close to the inner workings of the city's famous cable-car system. Here you're right in the middle of the action, feeling the vibrations and hearing the whirring mechanics of public transportation at work.

This is both a museum and the powerhouse of today's cable-car system *(p120)*. Anchored to the ground floor are the engines and wheels that wind the cables through the system of channels and pulleys beneath the streets. Observe them from the mezzanine, then descend to below street level in order to view the large underground chamber where the haulage cables are routed out to the street. The museum houses an early cable car and examples of the mechanisms that control the individual cars. The system is the last of its kind in the world, so after you're done getting a close-up look in the car barn don't miss a chance to hop on either the Powell-Mason or Powell-Hyde line right outside and experience a journey on one of these historic cars.

→ An old cable car stoplight on display at the museum

Timeline of events

1869

▲ Inventor Andrew Hallidie's desire to put a stop to the use of horse-drawn trams allegedly inspired the cable-car system.

1873

▲ Construction begins on San Francisco's first cable-car line in May, with regular service starting in September.

1906

▲ The San Francisco earthquake destroys most of the system's cars and lines, and electric streetcars replace most of the old cable-car lines when the city is rebuilt.

1947

▲ The mayor attempts to have the remaining lines closed, but a committee led by Friedel Klussmann succeeds in preserving the city's cable-car system.

↑ The Cable Car Museum, also home to the city's cable-car system

REBUILDING THE CABLE CARS

San Francisco's cable-car system was introduced in 1873, and remained in use even with the advent of more modern public transportation over the years. Despite regular maintenance, the aging system began to deteriorate to the point where drastic measures had to be taken, but as a beloved and iconic feature of the city there was no chance of simply closing the lines. Instead the city initiated the Cable Car System Rehabilitation Program, an immense and thorough upgrade that involved closing the whole cable-car system from 1982–4. The work involved replacing old tracks across 69 city blocks, tidying up the cars, and carrying out important upgrades at 1201 Mason St – both on the structure of the car barn as well as the mechanisms of the powerhouse. In June 1984 the system reopened and San Franciscans celebrated its return with four days of festivites.

SAN FRANCISCO'S CABLE CARS

In their heyday, cable cars ran on 23 lines throughout the city. While San Franciscans mostly use other public transport on their commute these days, the cable cars are still a beloved and iconic feature of the city.

The cable-car system was launched in 1873, with its inventor Andrew Hallidie riding in the first car. He was purportedly inspired to tackle the problem of transporting people up the city's steep slopes after seeing a horrible accident: a horse-drawn tram slipped down a hill, dragging the horses with it. His system was a great success, and by 1889 cars were running on eight lines. With the advent of the internal combustion engine, cable cars became almost obsolete, and in 1947 attempts were made to replace them with buses. However, after a public outcry – led by Friedel Klussmann's "Citizens' Committee to Save the Cable Cars" – the present three lines, using 17 miles (25 km) of track, were retained.

↑ Two of the 12 California Street cable cars passing by on the streets of San Francisco

Did You Know?

A cable-car bell-ringing contest is held in Union Square every July.

→ Cross-section illustration of a Powell Street car and cable-car tracks

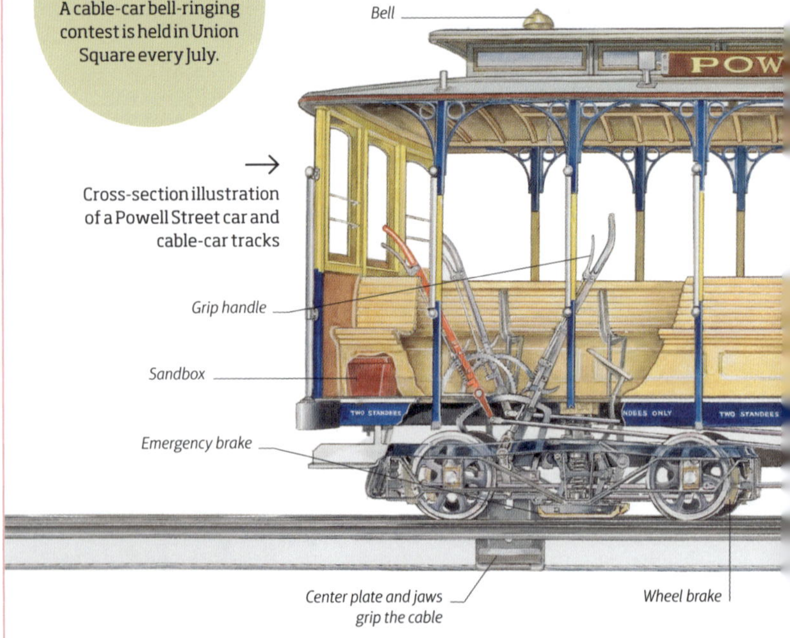

Bell

POW

Grip handle

Sandbox

Emergency brake

Center plate and jaws grip the cable

Wheel brake

HOW CABLE CARS WORK

Engines in the central powerhouse wind a looped cable under the city streets, guided by a system of grooved pulleys. When the gripman in the cable car applies the grip handle, the grip reaches through a slot in the street and grabs the cable. This pulls the car along at a steady speed of 9.5 mph (15.5 km/h). To stop, the gripman releases the grip and applies the brake. Great skill is needed at corners where the cable passes over a pulley. The gripman must release the grip to allow the car to coast over the pulley.

PRESERVING HISTORY

Maintenance and renovations on the cable cars are done with attention to historical detail, because they are designated historic monuments. A cable car celebration was held in 1984 after a two-year renovation of the system. Each car was restored, and all lines were replaced with reinforced tracks. The system should now work safely for 100 years.

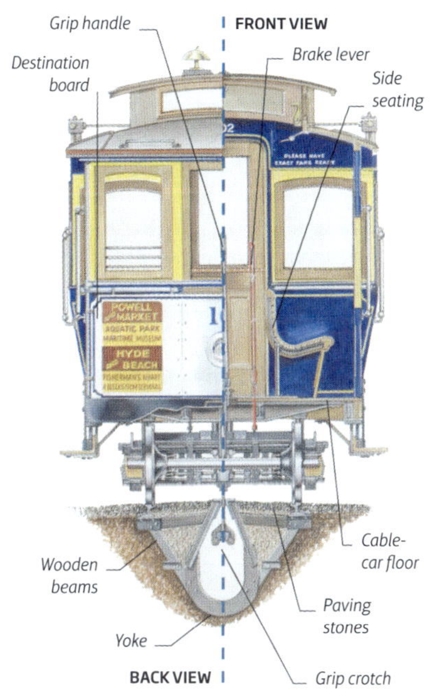

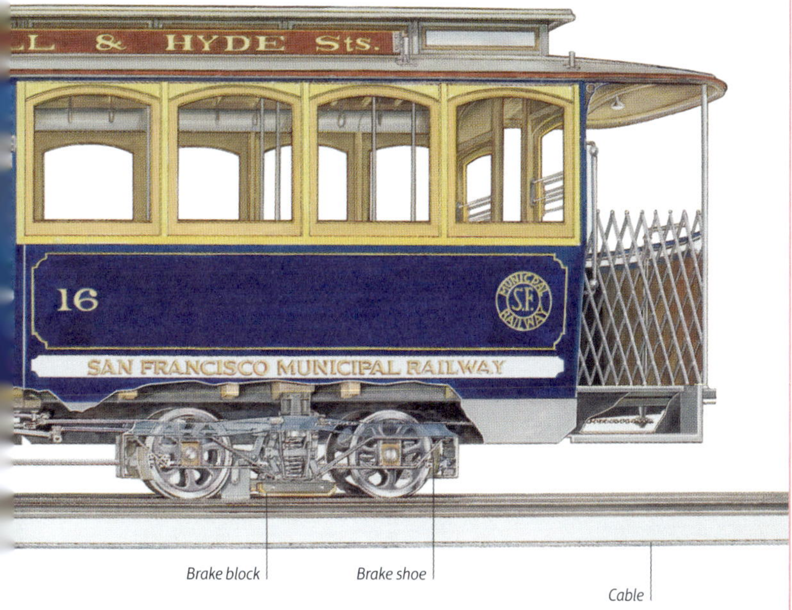

L & HYDE Sts.
16
SAN FRANCISCO MUNICIPAL RAILWAY
Brake block
Brake shoe
Cable

2

GRACE CATHEDRAL

S2 1100 California St 1 California St 10am-5pm Mon-Sat, 1-5pm Sun gracecathedral.org

Located on Nob Hill, the soaring Neo-Gothic Grace Cathedral has many stunning works of medieval-style art. The cathedral is committed to social justice and has a lively, all-inclusive program of services and events.

Designed by architect Lewis P. Hobart, Grace Cathedral is the third largest Episcopal Cathedral in the United States. Construction started in 1928, but it did not near completion until 1964; the interior vaulting remains unfinished. The cavernous building is inspired by the Notre Dame in Paris.

The cathedral's entrance doors are cast from Lorenzo Ghiberti's "Doors of Paradise." Made in the 15th century for the Baptistry in Florence, Ghiberti's creation was considered an early Italian Renaissance masterpiece. The cathedral has a rich collection of stained glass. The 34 leaded medieval-style windows were designed by Charles Connick, using the blue glass of Chartres as his inspiration. The rose window, designed by Lewis P. Hobart, is made of 1-inch- (2.5-cm-) thick faceted glass, which is illuminated from inside the building at night. Other windows were made by Marguerite Gaudin, Henry Willett, and Gabriel Loire. These include the Human Endeavour series, which depicts more than 1,000 figures in science, including Albert Einstein and astronaut John Glenn.

Historical artifacts held within the cathedral include a 13th-century Catalonian crucifix and a 16th-century Brussels tapestry. The AIDS Interfaith Memorial Chapel holds a gold-leaf three-part altarpiece by pop artist Keith Haring, his last work before his death in 1990.

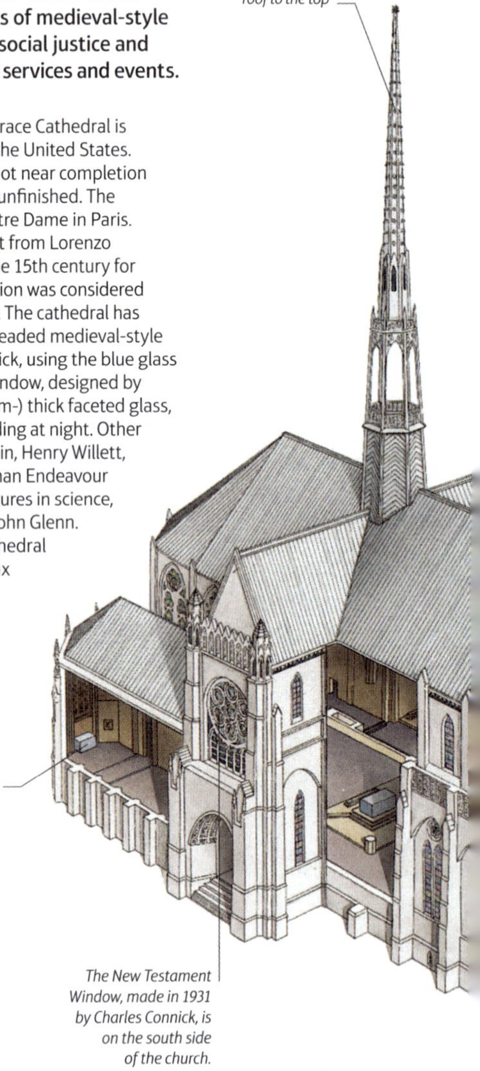

The spire is 117 ft (35 m) tall from the roof to the top

The Chapel of Grace, funded by the Crocker family, has a 15th-century French altarpiece.

The New Testament Window, made in 1931 by Charles Connick, is on the south side of the church.

↑ The elegant Grace Cathedral, built in the 20th century

Did You Know?

Grace Cathedral may look like it's built of stone, but it is, in fact, made of concrete.

1 The facade has replicas of Ghiberti's Baptistry bronze doors in Florence.

2 A medieval-style labyrinth decorates the floor inside the church.

3 *The Life of Christ* bronze-and-white-gold altarpiece by Keith Haring is one of the artist's few religious pieces.

INSIDER TIP
Events

Look up the varied events on the cathedral's website. These include spectacular choral Evensongs and gospel, classical, and jazz concerts. There are also regular candlelit meditation services and yoga classes. Every year there are exhibits or performances from the artist in residence, which range from art installations to spoken word to dance.

EXPERIENCE MORE

Chinatown Gateway

U2 Grant Ave at Bush St 8, 30, 45

Opened in 1970 and designed by Chinese American architect Clayton Lee, this portal spans the entrance to Chinatown's tourist street, Grant Avenue. Inspired by the ceremonial entrances of traditional Chinese villages, the three-arched gateway is capped with green roof tiles and a host of propitiatory animals – including two dragons and two carp chasing a large, round pearl – all of glazed ceramic. Village gateways are often commissioned by wealthy clans to enhance their status, and the names of these benefactors are inscribed on the gates. This structure was erected by the Chinatown Cultural Development Committee, and features depictions of 78 dragons and 58 mythical characters that pay homage to Chinese culture.

It is guarded by two stone lions that are suckling their cubs through their claws, in accordance with ancient lore. Once through the gate, you find yourself among some of the most elegant stores in Chinatown. Here you can buy antiques, silks, and gems, although sometimes at high prices.

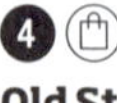

Old St. Mary's Cathedral

U2 660 California St 1, 15, 30 California St, Powell-Hyde, Powell-Mason 10am-4:30pm Tue-Fri, 11:30am-6pm Sat, 8:30am-noon Sun (summer: Hours vary, check website) oldsaintmarys.org

San Francisco's first Catholic cathedral, Old St. Mary's served a largely Irish-American congregation from 1854 to 1891, when a new St. Mary's Church was built on Van Ness Avenue. Owing to the shortage of suitable building materials in California, the bricks for the old church were imported from the East Coast, while the granite foundation stones came from China. The clock tower bears the inscription, "Son, observe the time and fly from evil," said to have been directed at the brothels that stood across the street. Twice damaged by fire, the church has its original foundations and walls.

Chinese street lamps and lanterns in San Francisco's Chinatown

Tin How Temple

U1 Top floor, 125 Waverly Pl 986-2520 1, 8, 8AX, 8BX, 30, 45 California St, Powell-Hyde, Powell-Mason 10am-3pm daily

This unique temple, the longest-operating Chinese temple in the United States, is dedicated to Tin How (Tien Hau), Queen of Heaven and protector of seafarers and visitors. Originally founded by the Cantonese Clan Association in 1852, it is situated at the top of three steep, wooden flights of stairs. The temple's narrow space is smoky with incense and burned paper offerings, and hung with hundreds of gold and red lanterns. Entry is free, though a donation is expected.

Grant Avenue and Stockton Street

U2 & T1 10, 12, 30, 45 California St sanfranciscochinatown.com

Grant Avenue, the main artery that runs through Chinatown, is

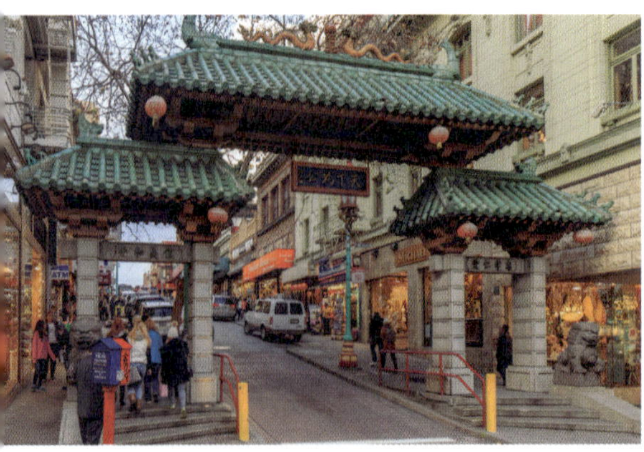

Chinatown Gateway at the entrance to Chinatown's main street, Grant Avenue

historically important for being the first street of Yerba Buena, the village that preceded San Francisco. An estimated 25,000 Chinese people settled in this area during the Gold Rush era.

Today, Grant Avenue is lined with a huge array of stores and is Chinatown's busiest street. Distinctive red lantern lights, installed in the 1930s, overhang the area. In between Grant Avenue and the parallel-running Stockton Street, are some of the most characterful streets in Chinatown – the Chinatown Alleys – containing many old buildings, temples, and traditional stores, such as Chinese herbalists. Throughout the alleys, small restaurants, both above and below street level, serve inexpensive, delicious, home-cooked food.

Golden Gate Fortune Cookie Factory

T/U1 56 Ross Alley 1, 8, 8AX, 8BX, 30, 45 California St, Powell-Hyde, Powell-Mason 9am-6:30pm daily (to 7pm Sat & Sun) goldengatefortunecookies.com

The Golden Gate Fortune Cookie Factory has been in business since 1962. The cookie-making machine nearly fills the tiny bakery, where dough is poured onto griddles and baked on a conveyor belt. An attendant inserts the "fortunes" (slips of paper bearing mostly positive predictions) before the cookies are folded.

Ironically, despite its association with Chinese culture, the fortune cookie is unknown in China. It was invented in 1909 in San Francisco's Japanese Tea Garden *(p198)*, by then chief gardener, Makota Hagiwara.

Portsmouth Square

U1 1, 8, 8AX, 8BX, 30, 45

San Francisco's original town square was laid out in 1839. Also known as the Portsmouth Plaza, it was once the social center for the small village of Yerba Buena. On July 9, 1846, less than a month after rebels declared California's independence from Mexico, a party of marines rowed ashore. They raised the American flag above the square, seizing the port as part of the United States. For a while the square was the hub of a dynamic city, but in the 1860s the business district shifted southeast and the plaza declined in civic importance.

Portsmouth Square today is very much the social center of Chinatown. In the morning, people practice *tai chi*, and others gather to play checkers and cards throughout the day.

EAT

China Live

Wash down beef noodle soup, pork dumplings, and Peking-style duck with cocktails made with ingredients such as lemongrass syrup and yuzu lemonade.

T/U1
644 Broadway
chinalivesf.com

$$$

Mister Jiu's

This inventive restaurant in a historic building serves thoughtfully sourced and beautifully presented food, including crunchy pork buns and seafood *cheong fun* (flat rice noodle rolls).

U2 28 Waverly Pl
Sun, Mon
misterjius.com

$$

Far East Café

The mostly Cantonese and American-Chinese menu at this restaurant has changed little since the 1920s; the egg *foo young* (omelet) is a favorite.

U2 631 Grant Ave
far-east-cafe.com

$$

Mee Mee Bakery

Open since 1950, Mee Mee is best known for mooncakes, and traditional pies stuffed with honey dew and red beans. Locals also queue for almond cookies and salty-sweet "cow ears."

T1 1328 Stockton St
meemeebakery.com

↑ An exhibition at the Chinese Historical Society of America

Chinese Historical Society of America

T2 965 Clay St 391-1188 Powell-Mason 1, 8, 8X, 8BX, 30, 45 11am-4pm Wed-Sun chsa.org

Founded in 1963, this is the oldest organization in the country dedicated to the interpretation, promotion, and preservation of the history and contributions of Chinese Americans. One of the exhibits is a multimedia display chronicling the complex history of the Chinese American experience. Look out for replicas of barracks and an interrogation room, at Angel Island, where the Chinese Exclusion Act of 1882 was enforced, controlling Chinese immigration into the United States.

The Chinese contribution to California's development was extensive. Chinese workers helped build the western half of the first transcontinental railroad and constructed dikes throughout the Sacramento River delta. The society sponsors oral history projects, an "In Search of Roots" program, and a monthly speakers' forum.

Pacific Heritage Museum

U1/2 608 Commercial St 399-1124 1, 8, 8AX, 8BX, 30X, 41 10am-4pm Tue-Sat

As elegant as the frequently changing collections of Asian arts displayed within, this is actually a synthesis of two distinct buildings. The US Sub-Treasury was built here in 1875–7 by William Appleton Potter, on the site of San Francisco's original mint. You can look into the old coin vaults through a cutaway section on the ground floor, or descend in the elevator for closer inspection. In 1984, architects Skidmore, Owings & Merrill designed the 17-story headquarters of the Bank of Canton (now East West Bank) above the existing building, incorporating the original street-level facade and basement.

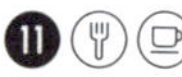

InterContinental Mark Hopkins Hotel

T2 999 California St 1 California St, Powell-Mason, Powell-Hyde ihg.com

At the behest of his wife Mary, Mark Hopkins, one of the founders of the Central Pacific Railroad, arranged for a fantastic wooden mansion, surpassing every other for ostentatious ornamentation, to be built on Nob Hill. When Mrs. Hopkins died, the house became home to the fledgling San Francisco Art Institute. It

SHOP

Chinatown Kite Shop
This store offers a little bit of everything, from Chinese clothing to homeware, but the real stars are the fantastic kites that hang like colorful decorations from the ceiling.

U2 717 Grant Ave chinatownkite.com

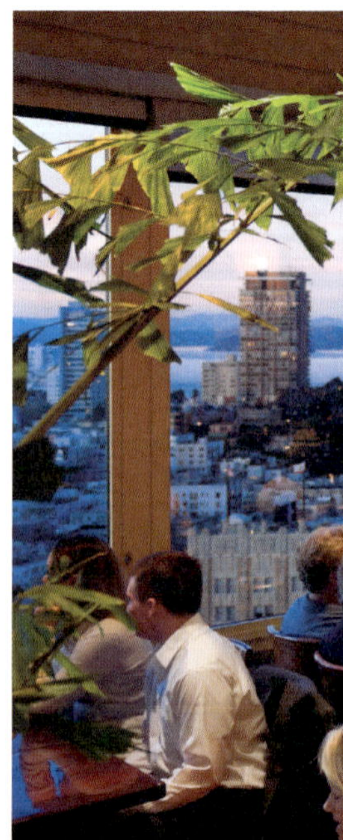

→ Top of the Mark rooftop bar, a perfect place to sip a cocktail and watch the sun set

burned in the fire after the earthquake of 1906, and only the granite retaining walls remain. The present 25-story tower, capped by a flag visible from all over the city, was built in 1925 by architects Weeks and Day. Top of the Mark, the glass-walled cocktail bar on the 19th floor, is one of San Francisco's most celebrated drinking establishments, enjoying spectacular panoramic views of the city. World War II servicemen customarily drank a farewell toast to the city here before leaving for overseas.

Fairmont Hotel

T2 950 Mason St 1 California St, Powell-Mason, Powell-Hyde fairmont.com/san-francisco

Commissioned by Tessie Fair Oelrichs (1871-1926), an American socialite and wife of steamship magnate Heinrich Oelrichs, this Beaux Arts building was completed on the eve of the 1906 major earthquake, and stood for two days before it was burned down. Rebuilt by architect Julia Morgan within the original white terracotta facade, it opened for business one year later. After World War II it was the scene of meetings that led to the founding of the United Nations. For some stunning views, ride the elevator to the city's highest observation point, the Fairmont Crown; or, enjoy a cocktail at the hotel's famed Tonga Room and Hurricane Bar, which serves Polynesian fusion cuisine and is well known for its extravagant tropical decor.

THE NOBS OF NOB HILL

"Nob" was one of the kinder names reserved for the unscrupulous entrepreneurs who amassed huge fortunes during the development of the American West. Many of the "nobs" who lived on Nob Hill acquired other nicknames that hint at the wild stories behind their vast wealth. "Bonanza King" James Flood formed a partnership with three Irish Americans and, in 1872, the four men bought controlling interests in some dwindling Comstock mines, sinking new shafts and striking a "bonanza" - a rich pocket of high-grade silver ore. Flood returned to San Francisco as a millionaire and bought a parcel of land on the summit of Nob Hill.

The Pacific-Union Club

T2 1000 California St 775-1234 1 California St, Powell-Mason, Powell-Hyde To the public

In 1885, Augustus Laver built this townhouse for one of the Nobs of Nob Hill – the "Bonanza King" James Flood. Its brown sandstone facade survived the 1906 fire, though the other mansions, built of wood, were destroyed. The gutted building was bought by the Pacific-Union Club, an exclusive gentlemen's club.

A SHORT WALK
CHINATOWN

Distance 1 mile (1.5 km) **Time** 20 minutes
Nearest buses 8, 30, 45, 91

Grant Avenue is the tourist Chinatown of dragon lampposts, upturned rooflines, and stores packed to the rafters with everything from kites to cooking utensils. Meanwhile, Stockton Street is where locals shop for fresh fish and other produce that spills over in boxes onto the sidewalk. The alleys in between have traditional temples, stores, and family-run restaurants.

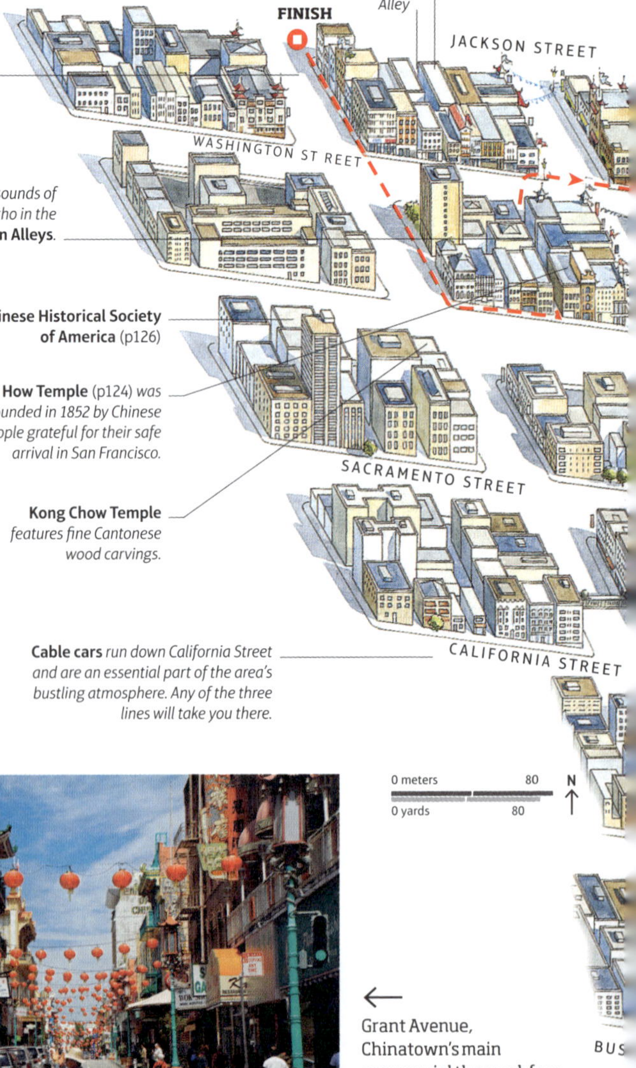

Watch cookies being made at **Golden Gate Fortune Cookie Factory** (p125).

Ross Alley

FINISH

JACKSON STREET

To bus nos. 8, 30, 45, 91

WASHINGTON STREET

The sights and sounds of the Far East echo in the busy **Chinatown Alleys**.

Chinese Historical Society of America (p126)

Tin How Temple (p124) *was founded in 1852 by Chinese people grateful for their safe arrival in San Francisco.*

SACRAMENTO STREET

Kong Chow Temple *features fine Cantonese wood carvings.*

Cable cars *run down California Street and are an essential part of the area's bustling atmosphere. Any of the three lines will take you there.*

CALIFORNIA STREET

0 meters 80
0 yards 80
N

BUS

Grant Avenue, Chinatown's main commercial thoroughfare

The elegant interior of Old St. Mary's Cathedral

Locator Map
For more detail see p116

Did You Know?

San Francisco's Chinatown is the oldest one in North America.

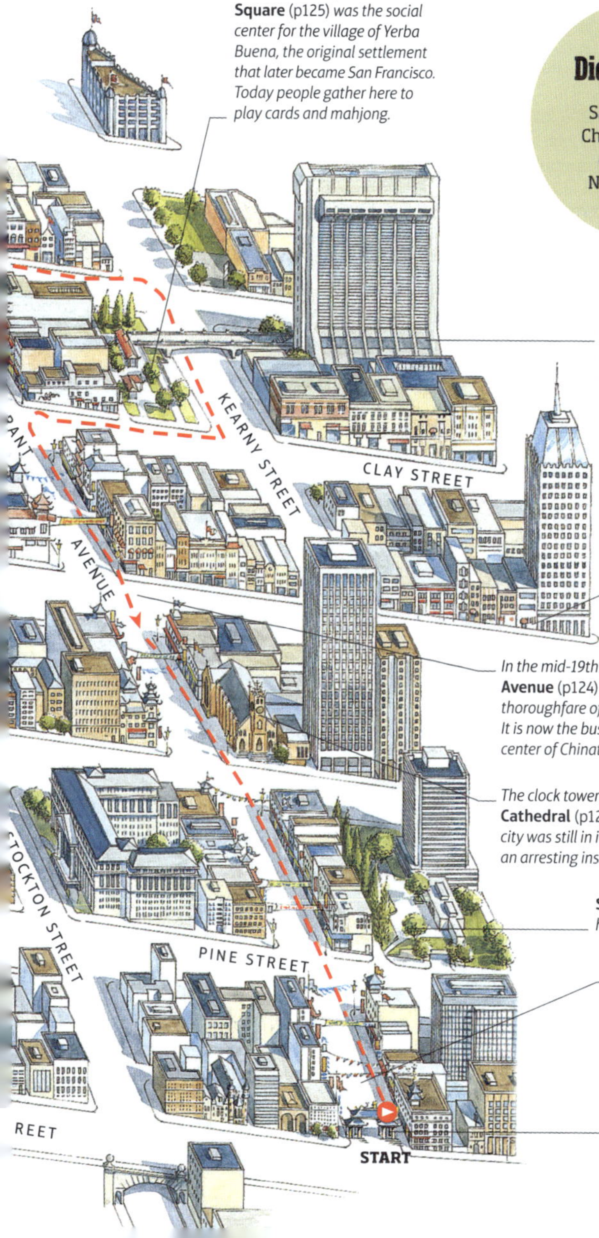

Laid out in 1839, **Portsmouth Square** (p125) *was the social center for the village of Yerba Buena, the original settlement that later became San Francisco. Today people gather here to play cards and mahjong.*

The Chinese Cultural Center *contains an art gallery and a small crafts store. It sponsors a lively series of lectures and seminars.*

Housed in an elegant building, the small **Pacific Heritage Museum** (p126) *has fine exhibitions of Asian art.*

In the mid-19th century, **Grant Avenue** (p124) *was the main thoroughfare of Yerba Buena. It is now the busy commercial center of Chinatown.*

The clock tower of **Old St. Mary's Cathedral** (p124), *built while the city was still in its infancy, bears an arresting inscription.*

St. Mary's Square *is a quiet haven in which to take a rest.*

To bus nos. 8, 30, 45, 91

Also known as the "Dragons' Gate," **Chinatown Gateway** (p124) *marks Chinatown's southern entrance.*

A SHORT WALK NOB HILL

Distance half a mile (1 km) **Time** 15 minutes
Nearest buses 1, 27

Nob Hill is the highest summit of the city center, rising 338 ft (103 m) above the bay, and affording splendid views of the city. Its steep slopes were treacherous for carriages and kept wealthier citizens away until the opening of the California Street cable car line in 1878. After that, the wealthy "nobs" soon built new homes on the peak of the hill. Though many of the grandiose mansions were burned down in the great fire of 1906 *(p53)*, Nob Hill still attracts the affluent to its many splendid hotels. A stroll through this well-heeled neighborhood will lead you past some of the most expensive real estate in the US.

The Pacific-Union Club (p127), *now an exclusive men's club, was once the mansion of Comstock millionaire James Flood.*

Huntington Park *is on the site of Collis P. Huntington's mansion.*

SACRAMENTO STREET

Grace Cathedral (p122) *is a replica of Notre Dame in Paris.*

TAYLOR STREET

START

JONES STREET

The Nob Hill Masonic Auditorium *honors Freemasons who died in American wars.*

Huntington Hotel *with its Big Four Bar and Restaurant exudes the opulent and urbane atmosphere of the Victorian era on Nob Hill.*

← The interior of Grace Cathedral with beautiful stained-glass windows

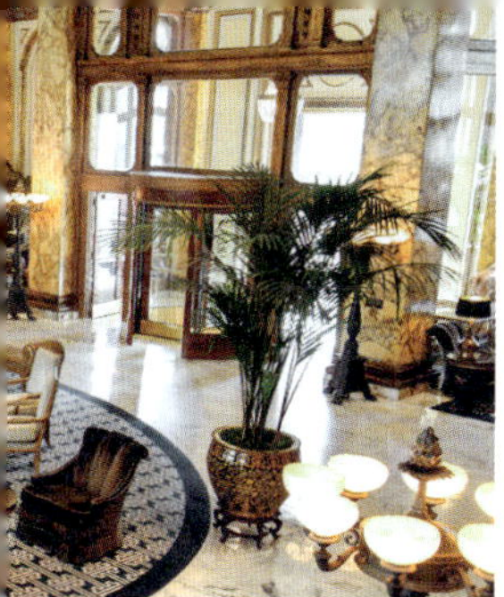

The lobby of the Fairmont Hotel, one of the grandest hotels on Nob Hill

CHINATOWN AND NOB HILL
Nob Hill

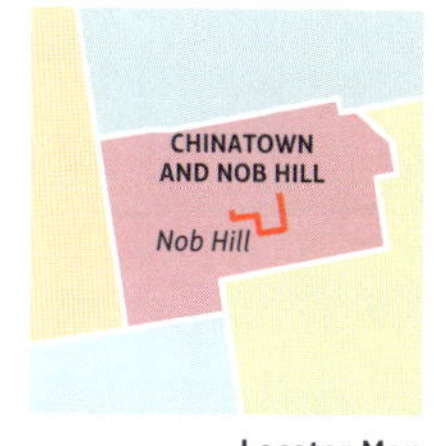

Locator Map
For more detail see p116

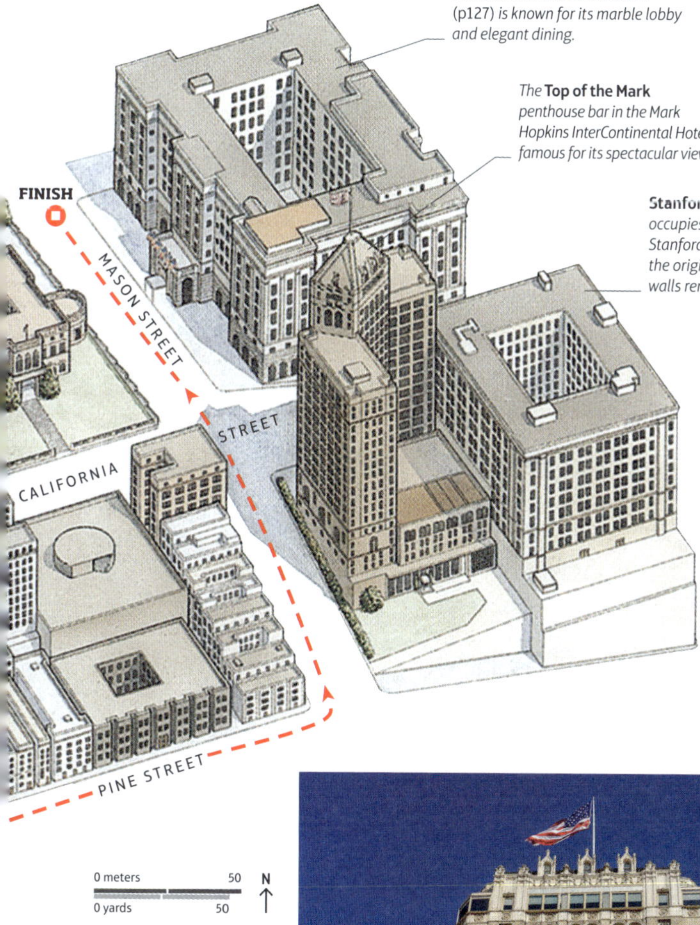

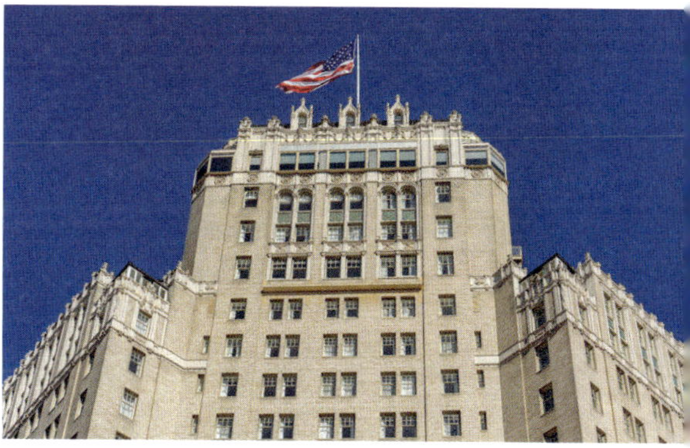

FINISH
MASON STREET
CALIFORNIA STREET
PINE STREET
0 meters 50
0 yards 50
N

The luxurious **Fairmont Hotel** (p127) *is known for its marble lobby and elegant dining.*

The **Top of the Mark** *penthouse bar in the Mark Hopkins InterContinental Hotel is famous for its spectacular views.*

Stanford Court Hotel *occupies the site of Stanford's mansion; the original boundary walls remain.*

The grand exterior of the 1920s Mark Hopkins InterContinental Hotel

Facade of SFMOMA on 3rd Street

DOWNTOWN AND SOMA

The original inhabitants of the San Francisco area were the Ohlone people. With the arrival of the Spanish in 1776, the effects of aggressive colonization combined with the spread of European diseases decimated the Ohlone within a few generations. The foundations of modern San Francisco were laid in 1835, when former English sailor William Richardson got permission to settle at what was then known as Yerba Buena Cove. The town developed slowly, its inhabitants trading hides and tallow with visiting ships. In 1849, San Francisco's population exploded, thanks to the California Gold Rush, and modern Downtown began to take shape along Montgomery Street, where miners came to weigh their gold dust. By the time the transcontinental railroad was completed in 1869, San Francisco was a rowdy boomtown.

In 1906 a massive earthquake, followed by three days of fire, destroyed three-quarters of the city. Rebuilding began immediately. Today, old-style banking halls from the early 20th century stand in the shadow of glass and steel skyscrapers. Bordering this high-profile hub is SoMa – "South of Market." Once a residential area, the neighborhood is now a contemporary and bustling district of galleries, fine dining, and tech companies.

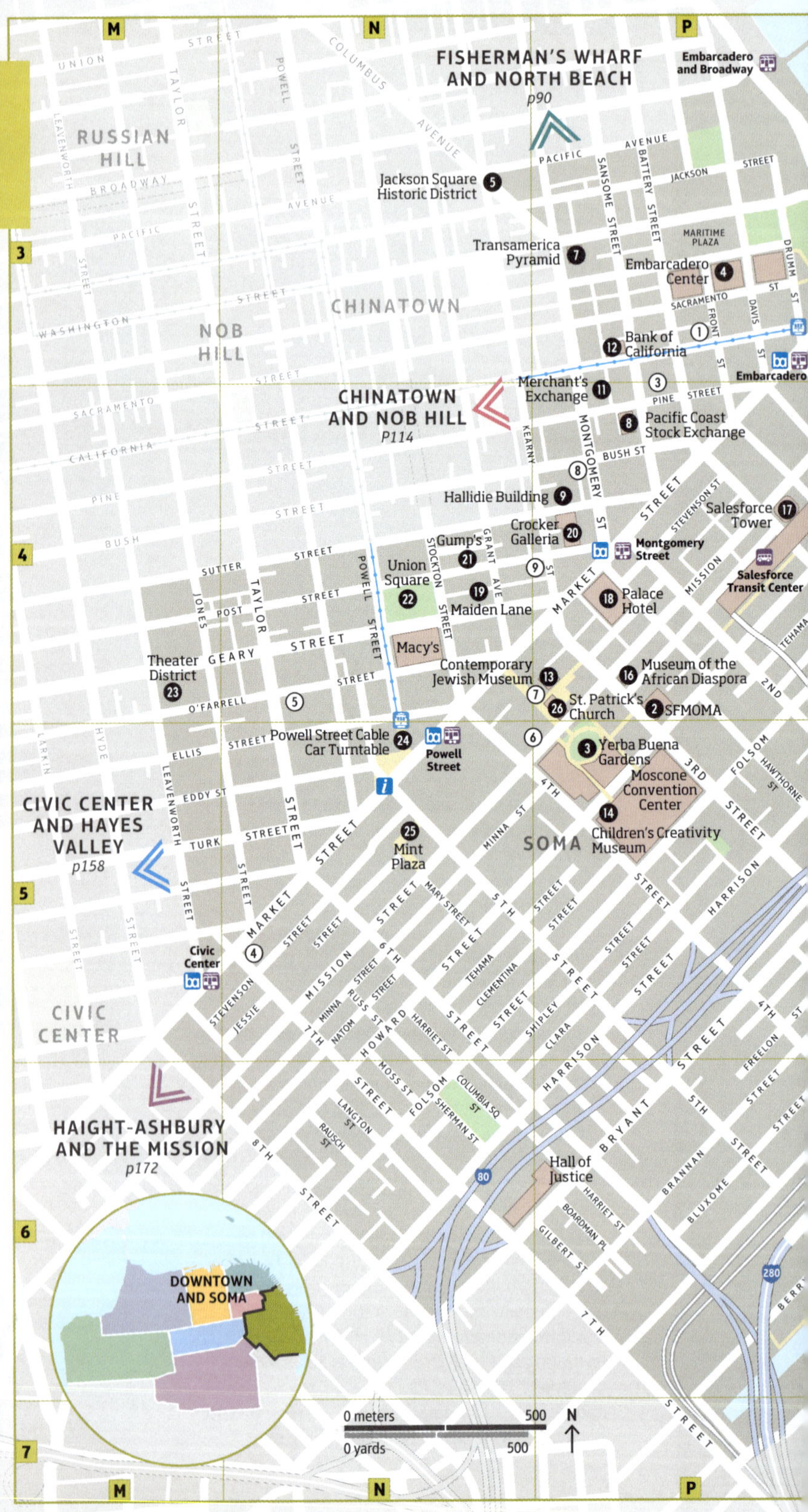

FISHERMAN'S WHARF AND NORTH BEACH
p90
CHINATOWN AND NOB HILL
P114
CIVIC CENTER AND HAYES VALLEY
p158
HAIGHT-ASHBURY AND THE MISSION
p172
DOWNTOWN AND SOMA
RUSSIAN HILL
NOB HILL
CHINATOWN
SOMA
CIVIC CENTER
Embarcadero and Broadway
Jackson Square Historic District 5
Transamerica Pyramid 7
Embarcadero Center 4
Bank of California 12
Embarcadero
Merchant's Exchange 11
Pacific Coast Stock Exchange 8
Hallidie Building 9
Salesforce Tower 17
Crocker Galleria 20
Gump's 21
Montgomery Street
Salesforce Transit Center
Union Square 22
Maiden Lane 19
Palace Hotel 18
Macy's
Theater District 23
Contemporary Jewish Museum 13
Museum of the African Diaspora 16
St. Patrick's Church 26
SFMOMA 2
Powell Street Cable Car Turntable 24
Powell Street
Yerba Buena Gardens 3
Moscone Convention Center
Children's Creativity Museum 14
Mint Plaza 25
Civic Center
Hall of Justice
0 meters 500
0 yards 500
N

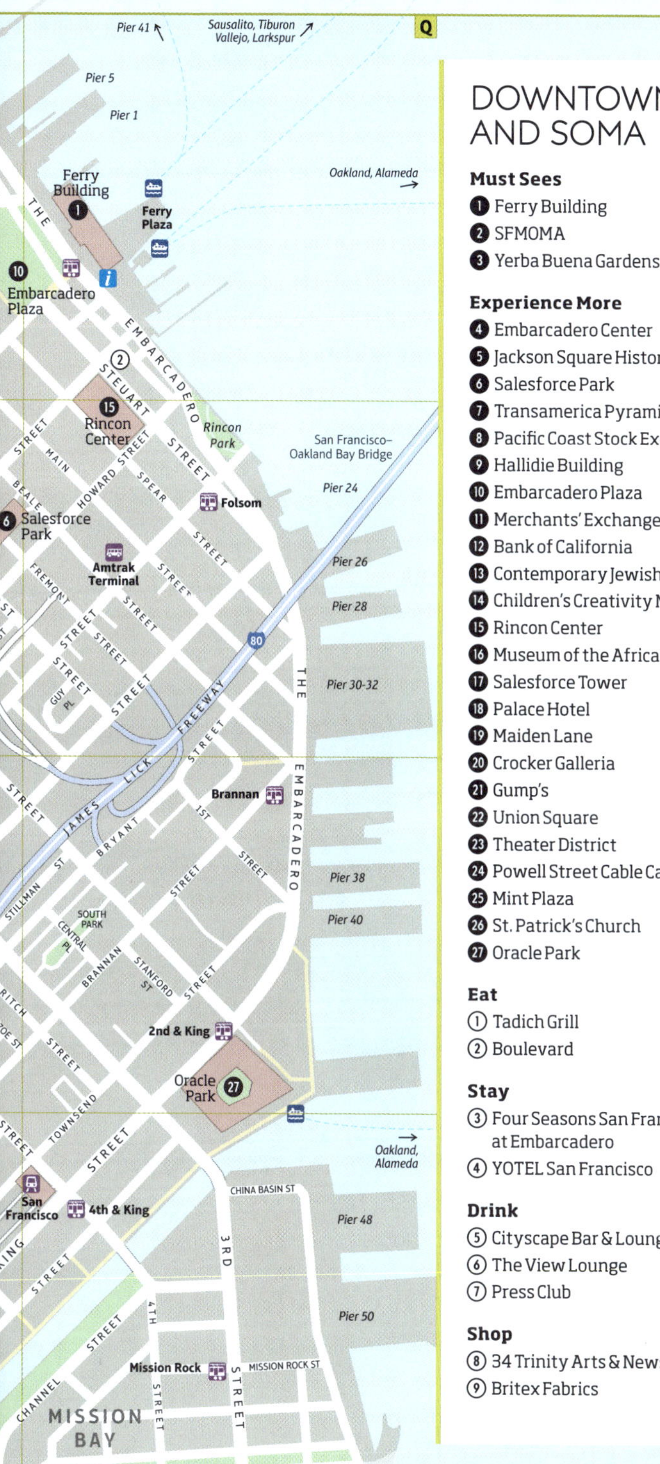

DOWNTOWN AND SOMA

Must Sees

1. Ferry Building
2. SFMOMA
3. Yerba Buena Gardens

Experience More

4. Embarcadero Center
5. Jackson Square Historic District
6. Salesforce Park
7. Transamerica Pyramid
8. Pacific Coast Stock Exchange
9. Hallidie Building
10. Embarcadero Plaza
11. Merchants' Exchange
12. Bank of California
13. Contemporary Jewish Museum
14. Children's Creativity Museum
15. Rincon Center
16. Museum of the African Diaspora
17. Salesforce Tower
18. Palace Hotel
19. Maiden Lane
20. Crocker Galleria
21. Gump's
22. Union Square
23. Theater District
24. Powell Street Cable Car Turntable
25. Mint Plaza
26. St. Patrick's Church
27. Oracle Park

Eat

① Tadich Grill
② Boulevard

Stay

③ Four Seasons San Francisco at Embarcadero
④ YOTEL San Francisco

Drink

⑤ Cityscape Bar & Lounge
⑥ The View Lounge
⑦ Press Club

Shop

⑧ 34 Trinity Arts & News
⑨ Britex Fabrics

1

FERRY BUILDING

Q3 Embarcadero at Market St 2, 6, 21, 31, 82 E, F, J, K, L, M, N California St SF Bay Ferry 7am–8pm daily ferrybuildingmarketplace.com

This historic entry point into the city is now a chic marketplace and food hall. Everything on offer is made with flair and care by local producers devoted to sustainability and traditional production techniques.

Once an important point of entry into the city, the Ferry Bulding is now a marketplace. It houses many gourmet stores, several restaurants and cafés, and hosts a farmers' market on Tuesdays and Saturdays. There's a distinctly northern California feel to the Ferry Building Marketplace in the way it celebrates popular modern principles like using regional produce, traditional farming, and local and artisan producers.

History

The Ferry Building, constructed between 1896 and 1903, survived the great fire of 1906 through the intercession of fireboats pumping water from the bay. The clock tower is 235 ft (71 m) high, and was inspired by the Moorish bell tower of Seville Cathedral. In the early 1930s, more than 50 million passengers a year passed through the building. With the opening of the Bay Bridge in 1936, the Ferry Building ceased to be the city's main point of entry, but even today ferries still cross the bay to Larkspur and Sausalito in Marin County and Alameda and Oakland in the East Bay.

The Ferry Building at night and *(inset)* the farmers' market ↑

← The Ferry Building's clock tower, an iconic feature of the local skyline

Inside the open and inviting Ferry Building Marketplace →

Did You Know?

The arched arcades of the Ferry Building were modeled on the aqueduct in Rome.

EAT

Gott's

Gott's is known for its award-winning classics, including cheeseburgers, grilled corn, and tacos.

gotts.com

\$

El Porteño

Argentinian empanadas passed down from an old family recipe.

elportenosf.com

\$

Señor Sisig

A beloved Filipino fusion restaurant famous for its one-of-a-kind burritos.

senorsisig.com

\$

Grande Crêperie

Offers delicious French-style crepes made with seasonal ingredients.

grandecreperie.com

\$

2

SFMOMA

P4 151 3rd St 5, 9, 12, 14, 30, 38, 45 J, K, L, M, N, T
Noon–8pm Thu, 10am–5pm Fri–Tue sfmoma.org

Standing proudly on the northeast side of the Yerba Buena Gardens art and entertainment complex, the San Francisco Museum of Modern Art (SFMOMA) houses innovative works of modern and contemporary art. It is one of the world's largest museums of its kind.

This museum forms the nucleus of San Francisco's reputation as a leading center of modern art. Opening in 1935 at the Veterans Building *(p167)*, it moved into its current quarters in 1995, and in spring 2016 reopened after a major three-year $365 million expansion that doubled its capacity. Designed by the international architecture firm Snøhetta, the 235,000-sq-ft (21,832-sq-m) expansion is seamlessly integrated with Swiss architect Mario Botta's 1995 modernist building. The museum offers a dynamic schedule of special exhibitions and permanent collection presentations.

Museum Highlights

SFMOMA is both an outstanding repository of modern and contemporary art and a powerhouse of inspiration and encouragement to the local art scene. With more than 33,000 works of art in the museum's permanent collection, you'll see works that include traditional paintings, media arts, architecture, and design. The museum's main strengths lie in US and Latin American modernism, Fauvism, Surrealism, Abstract Expressionism, Minimalism and post-Minimalism, Pop Art, postwar German art, and the art of California. The 2016 expansion brought a notable addition: the 15,000-sq-ft (1,393-sq-m) Pritzker Center for Photography, the largest space dedicated to this art form in any art museum in the country.

↑ The Howard Street entrance and visitors at a media arts exhibit *(inset)*

Gallery Guide

Level One

Here you'll find the excellent museum store, a theater, and large abstract works by Julie Mehretu.

Level Two

The permanent collection, Education Center, and library are housed on the second floor, interspersed with some temporary exhibits.

↑ The vibrant *Figures with Sunset* (1978) by Roy Lichtenstein

Level Three

▲ The fabulous Center for Photography sits on the third floor along with the Sculpture Terrace, Graphic Design Gallery, and the 30-ft- (9-m-) high Living Wall.

Level Four

▲ The Agnes Martin and Kelly Elsworth Galleries, event space, and many temporary exhibits.

Level Five

▲ The fifth floor houses a variety of museum highlights, including the Oculus Bridge, Andy Warhol gallery, and Sculpture Garden.

Level Six

▲ The Anselm Kiefer and Gerhard Richter Galleries.

Level Seven

Sculpture Terrace and temporary exhibits.

LOWER FLOORS

California Arts

On the second floor there are galleries dedicated to works by California artists. These painters and sculptors have drawn their inspiration from local materials and scenes to create an influential body of art that is unique to the West Coast. Collage and assemblage works by these artists, exhibited on rotation from the museum's collection, make use of everyday materials such as felt-tip pens, junkyard scraps, and old paintings, producing art with a distinctive West Coast flavor.

Photography

Drawing on its enormous permanent collection of more than 17,800 photographs, the museum presents wonderful exhibitions of the photographic arts in the Pritzker Center for Photography, located on the third floor.

The collection of Modernist American masters includes Berenice Abbott, Walker Evans, Edward Steichen, and Victoria Sambunaris, with special attention paid to California photographers. It has the finest collection of Japanese photography outside of Japan, as well as extensive collections from Latin America and Europe, including German avant-garde photographers of the 1920s, and European Surrealists of the 1930s.

Paintings and Sculpture

Included in the museum's permanent holdings are more than 8,000 paintings, sculptures ,and works on paper. American Abstract Expressionism is well represented at the museum by Philip Guston, Franz Kline, and Jackson Pollock, whose first ever museum exhibition took place here at SFMOMA.

Other prominent North and Latin American artists whose works are displayed in the museum collections include Frida Kahlo, Diego Rivera, and Georgia O'Keeffe. Another exhibition area permanently shows works by Jasper Johns, Robert Rauschenberg, and Andy Warhol, among others. There is a good collection of the European Modernists, including notable paintings by Pablo Picasso from various periods. A large collection of works by Paul Klee are accommodated in an individual gallery; works by the famous French painter of the Fauvist school, Henri Matisse, are found nearby on the second floor.

Did You Know?

SFMOMA includes works from the collection of Doris and Donald Fisher, founders of GAP.

A display in the Pritzker Center for Photography ↑

An actively changing schedule of contemporary art exhibits supplements the museum's historical collection and does much to encourage today's art scene.

↑ Alexander Calder sculptures; *Frieda and Diego Rivera* (1931), by Frida Kahlo *(inset)*

UPPER FLOORS

Architecture and Design

SFMOMA's Department of Architecture and Design was founded in 1983. Its function is to procure and maintain a collection of historical and contemporary architectural drawings, models, and design objects, and to examine and illuminate their influences on modern art. Its current holding of over 6,000 items focuses on architecture, furniture, product design, and graphic design, and is widely considered one of the most significant in the United States. The new sixth-floor galleries offer rotating exhibitions.

Among items included in the permanent collection are models, drawings, prints, and prototypes by well-known and emerging designers, including famous architect Bernard Maybeck, who was responsible for some of the most beautiful buildings in the Bay Area such as the Palace of Fine Arts Theatre *(p68)*. Other noted San Francisco Bay Area architects represented are Timothy Pflueger, William Wurster, and Willis Polk, known for his design of the glass and steel Hallidie Building *(p146)*, and the California design team of Charles and Ray Eames. The permanent collection also has works by Frank Lloyd Wright, Frank Gehry, and Fumihiko Maki.

Media Arts

Established in 1988, the Department of Media Arts collects, conserves, documents, and exhibits art of the moving image, including works in video, film, projected image, electronic arts, and time-based media. The seventh-floor galleries deploy state-of-the-art equipment to present photographic, multi-image and multimedia works, film, video, and selected programs of interactive media artwork.

The museum's growing permanent collection includes pieces by artists such as Nam June Paik, Don Graham, Peter Campus, Joan Jonas, Lynn Hershman Leeson, Bill Viola, Doug Hall, and Mary Lucier.

Contemporary Art and Special Exhibitions

The fourth floor features special exhibition galleries. An actively changing schedule of contemporary art exhibits supplements the museum's historical collection. It also organizes film screenings and public talks in the theater.

EAT

Grace

Open to all, Grace offers French-American fare.

P4 Level 1 sfoma.org/visit/dining-at-sfmoma/#grace

Cafe 5

A relaxed restaurant in the sculpture garden.

P4 Level 5 sfoma.org/visit/dining-at-sfmoma/#cafe-5

YERBA BUENA GARDENS

P5 Mission, 3rd, Folsom, 4th & Howard sts 9, 14, 30, 45, 76 J, K, L, M, N, T 6am-10pm daily yerbabuenagardens.com

Teeming with art installations, green spaces, and museums spread out across several modern buildings, the Yerba Buena Gardens feel like a mini artists' community. With so much to explore, it's the perfect location for both art lovers and urban adventurers.

The construction of the Moscone Center, San Francisco's largest venue for conventions, was just the first in a series of ambitious development plans for Yerba Buena Gardens. Housing, hotels, museums, galleries, gardens, and restaurants have all followed, and now the area is a vibrant hub of activity. Check the Yerba Buena Gardens website for information about hours and admission prices for the individual buildings on site.

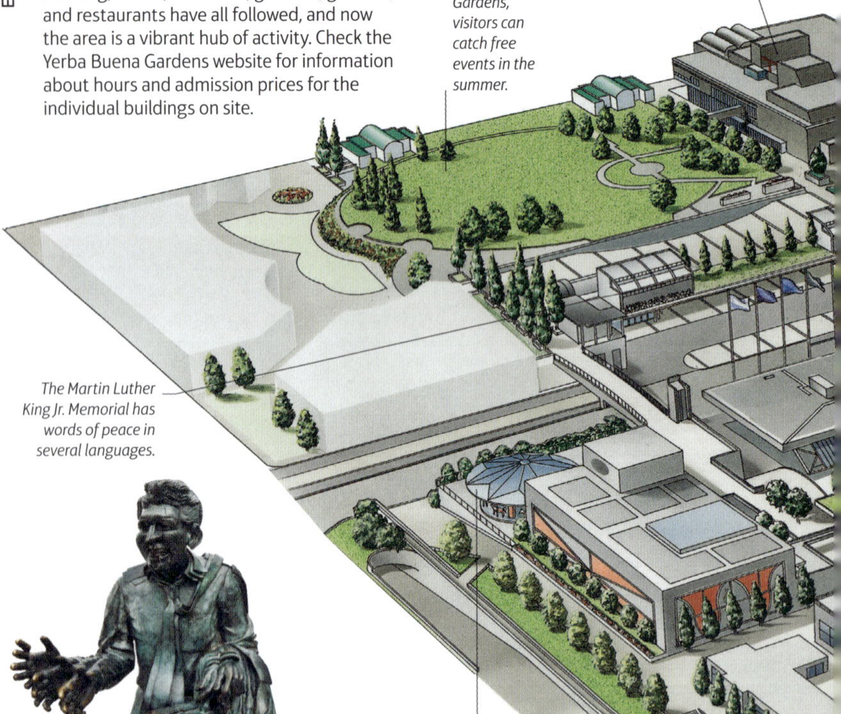

The Yerba Buena Center for the Arts is made up of the Galleries, Forum, and Theater buildings.

At the Esplanade Gardens, visitors can catch free events in the summer.

The Martin Luther King Jr. Memorial has words of peace in several languages.

The Children's Creativity Museum combines imagination with art and technology tools, and visitors can create animations, music videos, digital art, and more.

← *Shaking Man* (1993), a statue by Terry Allen at Esplanade Gardens

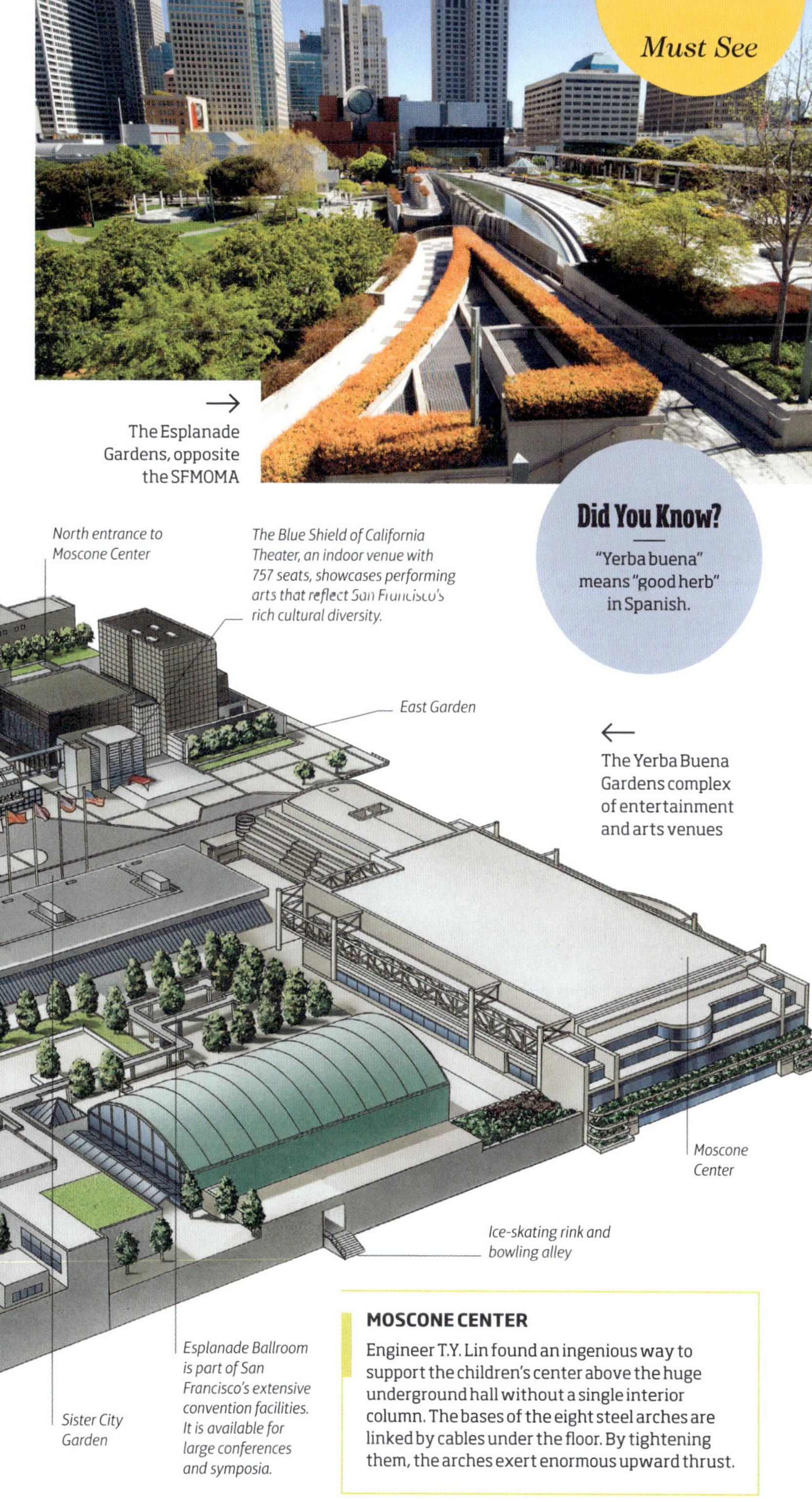

→ The Esplanade Gardens, opposite the SFMOMA

Did You Know?

"Yerba buena" means "good herb" in Spanish.

← The Yerba Buena Gardens complex of entertainment and arts venues

MOSCONE CENTER

Engineer T.Y. Lin found an ingenious way to support the children's center above the huge underground hall without a single interior column. The bases of the eight steel arches are linked by cables under the floor. By tightening them, the arches exert enormous upward thrust.

EXPERIENCE MORE

4 Embarcadero Center

P3 Many buses E, F, J, K, L, M, N, T California St

The Embarcadero Center was completed in 1981 after a decade of construction, the largest redevelopment project in the city's history. The complex of hotels and office and retail space reaches from Embarcadero Plaza *(p146)* to Battery Street. Four separate high-rise towers reach upward 35 to 40 stories above the landscaped plazas and elevated walkways.

Embarcadero Center's most spectacular interior is the lobby of the Hyatt Regency Hotel. Its 17-story atrium contains an immense sculptured globe, made up of 1,440 interlacing aluminum tubes, by Charles O. Perry, entitled *Eclipse* (1973). Glass elevators glide up and down one wall, carrying visitors to and from their rooms. Also housed in the center is an array of stores and a movie theater screening independent and foreign movies.

5 Jackson Square Historic District

N3 8AX, 8BX, 10, 12, 41, 82X

Renovated in the early 1950s, this low-rise neighborhood contains many historic ornate brick, cast-iron, and granite facades dating from the Gold Rush era. From 1850 to 1910, it was notorious for its red light district, and was known as the Barbary Coast. The Hippodrome at No. 555 Pacific Street used to be a theater; the bawdy relief sculptures in the recessed front recall the risqué shows that were performed there. Today the buildings of the Jackson Square Historic District are used as showrooms, law offices, top-notch restaurants, design and fashion boutiques, art galleries, and antiques stores; the most attractive buildings can be seen on Jackson Street, Gold Street, Hotaling Place, and Montgomery Street.

6 Salesforce Park

P4 425 Mission St 5, 5R, 7, 10, 12, 14, 14R, 25, 38, 38R Montgomery, Embarcadero 6am-8pm daily (summer: to 9pm) tjpa.org

Stretching across the entire almost four-block length of San Francisco's Transit Centre, this rooftop park, opened in 2018, is the crowning glory of one the city's most ambitious 21st-century urban development projects. Spread across 226,000 sq ft (21,000 sq m) of

↑ Aerial view of the extensive greenery in Salesforce Park

Charles O. Perry's dramatic sculpture, *Eclipse*, in the Hyatt Regency Hotel's lobby

lawns and gardens, it features hundreds of trees, flowers, and shrubs. The park is home to 13 botanical gardens, each representing a unique eco-system, including Chilean, South African, and Australian landscapes, all interconnected by scenic paths. Note, you can access the park from street level by taking the gondola from the corner of Mission and Fremont Streets, or using one of the elevators or escalators in the bus station. The Main Plaza, an open space surrounded by a bamboo grove, hosts events such as concerts, storytelling, fitness sessions, and children's activities. Towards the park's west end is an outdoor theater where live music and movie nights are held.

One of the park's quirkiest and site-specific attractions is the 1,000-ft (300-m) long Bus Fountain, designed by northern California artist Ned Kahn. It is driven by motion sensors located in the transport terminal below it, causing the water to spurt in rhythm with the comings and goings of the buses. Kahn himself likened it to a huge musical instrument played by the city's drivers.

7

Transamerica Pyramid

P3 600 Montgomery St 1, 8AX, 8BX, 10, 12, 41 To the public pyramidcenter.com

Capped with a pointed spire on top of its 48 stories, the pyramid reaches 853 ft (256 m) above sea level. It is one of the most recognized buildings in the city and was the tallest until it was overtaken by the Salesforce Tower *(p149)*, which was completed in 2018.

Although San Franciscans disliked it when it opened in 1972, they have since accepted it as part of their city's skyline. Designed by William Pereira & Associates, the pyramid houses 1,500 office workers on a historically rich site. The Montgomery Block was built here in 1853. In the basement was the Exchange Saloon, frequented by Mark Twain. In the 1860s artists and writers took up residence in the Montgomery Block. The Pony Express terminus, marked by a plaque, was at Merchant Street opposite the pyramid.

The building has been closed to the public since September 11, 2001, though there is a visitors' center in the lobby.

56

skyscrapers in San Francisco are over 400 ft (122 m) tall.

The Transamerica Pyramid, one of San Francisco's most recognizable sights

↑ The grand colonnaded facade of the Pacific Coast Stock Exchange building

8

Pacific Coast Stock Exchange

P4 301 Pine St 3, 8, 30X, 41 To the public

This was once America's largest stock exchange outside New York. Founded in 1882, it occupied these buildings, which were remodeled by Miller and Pflueger in 1930 from the existing US Treasury. The monumental granite statues that flank the Pine Street entrance to the building were made by the renowned San Francisco sculptor, painter, and muralist Ralph Stackpole, also in 1930. No longer a stock exchange, the building is now a fitness club.

INSIDER TIP

Naming the Plaza

In 2017 city officials voted to change the name of the Justin Herman Plaza. Embarcadero Plaza is its current title, and as of now there are no plans to change it in the foreseeable future.

9

Hallidie Building

P4 130 Sutter St 3, 8, 30, 45 K, L, M, N California St Montgomery Embarcadero To the public

A unique and important architectural achievement, the Hallidie Building was the first building in the United States to use the glass-curtain style, in which glass panes are suspended in a steel-mullion grid. When constructed in 1918 by Willis Polk, the seven-floor building was incredibly modern. It juxtaposes minimalist elements like the glass curtain with classic Gothic architectural details such as embellished cornices, balconies, fire escapes, and thin zinc panels adorned with birds and flowers. A major restoration of the facade was completed in 2013.

10

Embarcadero Plaza

P3 Many buses E, F, J, K, L, M, N California St

Formerly known as the Justin Herman Plaza, this open square is popular with lunchtime crowds from the nearby Embarcadero Center and other offices. The plaza is mostly known for its avant-garde Vaillancourt Fountain, made in 1971 by Canadian artist Armand Vaillancourt. The fountain is modeled from huge concrete blocks, and some

find it ugly, especially when it runs dry in times of drought. However, you can climb on and through it, and its pools and columns of falling water make it an intriguing public work of art when functioning as intended.

11

Merchants' Exchange

P4 465 California St 1, 3, 8, 30X, 41 California St By appointment only mxbuilding.com

The exchange, designed by Willis Polk in 1903, survived the great fire of 1906 with little damage. Inside, fine seascapes by the Irish painter William Coulter line the walls. These depict epic maritime scenes from the age of steam and sail. The building was the focal point of San Francisco's commodities exchange in the early 20th century, when lookouts in the tower relayed news of ships arriving from abroad. The building is now an office and events space.

Did You Know?

California architect Julia Morgan helped to redesign parts of the Merchants' Exchange.

12

Bank of California

P3 400 California St 765-0400 1, 30X, 41 California St

William Ralston and Darius Mills founded this bank in 1864. Ralston, known as "the man who built San Francisco," invested profitably in Comstock mines, and used the bank and his personal fortune to finance many civic projects in San Francisco. These included the city's water company, a theater, and the Palace Hotel *(p149)*. However, when economic depression struck in the 1870s, Ralston's empire also collapsed. The present colonnaded building was completed in 1908. In the basement there is a pleasant arcade of shops, restaurants, and art exhibits.

EAT

Tadich Grill

Operating since 1849, this old-school favorite pulls in the after-work crowds for famously large portions of seafood.

P3 240 California St Sun tadichgrillsf.com

$$$

Boulevard

Indulgent ingredients from Pacific swordfish to Burgundy truffles are used to create refined, regionally focused dishes. The waterfront setting and low lighting make this a favorite date spot.

Q3 1 Mission St boulevardrestaurant.com

$$$

↓ The Vaillancourt Fountain in the Embarcadero Plaza

18

A lucky number in Jewish culture - which is why 18 steps lead up to the Contemporary Jewish Museum.

Contemporary Jewish Museum

P4 736 Mission St 8, 14, 30, 45, 81X J, K, L, M, N, T 11am-5pm Thu-Sun thecjm.org

This museum partners with national and international cultural institutions to present a variety of art forms, photography, and installations celebrating and exploring Judaism.

The museum is housed in an early 20th-century Pacific Gas & Electric (PG&E) Power Substation, adapted and redesigned by world-renowned architect Daniel Libeskind and unveiled in 2005. The space features more than 10,000 sq ft (930 sq m) of exhibition space and an impressive education center.

Children's Creativity Museum

P5 221 4th St 9, 14, 30, 45, 76 J, K, L, M, N, T 10am-4pm Fri-Sun creativity.org

More of a hands-on creative workshop than a tradtional museum, this lively non-profit center encourages kids of all ages to dive in and get involved in a variety of fun activities, including painting, clay modelling, composing music, and digital animation. Visitors can also collaborate on group projects and explore storytelling through interactive exhibits.

Rincon Center

Q4 121 Spear St 14

This shopping center, with its soaring atrium, was added on to the old Rincon Annex Post Office Building in 1989. The Rincon Annex is known for 27 painted panels titled *The History of California*, executed in Social Realist style by Russian-born Anton Refregier between 1940 and 1948.

Museum of the African Diaspora

P4 685 Mission St 8, 14, 30, 45, 81X J, K, L, M, N, T 11am-6pm Wed-Sat, noon-5pm Sun moadsf.org

Founded in 2005, the Museum of the African Diaspora (MoAD) explores the diverse cultural heritage of Africa and African descendant cultures around the world. Four universal themes – Origins, Movement, Adaptation, and Transformation – provide inspiration for the museum's rotating exhibitions, which highlight the work of local and international artists, as well as examine contemporary issues arising from historical movements and events.

Works on display range across a variety of mediums, including visual arts and crafts, music, and dance. The museum also hosts regular film screenings, poetry readings, and artists' talks.

↓ The Contemporary Jewish Museum, redesigned by D. Libeskind

17    

Salesforce Tower

P4 415 Mission St To the public salesforcetower.com

Rising an impressive 1,070 ft (326 m) above the East Cut neighborhood, the gleaming Salesforce Tower (formerly the Transbay Tower) has been the tallest building in San Francisco since 2018, when it overtook the 853-ft- (260-m-) high iconic Transamerica Pyramid *(p145)* – a prominent part of the city's skyline.

In a city with relatively few tall buildings, the Salesforce Tower certainly stands out, even though it's just 7 ft (2 m) taller than the Eiffel Tower. Its top floors are adorned with a public art installation by local artist Jim Campbell, made up of 11,000 LED lights. Together, they form a gigantic video screen projecting abstract imagery by local artists, or footage recorded remotely in the city on the same day.

↑ The magnificent Garden Court restaurant at the Palace Hotel, dating from 1909

18 

Palace Hotel

P4 2 New Montgomery St 8, 12, 14, 30, 45, 81X J, K, L, M, N, T marriott.com

The original Palace Hotel was opened by William Ralston, one of San Francisco's best-known financiers, in 1875. It was the most luxurious of San Francisco's early hotels and was regularly frequented by the rich and famous. Among its patrons were writers Oscar Wilde and Rudyard Kipling, and actor Sarah Bernhardt. The celebrated tenor Enrico Caruso was a guest at the time of the earthquake of 1906, when the hotel caught fire. It was rebuilt by the architect George Kelham, and reopened in 1909. It is best known for the Garden Court, its fabulous, glass-ceilinged, colonnaded restaurant, and its Pied Piper bar. The bar is decorated with a beautiful mural by Maxfield Parrish. The hotel's palm-filled Garden Court also provides a memorable brunch or high tea experience.

STAY

Four Seasons San Francisco at Embarcadero

This hotel occupies the top floors of a high-rise and has a lofty perch with a lounge. Some of the rooms have great views of Alcatraz.

P3/4 222 Sansome St fourseasons.com/embarcadero

$$$

YOTEL San Francisco

Compact, high-tech rooms, a rooftop terrace, and social spaces are housed in one of the few buildings to survive the 1906 earthquake.

N5 1095 Market St yotel.com

Pedestrianized Maiden Lane, a pretty, tranquil haven away from the city bustle

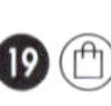

Maiden Lane

N4 Between Stockton & Kearny sts 3, 30, 38R Powell-Mason Powell

In the heady days of the Gold Rush, this prim-sounding street played host to San Francisco's most popular red light district. Today, its name is associated with its high-end boutiques, opera-singing buskers, and art galleries. A traffic-free corridor located just off Union Square, lined with stores and open-air cafés, the street offers a respite from the hustle and bustle just a block away. One notable building, the V. C. Morris Gift Shop, is a designated San Francisco landmark, since it's the only Frank Lloyd Wright-designed structure in the city. Movie buffs will get a kick out of touring one of the city spots where Alfred Hitchcock shot a scene for his movie *The Birds*.

HIDDEN GEM

Frank Lloyd Wright

Architect Frank Lloyd Wright experimented with the use of ramps in the small V. C. Morris Gift Shop at 140 Maiden Lane. It is considered one of his most influential works.

Crocker Galleria

P4 Between Post, Kearny, Sutter, & Montgomery sts (415) 393-1505 3, 5, 6, 8, 21, 30, 38, 45 J, K, L, M, N, T Montgomery Sun

The Crocker Galleria was built in 1982, by the architects Skidmore, Owings & Merrill. Inspired by the Galleria Vittorio Emanuele in Milan, this building features a central plaza underneath a vaulting skylight glass roof.

A rooftop garden, farmers' market, food court, and dozens of stores, from gourmet patisseries to one-off homeware and fashion boutiques, are housed here on three floors.

Gump's

N4 250 Post St 3, 5, 6, 8, 9, 21, 30, 38, 45 J, K, L, M, N, T Powell-Mason, Powell-Hyde 11am-5pm Mon-Sat gumps.com

Founded in 1861 by German immigrants, this homegrown San Francisco department store is an institution. Many local couples register their wedding present list with the

DRINK

Cityscape Bar & Lounge

Craft cocktails and a vast selection of wines are served up with views of the Golden Gate Bridge at this chic rooftop bar.

N4 333 O'Farrell St cityscapesf.com

The View Lounge

Those in the know head to this rooftop before sunset to grab a cocktail and a seat for one of the city's best views over skyscrapers toward the San Francisco Bay.

N/P5 780 Mission St sfviewlounge.com

Press Club

This underground bar is the place to be for happy hour, offering generous discounts on local craft brews and wines by the glass.

P4 20 Yerba Buena Lane pressclubsf.com

store. Gump's has the largest collection of fine china and crystal in the US.

The store is also celebrated for its Asian-inspired treasures, furniture, and the rare works in the art department. The Asian art is particularly fine, especially the remarkable jade collection, which enjoys a worldwide reputation. In 1949 Gump's imported the great bronze Buddha and presented it to the Japanese Tea Garden *(p198)*. Gump's has an exclusive, refined atmosphere and is frequented by the rich and famous. It is also renowned for its colorful and extravagant window displays.

Union Square

N4 2, 3, 5, 6, 8, 9, 21, 30 J, K, L, M, N, T Powell-Mason, Powell-Hyde

Union Square was named for the big, pro-Union rallies held there during the Civil War of 1861–5. The rallies galvanized popular support in San Francisco for the Northern cause, and this was instrumental in bringing California into the war on the side of the Union. The square is at the heart of the city's shopping district; large department stores can be found here, including Macy's and Sak's Fifth Avenue, as well as major flagship stores. The square is bordered on the west side by the famous Westin St. Francis Hotel, and at the center there is a statue of *Victory* atop a 90-ft (27-m) column. This monument commemorates Admiral Dewey's victory at Manila Bay during the Spanish–American War of 1898.

Theater District

M4 2, 3, 27, 38, 45 J, K, L, M, N, T Powell-Mason, Powell-Hyde

Several theatres are located near Union Square, all within a six-block area, giving the area the title of San Francisco's theater district. The two biggest venues are on Geary Boulevard, two blocks west of the square. These are the Curran Theatre – which was built in 1922 and sports a grand carved ceiling and glass chandelier – and the Geary Theater, built in 1909 and now the home of the American Conservatory Theater (ACT). Drama has flourished in San Francisco since the days of the Gold Rush, and great actors and opera stars have been attracted to the city. Isadora Duncan, the innovative 1920s dancer, was born nearby on Taylor Street.

Did You Know?

Union Square was once covered by a huge sand dune that stood 60-80 ft (18-24 m) tall.

↑ Union Square surrounded by stores such as Saks Fifth Avenue and Tiffany & Co

SHOP

34 Trinity Arts & News

Browse local print media at this independent bookstore known for its great selection of second-hand books. Sometimes, there are also occasional sidewalk concerts outside its doors.

P4 34 Trinity Place Noon-6pm Tue-Fri 34trinity.com

Britex Fabrics

This long-established, family-run shop provides a wide array of fabrics in various colors, patterns, and textures, along with buttons, sequins, and lace. It also offers a customized swatch service and personalized gift cards.

N4 117 Post St britexfabrics.com

24

Powell Street Cable Car Turntable

N5 Hallidie Plaza, Powell St at Market St Many buses J, K, L, M, N, T Powell-Mason, Powell-Hyde

The Powell-Hyde and the Powell-Mason cable-car lines are the most spectacular routes in San Francisco. They start and end their journeys to Nob Hill, Chinatown, and Fisherman's Wharf at the corner of Powell Street and Market Street. Unlike the double-ended cable cars on the California Street line, the Powell Street cable cars were built to move in one direction only – hence the need for a turntable at every terminus.

After the car's passengers have disembarked, it is pushed onto the turntable and rotated manually by the conductor and grip-man (the person who operates the "grip," which by grasping or releasing the cable, starts or stops the car). Prospective customers for the return journey wait amid an ever-moving procession of street musicians, shoppers, tourists, and office workers.

Did You Know?

Both the Powell-Mason and Powell-Hyde lines end near Fisherman's Wharf, but in different areas.

A cable car at the Powell Street cable car turntable

Oracle Park, the home of the San Francisco Giants and *(inset)* a statue of Hall of Famer, Willie Mays

25

Mint Plaza

N5 8AX, 9R, 14, 27, 45, 88X J, K, L, M, N, T Powell

With plenty of outdoor chairs scattered about, this public plaza offers a comfortable space to rest your feet or to grab a bite after sightseeing near Union Square. Tucked away off Market Street, the square is framed by trees, flower beds, and historic buildings. The plaza is a popular conduit for San Franciscans walking to work during rush hour and makes for excellent people-watching. During the summer months, you will frequently find live music being played. The original Blue Bottle Coffee, renowned for its quality coffee, is located just off the plaza, and sandwich shops and lunch spots abound. You'll also find popular restaurants and wine bars for happy hour.

St. Patrick's Church

P4 756 Mission St stpatricksf.org

Built in Flamboyant Gothic style, this red-brick Catholic church offers an attractive contrast to the surrounding high-rise buildings. It was built in 1851 and is named for Ireland's patron saint. The church's Tiffany-style windows depict Irish traditions and each of the patron saints of the 32 Irish counties. Even the interior columns, made from green Connemara and gold and white Botticino marble, reflect the colors of the Irish flag. Damaged in the earthquake of 1906, the church was repaired in the same distinctive style that made it a landmark in 1968.

For baseball fans, no trip to the Bay Area would be complete without catching a game at Oracle Park.

27   

Oracle Park

Q5 24 Willie Mays Plaza 10, 30, 45, 47, 81, 82, 83 E, N, T mlb.com/giants/ballpark

Oracle Park is the home of the World Series-winning San Francisco Giants. For baseball fans, no trip to the Bay Area would be complete without catching a game at Oracle Park. The stadium is located right on the water in the southwest quadrant of the city; spectators at afternoon games are treated to spectacular views and plenty of sunshine. Like everything in San Francisco, the food options are top-notch for stadium cuisine, with many local chefs collaborating on independent food stands.

Outside of baseball season, visitors can come to enjoy other events at the park, from Cirque du Soleil productions to food festivals.

A SHORT WALK FINANCIAL DISTRICT

Distance half a mile (1 km) **Time** 15 minutes
Nearest buses 1, 8AX, 8BX, 10, 12, 41

San Francisco's economic engine is fueled largely by the Financial District, one of the chief commercial centers in the US. It reaches from the imposing modern towers and plazas of the Embarcadero Center to staid Montgomery Street, sometimes known as the "Wall Street of the West." All the principal banks, brokers, exchanges, and law offices are situated within this compact area. The Jackson Square Historical District, north of Washington Street, was once the heart of the business community.

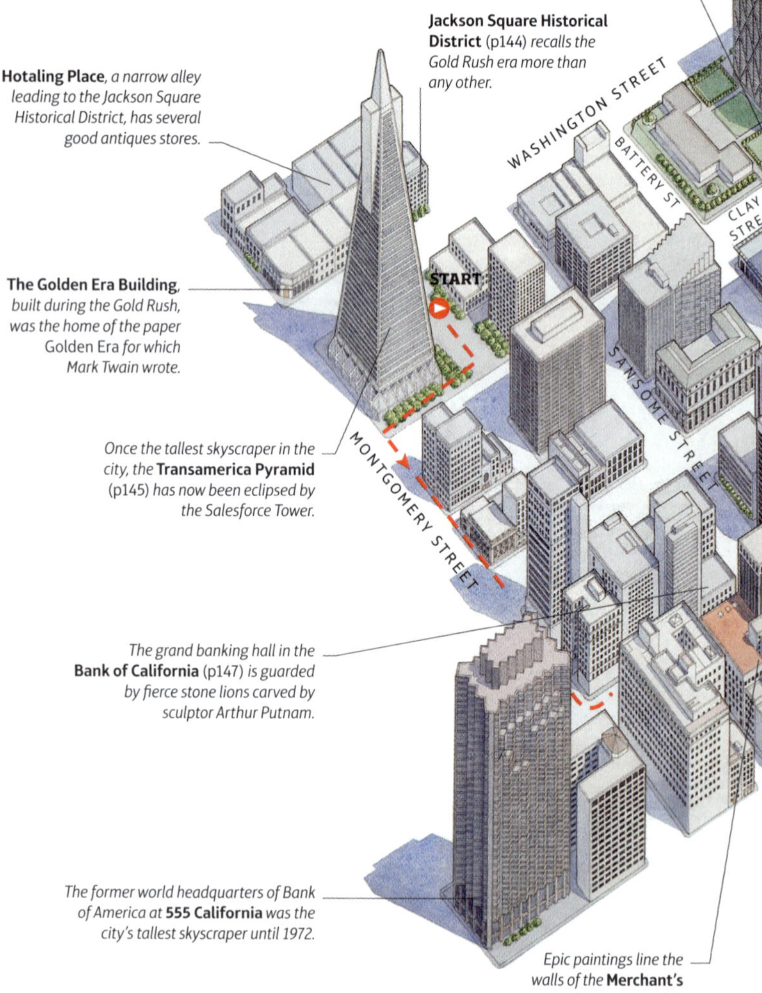

Embarcadero Center (p144) *houses both commercial outlets and offices. A shopping arcade occupies the first three tiers of the towers.*

Jackson Square Historical District (p144) *recalls the Gold Rush era more than any other.*

Hotaling Place, *a narrow alley leading to the Jackson Square Historical District, has several good antiques stores.*

The Golden Era Building, *built during the Gold Rush, was the home of the paper* Golden Era *for which Mark Twain wrote.*

Once the tallest skyscraper in the city, the **Transamerica Pyramid** (p145) *has now been eclipsed by the Salesforce Tower.*

The grand banking hall in the **Bank of California** (p147) *is guarded by fierce stone lions carved by sculptor Arthur Putnam.*

The former world headquarters of Bank of America at **555 California** *was the city's tallest skyscraper until 1972.*

Epic paintings line the walls of the **Merchant's Exchange** (p147).

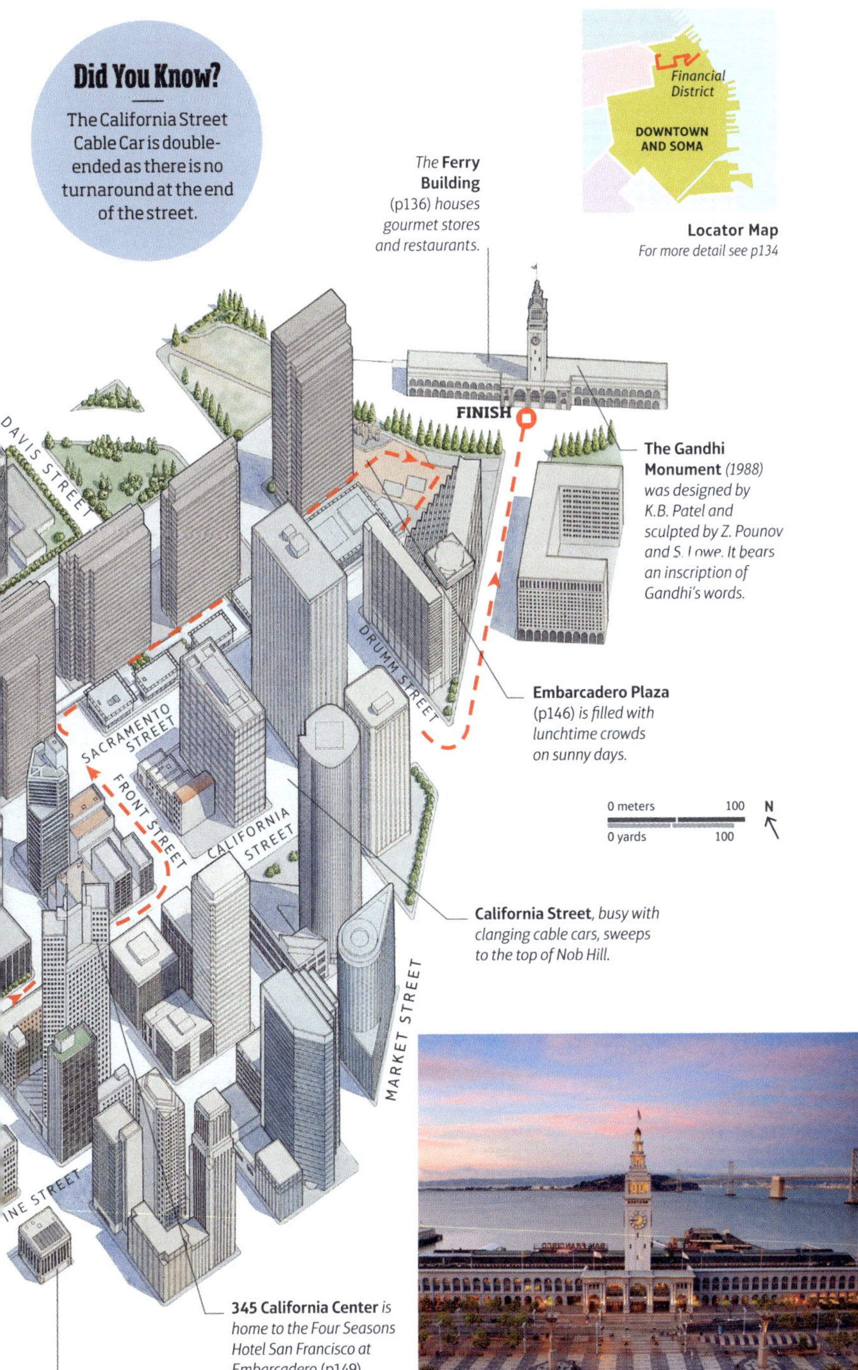

The **Pacific Coast Stock Exchange** (p146) was once the focal point of the city's trade.

↑ The iconic Ferry Building at sunset, a San Francisco landmark

A LONG WALK AROUND SOMA

Distance 2.5 miles (4 km) **Time** 45 minutes **Terrain** Flat streets, busy with pedestrians and traffic **Nearest Bay Area Rapid Transit (BART) station** Powell Street

Once a grubby warehouse district, SoMa (a contraction of "South of Market") is a model of urban revitalization. This was once the "wrong side" of the Market Street cable-car tracks when Gold Rush-era immigrants worked in the factories here in the 19th century. Today, a four-block square area surrounding the Moscone Convention Center *(p143)* is packed with major art galleries and history museums, high-rise hotels, and stores, and on this walk you will encounter vestiges of the city's lively past among its dazzling 21st-century architecture.

↑ Lush greenery at the Yerba Buena Gardens

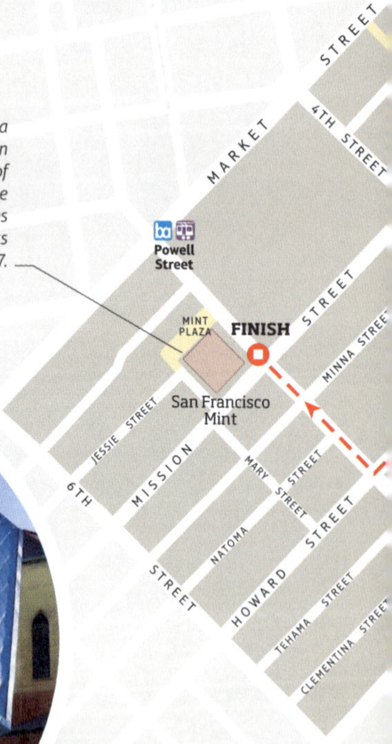

Turn left onto Howard Street, then take a right onto 5th Street. At the corner of Mission Street, you will see the magnificent facade of the "Granite Lady," the Greek Revival-style **Old Mint**, *erected in 1869–74 to make coins from California gold and Nevada silver. Its last coins were produced in 1937.*

Powell Street
MINT PLAZA
FINISH
San Francisco Mint
MARKET STREET
4TH STREET
5TH STREET
6TH STREET
JESSIE STREET
MISSION STREET
MINNA STREET
MARY STREET
NATOMA STREET
HOWARD STREET
TEHAMA STREET
CLEMENTINA STREET

← Daniel Libeskind's extension to the Contemporary Jewish Museum, unveiled in 2005

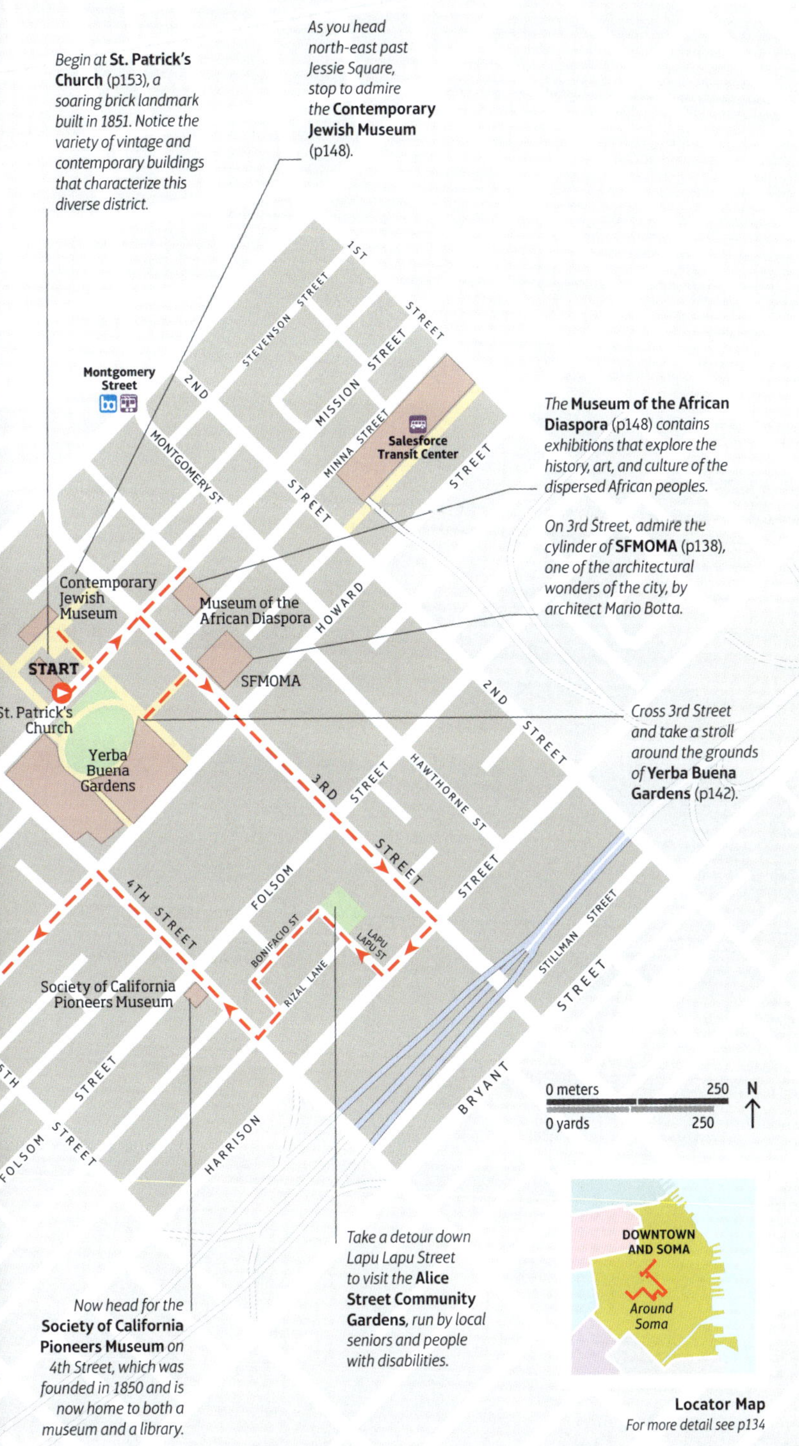
Begin at St. Patrick's Church (p153), a soaring brick landmark built in 1851. Notice the variety of vintage and contemporary buildings that characterize this diverse district.
As you head north-east past Jessie Square, stop to admire the Contemporary Jewish Museum (p148).
The Museum of the African Diaspora (p148) contains exhibitions that explore the history, art, and culture of the dispersed African peoples.
On 3rd Street, admire the cylinder of SFMOMA (p138), one of the architectural wonders of the city, by architect Mario Botta.
Cross 3rd Street and take a stroll around the grounds of Yerba Buena Gardens (p142).
Now head for the Society of California Pioneers Museum on 4th Street, which was founded in 1850 and is now home to both a museum and a library.
Take a detour down Lapu Lapu Street to visit the Alice Street Community Gardens, run by local seniors and people with disabilities.
Montgomery Street
Salesforce Transit Center
Contemporary Jewish Museum
Museum of the African Diaspora
SFMOMA
START
St. Patrick's Church
Yerba Buena Gardens
Society of California Pioneers Museum
1ST STREET
STEVENSON STREET
MISSION STREET
MINNA STREET
2ND STREET
MONTGOMERY ST
HOWARD STREET
3RD STREET
HAWTHORNE ST
4TH STREET
FOLSOM STREET
BONIFACIO ST
LAPU LAPU ST
RIZAL LANE
STILLMAN STREET
BRYANT STREET
5TH STREET
HARRISON
0 meters 250
0 yards 250
N
DOWNTOWN AND SOMA
Around Soma
Locator Map
For more detail see p134

The beautiful Beaux Arts City Hall

CIVIC CENTER AND HAYES VALLEY

After the old City Hall was destroyed in the 1906 earthquake and fire, the Civic Center was built to the south of Pacific Heights to a masterplan by local architects chaired by John Galen Howard. It contains many of the city's important cultural and government institutions. The 50 United Nations Plaza Federal Office Building, completed in 1934, was where the UN Charter was signed in 1945, as was the Treaty of San Francisco in 1951, which officially ended the Pacific War. Today the Civic Center remains the home of the Supreme Court of California, and the seat of government for the City and County of San Francisco.

Adjoining this historic government district, Hayes Valley has a much more humble history, originally being used as farmland during the mid-19th century. It was subsequently developed into a residential neighborhood, which went into decline following the construction of a freeway through the area in the mid-20th century – Hayes Valley suffered serious problems with crime and for many years was considered one of the city's most dangerous districts. However, the demolition of the freeway following the Loma Prieta earthquake in 1989 enabled major redevelopments to the area, and Hayes Valley is today an upscale district full of charming houses, boutiques, and restaurants.

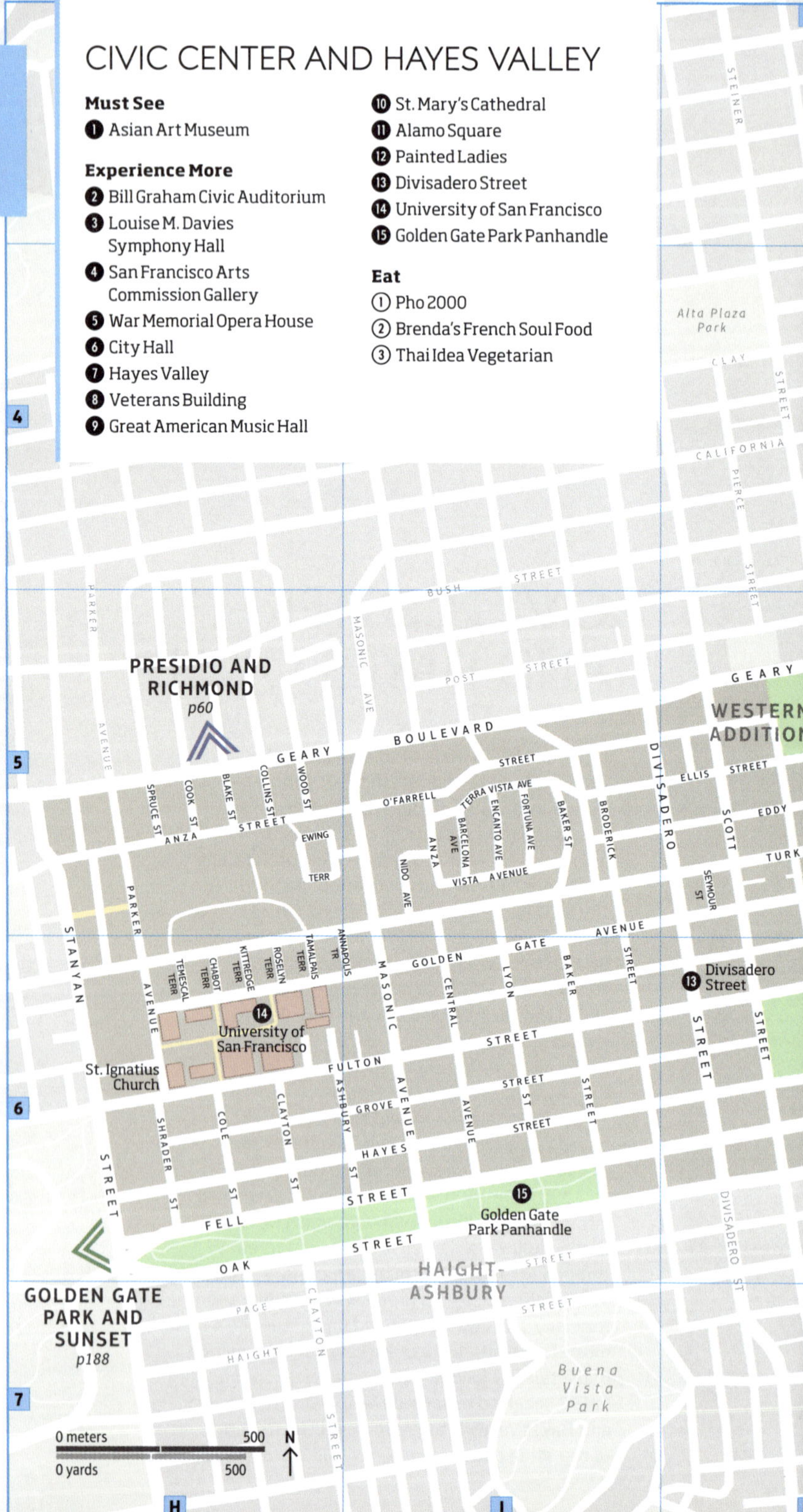
CIVIC CENTER AND HAYES VALLEY
Must See
1 Asian Art Museum
Experience More
2 Bill Graham Civic Auditorium
3 Louise M. Davies Symphony Hall
4 San Francisco Arts Commission Gallery
5 War Memorial Opera House
6 City Hall
7 Hayes Valley
8 Veterans Building
9 Great American Music Hall
10 St. Mary's Cathedral
11 Alamo Square
12 Painted Ladies
13 Divisadero Street
14 University of San Francisco
15 Golden Gate Park Panhandle
Eat
① Pho 2000
② Brenda's French Soul Food
③ Thai Idea Vegetarian
PRESIDIO AND RICHMOND
p60
WESTERN ADDITION
GOLDEN GATE PARK AND SUNSET
p188
HAIGHT-ASHBURY
Alta Plaza Park
Buena Vista Park
St. Ignatius Church
University of San Francisco
Divisadero Street
Golden Gate Park Panhandle
GEARY BOULEVARD
BUSH STREET
POST STREET
O'FARRELL STREET
ELLIS STREET
EDDY
TURK
GOLDEN GATE AVENUE
FULTON STREET
GROVE STREET
HAYES STREET
FELL STREET
OAK STREET
PAGE STREET
HAIGHT
CLAY
CALIFORNIA
STEINER
PIERCE STREET
PARKER AVENUE
STANYAN STREET
MASONIC AVE
DIVISADERO
SCOTT STREET
BRODERICK
BAKER ST
LYON
CENTRAL
ASHBURY
CLAYTON ST
COLE ST
SHRADER ST
ANZA STREET
SPRUCE ST
COOK ST
BLAKE ST
COLLINS ST
WOOD ST
EWING TERR
TERRA VISTA AVE
ENCANTO AVE
FORTUNA AVE
BARCELONA AVE
ANZA VISTA AVENUE
NIDO AVE
SEYMOUR ST
TEMESCAL TERR
CHABOT TERR
KITTREDGE TERR
ROSELYN TERR
TAMALPAIS TERR
ANNAPOLIS TR
DIVISADERO ST
0 meters 500
0 yards 500
N
4
5
6
7
H
J
K

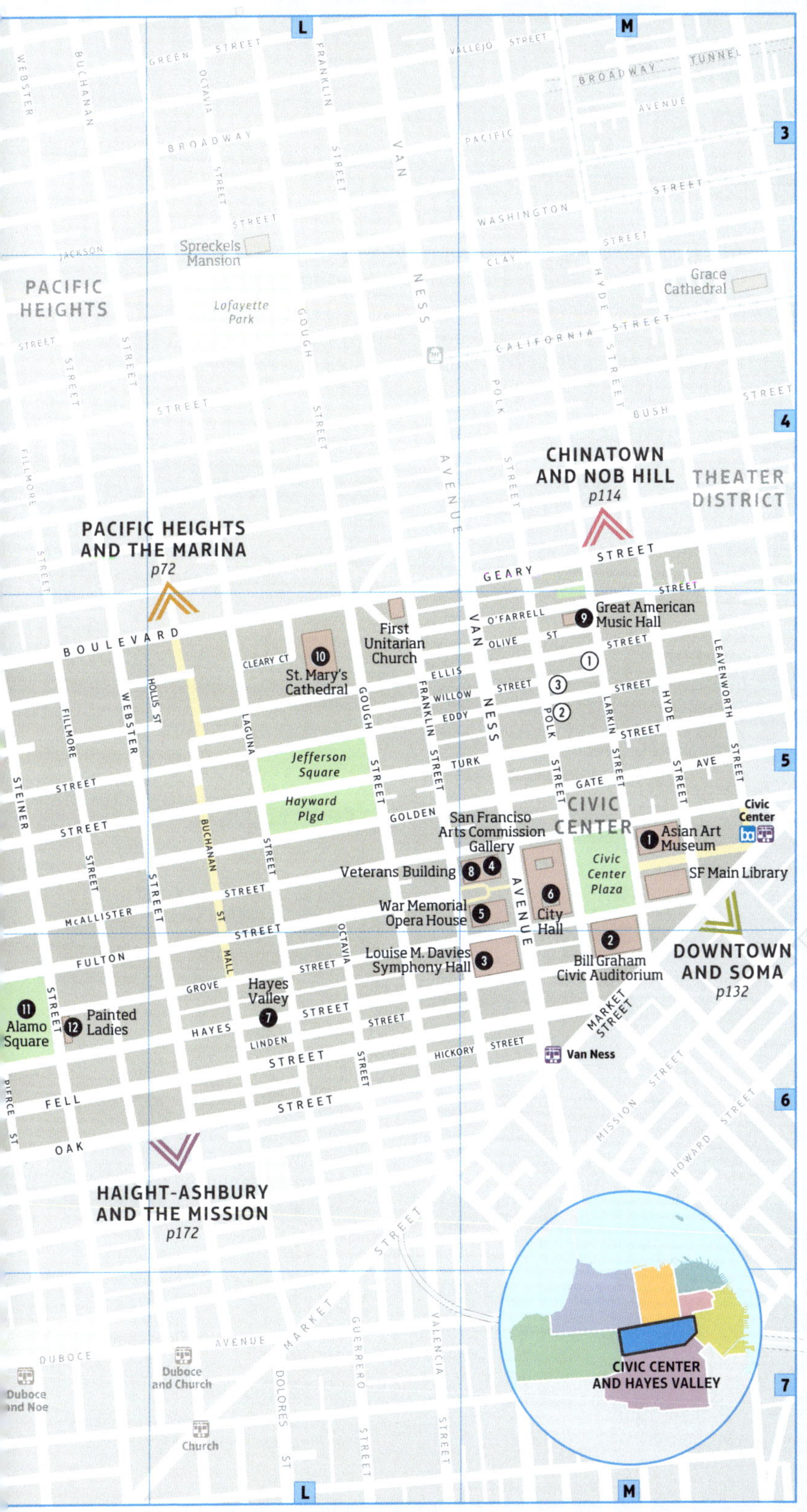
PACIFIC HEIGHTS
Spreckels Mansion
Lafayette Park
Grace Cathedral
CHINATOWN AND NOB HILL p114
THEATER DISTRICT
PACIFIC HEIGHTS AND THE MARINA p72
Great American Music Hall
First Unitarian Church
St. Mary's Cathedral
Jefferson Square
Hayward Plgd
CIVIC CENTER
San Francisco Arts Commission Gallery
Asian Art Museum
Civic Center
Veterans Building
Civic Center Plaza
SF Main Library
War Memorial Opera House
City Hall
Louise M. Davies Symphony Hall
Bill Graham Civic Auditorium
DOWNTOWN AND SOMA p132
Hayes Valley
Painted Ladies
Alamo Square
Van Ness
HAIGHT-ASHBURY AND THE MISSION p172
Duboce and Noe
Duboce and Church
Church
CIVIC CENTER AND HAYES VALLEY

1

ASIAN ART MUSEUM

M5 200 Larkin St 5, 7X, 9, 19, 21, 31, 47, 49 F, J, K, L, M, N, T Civic Center 1-8pm Thu, 10am-5pm Mon-Wed & Fri-Sun, 1-8pm Thu asianart.org

Heading up the grand staircase of the Asian Art Museum is like setting out on a historical and cultural tour of the world's largest continent. The 2,000 works on display celebrate both tradition and history as well as the contemporary cultures of many Asian nations.

The Asian Art Museum is located on Civic Center Plaza in a building that was the crown jewel of the Beaux Arts movement in San Francisco. The former Main Library, built in 1917, underwent major renovation in 2001 to create the largest museum outside of Asia devoted exclusively to Asian art. The museum has more than 18,000 art objects spanning 6,000 years of history and representing cultures and countries throughout Asia. It hosts festivals and performances, and has a library, hands-on exhibits, and a unique store that sells artisanal items from Bay Area makers. The museum's East West Bank Art Terrace – an outdoor platform designed to display contemporary artworks by both emerging and well-known artists – opened to the public in 2021.

Facade of the Asian Art Museum, a Beaux Arts building dating back to 1917

GALLERY GUIDE

Temporary exhibits are housed on the first floor. The second and third floors feature over 2,000 artworks from all major Asian cultures. These works are regularly rotated, so don't be surprised if you see different pieces on display if you visit more than once.

Observing a statue on display at an exhibition in the museum

Highlights

1000 BCE

The museum's pair of sculptures of Shiva and Parvati are from the inner sanctuary of a Hindu temple in Cambodia.

c. 1500

◀ This complex Buddha sculpture from China's Ming Dynasty is made of many small pieces that were fitted together before firing.

1870

▲ This watercolor portrait of Maharaja Mahinder Singh of Patiala was copied from a photograph, which was a common practice.

2014

▲ Melding motifs from folk art with vibrant Pop Art colours, Hung Yi's *Dragon Fortune* is a photogenic sculpture outside the museum.

Admiring some of the museum's more modern artworks

EXPERIENCE MORE

EAT

Pho 2000

Tucked unassumingly in the area known as "Little Saigon," this Vietnamese place is a favorite with locals.

M5 637 Larkin St Tue 474-1188

Brenda's French Soul Food

New Orleans classics made with regionally sourced ingredients.

M5 652 Polk St frenchsoulfood.com

Thai Idea Vegetarian

A bright and breezy café with a meat-free menu of Thai specialties. Vegan options are also on offer.

M5 710 Polk St thaiideasf.com

2

Bill Graham Civic Auditorium

M6 99 Grove St 5, 7X, 9, 19, 21, 31, 47, 49 J, K, L, M, N, T Civic Center billgrahamcivic.com

This venue was designed in Beaux Arts style *(p36)* by architect John Galen Howard to form a major part of the Panama-Pacific International Exposition. Orignally named the San Francisco Civic Auditorium, the venue opened in 1915 and was inaugurated by the French composer and pianist Camille Saint-Saëns. The building was completed along with City Hall, in the course of the massive architectural renaissance that followed the natural disasters of 1906. It was built, together with the adjoining Brooks Exhibit Hall, beneath the Civic Center Plaza.

The Civic Auditorium now serves as the city's main conference center, and has the capacity to seat 7,000 people. In 1992 its name was changed in honor of Bill Graham, the local rock music impresario who was a pivotal figure in both the development and promotion of the city's trademark psychedelic sound.

Louise M. Davies Symphony Hall

M6 201 Van Ness Ave 7X, 19, 21, 47, 49 J, K, L, M, N, T Civic Center sfsymphony.org

Loved and loathed in equal measure by the citizens of San Francisco, this curving, glass-fronted concert hall was constructed in 1980 – the creation of architects Skidmore, Owings & Merrill. The ultra-modern hall is named for the prominent philanthropist who donated $5 million of the $35 million construction cost. It is home to the San Francisco

Symphony Orchestra and also welcomes many visiting orchestras and artists.

The acoustics of the building were disappointing when it first opened, but measures were taken to improve them. After many years of negotiations a new sound system was installed. The interior was also redesigned, and the walls were resculptured to better reflect sound.

San Francisco Arts Commission Gallery

M5 401 Van Ness Ave 5, 7X, 19, 21, 47, 49 J, K, L, M, N, T Noon-5pm Wed-Sat sfartscommission.org/gallery

Located in the Veterans Building *(p167)*, this dynamic gallery shows paintings, sculptures, and multimedia works made by local artists. Their website also lists public artworks that can be found throughout the city, including some photography exhibitions at City Hall.

An orchestral performance at the Louise M. Davies Symphony Hall

5 

War Memorial Opera House

M5 301 Van Ness Ave 5, 7X, 9, 19, 21, 47, 49 J, K, L, M, N, T Civic Center sfwarmemorial.org

Opened in 1932, the War Memorial Opera House, designed by Arthur Brown, was dedicated to the memory of World War I soldiers. It was a key venue during the 1945 conference which led to the creation of the United Nations Charter, and in 1951 it was used for the signing of the peace treaty between the US and Japan. It is now home to the San Francisco Opera and San Francisco Ballet.

↑ The War Memorial Opera House, with its impressive colonnaded facade

THE SOUNDS OF 1960S SAN FRANCISCO

During the Flower Power years of the late 1960s, and most notably during the 1967 Summer of Love, young people from all over the US flocked to San Francisco. They came not just to "turn on, tune in, and drop out," but also to listen to music. Janis Joplin, Jimi Hendrix, and the Grateful Dead all emerged out of a seminal music scene. The Avalon Ballroom was the first and most significant rock venue pioneering the use of colorful psychedelic posters.

PICTURE PERFECT
A City Landmark

Towering at 307 ft (94 m) above street level, City Hall's dome makes the perfect subject for a memorable photo - especially during one of the light shows that illuminate the exterior for events and holidays.

6 

City Hall

M5 400 Van Ness Ave 5, 7X, 9, 19, 21, 47, 49 J, K, L, M, N, T 8am-6pm Mon-Fri sf.gov

City Hall, completed in 1915, just in time for the start of the Panama-Pacific International Exposition, was designed by Arthur Brown when he was at the height of his career. The original building was completely destroyed in the 1906 earthquake. Its grand Baroque golden dome was modeled on St. Peter's Church in Rome and is higher than the US Capitol in Washington, DC. The upper levels of the dome are open to the public.

The restored building is at the heart of the Civic Center complex and is a magnificent example of the Beaux Arts style *(p36)*. Allegorical figures evoking the city's Gold Rush past can be seen in the pediment above the main Polk Street entrance, which leads into the marble-floored Rotunda. Guided tours of City Hall are available on weekdays; see the website for details on booking.

Hayes Valley

L6 6, 7, 21, 22

Just west of City Hall, Hayes Valley became one of San Francisco's trendier leisure districts after the US 101 highway was badly damaged in the Loma Prieta earthquake of 1989. The road was then torn down, having previously cut Hayes Valley off from the wealthy power brokers and theater-goers of the Civic Center. A few of the local cafés and restaurants, such as Hayes Street Grill, had already begun to mix in with the Hayes Street second-hand furniture and thrift stores. This was followed by an influx of art galleries, interior design stores, top-notch restaurants, trendy nightspots, craft coffee roasters, and clothing boutiques – all of which has transformed the area into one of San Francisco's coolest neighborhoods.

↑ Brandon Flowers performing with The Killers at the Great American Music Hall

Veterans Building

M5 401 Van Ness Ave 5, 7X, 9, 19, 21, 47, 49 J, K, L, M, N, T sfwarmemorial.org

Like the War Memorial Opera House *(p165)*, this building was designed by Arthur Brown and built in 1932 to honor World War I soldiers. It was rededicated in 2015 after the opening of a 3,000-sq-ft (280-sq-m) art gallery. In addition to displays of historic weapons, there are showcases of military memorabilia. The building is also home to the Herbst Theater, a 928-seat classical music concert hall. The theater was the site of the signing of the United Nations Charter during the San Francisco Conference of 1945.

Great American Music Hall

M5 859 O'Farrell St 19, 31, 38, 47, 49 gamh.com

Built in 1907 as a place for bawdy comedy shows, the Great American Music Hall is now an excellent performance space, with a rich interior containing tall marble columns and elaborate balconies, adorned with ornate gilt plasterwork. The venue is intimate and stylish, and the views are good from almost every table. Famous artists such as Carmen McCrae, B. B. King, Duke Ellington, Van Morrison, and Tom Paxton have played every kind of music here, from blues to rock 'n' roll, and even jazz.

St. Mary's Cathedral

L5 1111 Gough St 2, 3, 31, 38 8am-5pm daily (from 7:30am Sun) smcsf.org

Situated at the top of Cathedral Hill, the ultra-modern St. Mary's is the city's principal Roman Catholic church and one of its most prominent landmarks. Designed by architect Pietro Belluschi and engineer Pier Luigi Nervi, the church was completed in 1971. The four-part arching paraboloid roof stands out like a white-sailed ship on the horizon. The 200-ft- (60-m-) high concrete structure, which supports a cross-shaped stained-glass ceiling, seems to hover effortlessly over the nave. A sunburst canopy made of aluminum rods sparkles above the plain stone altar.

San Francisco's City Hall, built in Beaux Arts style and topped with a splendid dome

Did You Know?

"Painted Ladies" refers to any Victorian and Edwardian houses repainted in three or more colors.

Alamo Square

K6 5, 21, 22, 24

San Francisco's most photographed row of colorful Victorian houses, the so-called "Seven Sisters" or "Painted Ladies," lines the eastern side of this sloping green square, which is located some 225 ft (68 m) above the Civic Center, giving grand views of City Hall backed by the Financial District skyscrapers. Alamo Square was laid out at the same time as the pair of Pacific Heights squares, but it was developed later and much more quickly, with speculators building large numbers of very nearly identical houses.

So many grand old Victorian houses line the streets around Alamo Square that the area has been declared a historic district.

Painted Ladies

K6 710-720 Steiner St & Hayes St 5, 21, 22, 24

These grand Victorian homes from the Queen Anne era, set against the backdrop of the downtown city skyscrapers, are a wonderful visual treat, and one of the most photogenic spots in the city. Also called "Postcard Row" and mistakenly known as the "Full House" house, the seven Painted Ladies are found on the east side of grassy Alamo Square.

Designed by Matthew Kavanaugh, with the last house completed in 1896, the houses are still private residences and tourists should be mindful not to trespass when coming by to admire the architecture and snap that perfect photo.

Divisadero Street

K6 5, 21, 24, 31

A San Francisco hotspot that delights locals and visitors alike, Divisadero Street has seen tremendous change in recent decades. Once a rather dull, middle-class street lined with cheap stores, Divisadero is now full of trendy lunch spots, restaurants, lovely independent boutiques, bakeries, and more. The street has a fresh, creative vibe, with plenty of art and music, a weekly farmers' market, and lots of community events.

The strip is the perfect place to spend the better part of a day. Start with brunch and window-shop your way down the street, enjoying the unique stores and people-watching. Or stop at Bi-Rite, the famous upscale grocer, to grab homemade ice cream or a picnic lunch and head a couple of blocks over to Alamo Square to take in the jaw-dropping views.

Divisadero is now full of trendy lunch spots, restaurants, lovely independent boutiques, bakeries, and more.

University of San Francisco

H6 2130 Fulton St 5, 21, 33, 43 usfca.edu

Estabished back in 1855 as St. Ignatius College, the University of San Francisco (USF) is still a Jesuit-run institution, though classes are now coeducational and non-denominational. The land-mark of the campus is the striking St. Ignatius Church, which serves as the chapel for the university and as a parish church. It was completed in 1914 and built in exuberant Italian Baroque style, with liberal use of columns and pilasters.

↑ The verdant campus of the University of San Francisco, on the site of a former cemetery

Its buff-colored twin towers are visible from all over the western half of San Francisco, especially when lit up at night. The church is regularly used for student graduation and convocation ceremonies. The university campus and residential neighborhood that surrounds it occupy land that historically formed San Francisco's main cemetery district, on and around Lone Mountain.

Golden Gate Park Panhandle

J6 5, 6, 7, 7X, 21, 24, 33, 43 N

This stretch of parkland, one block wide and eight blocks long, forms the narrow "Panhandle" to the giant rectangular pan that is Golden Gate Park *(p206)*. It was the first part of the park to be reclaimed from the sand dunes that rolled across west San Francisco, and its stately eucalyptus trees are among the oldest and largest in the city. The Panhandle's winding bicycle lanes and bridle paths were first laid out in the 1870s, when the upper classes came here to walk and ride. They built large mansions on the outskirts of the park; many can still be seen today. In 1906 the Panhandle was a refuge for families made homeless by the earthquake. Today the old roads and paths are used regularly by joggers and cyclists.

The Panhandle is still remembered for its "Flower Power" heyday of the 1960s *(p165)*, when bands gave impromptu concerts here.

The eye-catching "Painted Ladies" Victorian houses, facing onto Alamo Square

VICTORIAN HOUSES IN SAN FRANCISCO

Despite earthquakes, fires, and the inroads of modern life, thousands of ornate, late 19th-century houses still line the streets of San Francisco. In fact, in many neighborhoods they are by far the most common type of housing. Victorian houses are broadly similar, in that they all have wooden frames, elaborately decorated with mass-produced ornament. Most were constructed on narrow plots to a similar floor plan, but they differ in the features of the facade. Four main styles prevail in the city, although in practice many houses, especially those built in the 1880s and 1890s, combine aspects of two or more styles.

Balustrades on the porch betray the origins of the style in the Deep South.

Wide porches can be reached by a central staircase.

A gabled roof with decorated vergeboards is the clearest mark of Gothic Revival.

The pitched roof over the main facade often runs lengthwise, allowing the use of dormer windows.

Tall cornices, often with decorative brackets above bay windows, conceal a pitched roof.

Architectural Styles

Gothic Revival (1850–80)

These houses are the easiest to identify, since they always have pointed arches over the windows, and sometimes over the doors. Other features are pitched gabled roofs, decorated vergeboards, and porches that run the width of the building. The smaller, simpler houses of this type are usually painted white, rather than the vibrant colors often associated with later styles.

Italianate (1850–85)

The Italianate style was more popular here than elsewhere in the US, perhaps because the compact form was suited to San Francisco's high building density. The most distinctive feature of the Italianate style is the tall cornice, usually with a decorative bracket, which adds a palatial air even to modest homes. Elaborate decoration around doors and windows is another typical feature.

↑ Neo-Classical doorways on an Italianate house

Stick (1860–90)

This style is perhaps the most prevalent among Victorian houses in the city. Sometimes also called "Stick-Eastlake" after London furniture designer Charles Eastlake, the style was intended to be architecturally "honest." Vertical lines are emphasized, both in the wood-frame structure and in ornamentation. Bay windows, false gabled cornices, and square corners are key identifiers.

Queen Anne (1875–1905)

The name "Queen Anne" does not refer to a historical period; it was coined by the English architect Richard Shaw. Queen Anne houses freely combine elements from many decorative traditions, but are marked by their turrets and towers and large, often decorative, panels on wall surfaces. Most houses also display intricate spindle-work on balustrades, porches, and roof trusses.

WHERE TO FIND THEM

Haas-Lilienthal House *(p83)*

Octagon House *(p83)*

Pacific Heights *(p86)*

Painted Ladies *(p168)*

(Richard) Spreckels Mansion *(p180)*

Clarke's Folly *(p182)*

Colorful exteriors of Haight-Ashbury's Victorian houses

HAIGHT-ASHBURY AND THE MISSION

With its rows of beautiful late Victorian houses, Haight-Ashbury was once a typical San Franciscan neighborhood, developed after the cable car connected the area with Downtown in the 1880s. After World War II, its wealthy upper-middle classes fled to the suburbs, resulting in low rents, which made the area a haven for hippies in the 1960s. This was the epicenter of the "Summer of Love" in 1967, home to the Grateful Dead, Janis Joplin, the Hell's Angels, and a host of counterculture icons. Though that rebellious past is long over, Haight-Ashbury has kept its alternative subculture vibe. The Castro District, to the east, is the nexus of San Francisco's LGBTQ+ community and has the largest number of gay bars in the city. Well known for its wild hedonism in the 1970s, the area retains its liveliness, albeit on a smaller scale.

The Mission District, farther east still, takes its name from the Mission San Francisco de Asís, founded by Spanish Franciscans in 1776. From the 1940s to 1960s, Central and South American immigrants moved into the neighborhood. Latin American artistic and cultural institutions, including vibrant street murals, still flourish here, despite the gentrification of the 1990s.

HAIGHT-ASHBURY AND THE MISSION
Must Sees
1 Castro Street
2 Haight-Ashbury
Experience More
3 (Richard) Spreckels Mansion
4 Buena Vista Park
5 Vulcan Street Steps
6 Randall Museum
7 Lower Haight Neighborhood
8 GLBT Historical Society Museum
9 Clarke's Folly
10 Dolores Street
11 Mission Dolores
12 Dolores Park
13 Sutro Tower
14 Twin Peaks
15 Mission Cultural Center for Latino Arts
16 Noe Valley
17 Carnaval Mural
Eat
① Loló
Shop
② Relic Vintage
③ Paxton Gate
④ Wasteland
⑤ 826 Valencia Pirate Supply Store
GOLDEN GATE PARK AND SUNSET
p188
Conservatory of Flowers
Panhandle
Haight-Ashbury
(Richard) Spreckels Mansion
Buena Vista Park
Duboce Park
Duboce and Noe
Carl and Cole
Irving and 2nd Ave
Randall Museum
Vulcan Street Steps
Castro Street
Castro Theater
Tank Hill Park
GLBT Historical Society Museum
Clarke's Folly
Mount Sutro
Sutro Tower
Reservoir
Twin Peaks Reservoir
Laguna Honda
Twin Peaks
Forest Hill
0 meters 800
0 yards 800
N

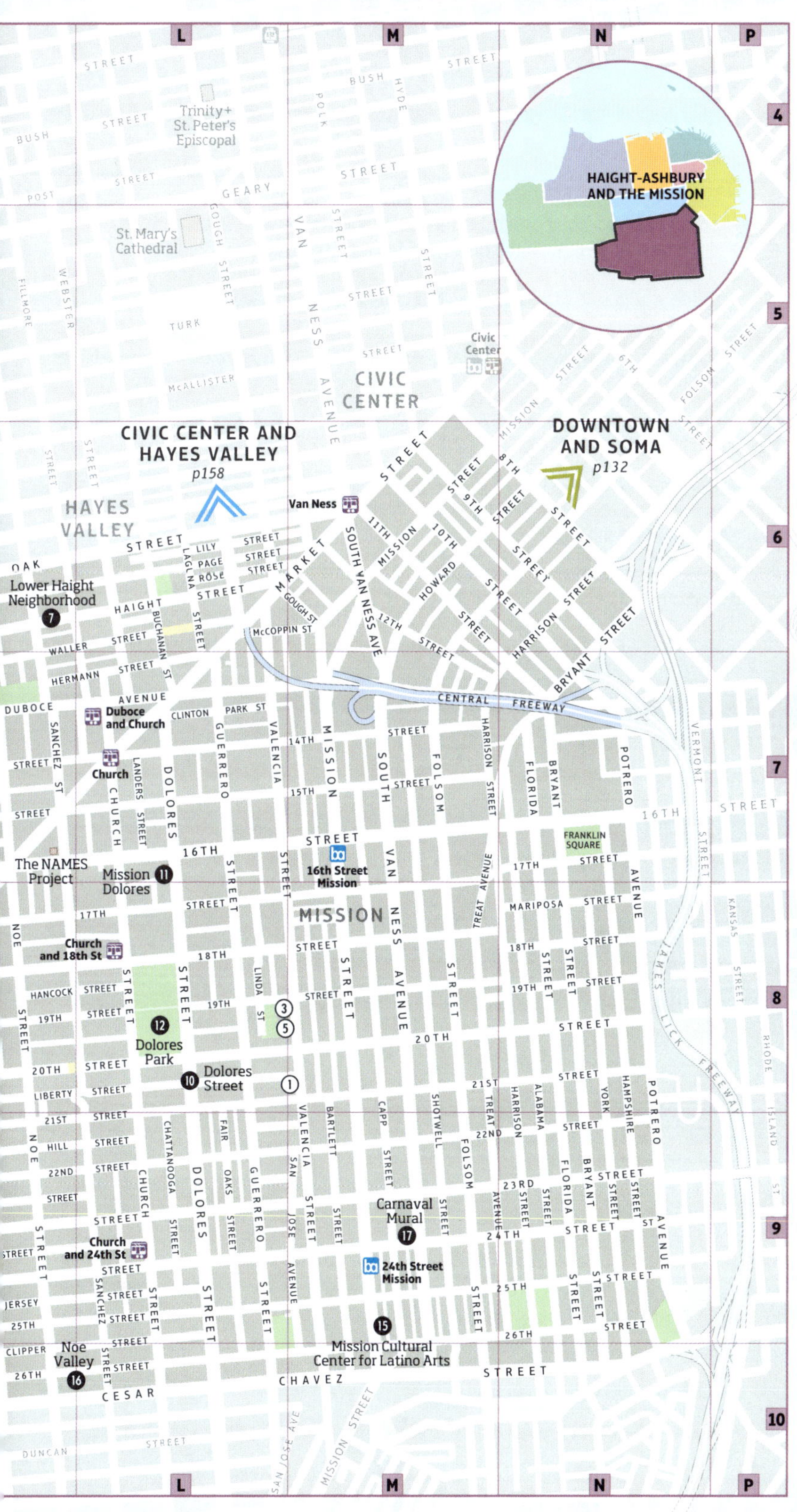

L
M
N
P
4
5
6
7
8
9
10
HAIGHT-ASHBURY AND THE MISSION
Trinity+ St. Peter's Episcopal
St. Mary's Cathedral
CIVIC CENTER
Civic Center
CIVIC CENTER AND HAYES VALLEY
p158
DOWNTOWN AND SOMA
p132
HAYES VALLEY
Van Ness
Lower Haight Neighborhood
7
Duboce and Church
Church
CENTRAL FREEWAY
FRANKLIN SQUARE
The NAMES Project
Mission Dolores
11
16th Street Mission
MISSION
Church and 18th St
12
Dolores Park
3
5
10
Dolores Street
1
Carnaval Mural
17
Church and 24th St
24th Street Mission
15
Mission Cultural Center for Latino Arts
Noe Valley
16
JAMES LICK FREEWAY
BUSH STREET
POST STREET
GEARY STREET
TURK STREET
McALLISTER STREET
FILLMORE
WEBSTER
GOUGH STREET
POLK
HYDE
VAN NESS AVENUE
OAK STREET
LILY
PAGE STREET
ROSE STREET
HAIGHT STREET
WALLER STREET
HERMANN STREET
DUBOCE AVENUE
MARKET STREET
MISSION STREET
SOUTH VAN NESS AVE
HOWARD STREET
FOLSOM STREET
HARRISON STREET
BRYANT STREET
MCCOPPIN ST
GOUGH ST
LAGUNA
BUCHANAN ST
CLINTON
PARK ST
GUERRERO STREET
VALENCIA STREET
DOLORES STREET
CHURCH STREET
SANCHEZ ST
LANDERS STREET
NOE STREET
14TH
15TH STREET
16TH STREET
17TH STREET
18TH STREET
19TH STREET
20TH STREET
21ST STREET
22ND STREET
23RD STREET
24TH STREET
25TH STREET
26TH STREET
CESAR CHAVEZ STREET
MARIPOSA STREET
POTRERO AVENUE
FLORIDA STREET
TREAT AVENUE
HAMPSHIRE STREET
YORK STREET
ALABAMA STREET
SHOTWELL STREET
CAPP STREET
BARTLETT STREET
SAN JOSE AVENUE
OAKS STREET
FAIR
CHATTANOOGA STREET
LINDA ST
HANCOCK STREET
LIBERTY STREET
HILL STREET
JERSEY STREET
CLIPPER STREET
DUNCAN STREET
VERMONT STREET
KANSAS STREET
RHODE ISLAND ST
8TH STREET
9TH STREET
10TH
11TH
12TH STREET
6TH STREET

1

CASTRO STREET

K9 24, 33, 35, 37 F, K, L, M, T

The hilly neighborhood around Castro Street between Twin Peaks and the Mission District is the heart of San Francisco's high-profile LGBTQ+ community. It's a lively district of entertainment venues and nightlife with a side of beautiful architecture and proud history.

Focused on the intersection of Castro Street and 18th Street, the self-proclaimed "Gayest Four Corners of the World" emerged as an LGBTQ+ nexus during the 1970s. Gay people of the Flower Power generation moved into this predominantly working-class district and began restoring Victorian houses and setting up businesses. They also opened gay bars, including Mary Ellen Cunha and Peggy Forster's Twin Peaks Tavern on the corner of Castro Street and 17th Street. Unlike earlier bars, where gay people had to hide in dark corners out of public view, the Twin Peaks Tavern had large windows that made it the first gay bar where passersby could see inside. Today, many stores and restaurants in the Castro are among the most popular in San Francisco, often owned and operated by members of the LGBTQ+ community. Castro's most influential resident, Harvey Milk *(p47)*, the first openly gay man elected to public office in California, is remembered with a plaza outside the Muni stop on Market Street.

Today, many stores and restaurants in the Castro are owned and operated by members of the LGBTQ+ community.

A rainbow-colored street crossing and *(inset)* the famous Twin Peaks Tavern

THE CASTRO THEATER

Completed in 1922, this brightly lit neon marquee is a Castro Street landmark. It is the most sumptuous and best preserved of San Francisco's neighborhood film palaces, with a lavish interior inspired by *The Arabian Nights* and a glorious Wurlitzer organ that rises from the floor between screenings. The venue hosts the San Francisco International LGBTQ+ Film Festival, held each June.

Rainbow Honor Walk

Bronze plaques on the Castro Street sidewalk commemorate important figures in the international LGBTQ+ community. While the honorees come from various backgrounds, they all shared in the battle for equality and are held up as inspirational figures in this walk of fame. Names range from famous artists like Freddie Mercury to local heroes like Major League Baseball's Glenn Burke, who is credited with inventing the high five.

2

HAIGHT-ASHBURY

J7 5, 6, 7, 24, 31, 33, 37, 43 N

The birthplace of hippie counterculture in the 1960s, the Haight retains its anti-establishment atmosphere, and an aura of the past can still be found in its congenial cafés and vintage clothing stores.

Taking its name from the junction of two main streets – named after the San Francisco pioneers Henry Haight and Munroe Ashbury – this district contains independent bookstores, large Victorian houses, cafés, and hip clothing boutiques. The neighborhood's origins date back to the 1890s, when the area was rapidly built up following the reclamation of Golden Gate Park *(p199)* and the opening of a large amusement park called The Chutes. The district became a middle-class suburb – hence the dozens of elaborate Queen Anne-style houses *(p171)* lining its streets.

The Hippie Haight

After the streetcar tunnel under Buena Vista Park was completed in 1928, the middle classes began their exodus to the suburbs in the Sunset district. After World War II the area reached its lowest ebb, and the big Victorian houses were divided into apartments offering low rents. While North Beach became the place for the beatniks in the 1950s, many creatives and free-thinkers began to venture to Haight-Ashbury, as it was the cheaper place to live. By the 1960s the Haight had become host to a creative community that was a hotbed of alternative culture. A component of this "hippie scene" was rock music, but the area stayed low-key until 1967. Then the media-fueled "Summer of Love" brought some 75,000 young people in search of free love, music, and drugs, and the area became the focus of a worldwide youth movement.

← Street-side seating at Cafe Cole in the Haight

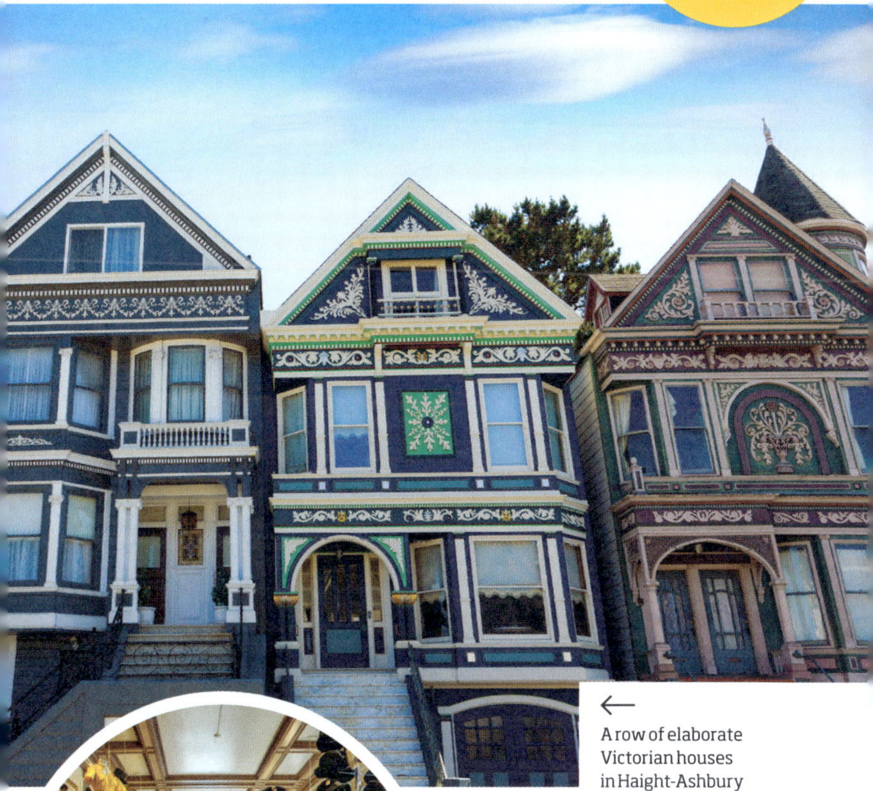

← A row of elaborate Victorian houses in Haight-Ashbury

While North Beach became the place for the beatniks in the 1950s, many creatives and free-thinkers began to venture to Haight-Ashbury, as it was the cheaper place to live.

← Vintage secondhand clothing at the Decades of Fashion store

FAMOUS FACES OF HAIGHT-ASHBURY

Famous residents of Haight-Ashbury include American singer Janis Joplin *(right)*, who moved to her second-floor apartment at 635 Ashbury Street with her lover Peggy Caserta in 1967. Band members of the Grateful Dead lived at 710 Ashbury Street from 1965–68 but left after the scene became too intense. Graham Nash, the singer-songwriter, also lived in "The Haight" in the 1960s and '70s, in a house opposite Buena Vista Park.

EXPERIENCE MORE

(Richard) Spreckels Mansion

J7 737 Buena Vista West 6, 7, 24, 33, 37, 43 To the public

This house should not be confused with the larger and grander Spreckels Mansion on Washington Street *(p80)*. It was, however, also built by the millionaire "Sugar King" Claus Spreckels, for his nephew Richard. The elaborate Queen Anne-style house *(p171)*, built in 1897, is a typical late-Victorian Haight-Ashbury home. It was once a recording studio, and later a guesthouse, but is now in private hands. Guests have included the journalist and ghost-story writer Ambrose Bierce, and Jack London, who wrote *White Fang* here in 1906.

The mansion is situated on a hill near Buena Vista Park. Rows of Victorian houses, many of them well preserved and some palatial, are nearby. One of these, a block away at 1450 Masonic Street, is an onion-domed house, one of the most unusual of the many eccentric mansions built in the Haight since the 1890s.

Did You Know?

Claus Spreckels immigrated from Germany to the US in 1846 with just one coin in his pocket.

Buena Vista Park

J7 6, 7, 24, 33, 37, 43

This park rises steeply, 569 ft (18 m) above the geographical center of San Francisco. First landscaped in 1894, it is a pocket of land left to nature. A network of paths winds up from Haight Street to the crest, where trees frame views of the Bay Area. Many of the trails are overgrown, but there is a paved route up to the summit from Buena Vista Avenue. It is best to avoid the park at night.

Vulcan Street Steps

J8 Vulcan St 37

Apart from a tiny figure of Spock – the famous alien from the fictional planet Vulcan – standing on the mailbox of one of the houses, there is no connection between the popular *Star Trek* series and this block of houses.

Like the Filbert Steps on Telegraph Hill *(p107)*, however, Vulcan Street Steps does feel light years away from the busy streets of the Castro District below. The gardens of the

Guests have included the journalist and ghost-story writer Ambrose Bierce, and Jack London, who wrote *White Fang* here in 1906.

→ Splendid views of the city from Corona Heights, home of the Randall Museum

←
Leaves strewn across the Vulcan Street Steps

houses spill out and a canopy of pines muffles the city sounds. There are grand views of the Mission District and beyond for those who take on the climb.

Randall Museum

K7 199 Museum Way 24, 37 10am-5pm Tue-Sat randallmuseum.org

Clinging to the side of Corona Heights Park, a dusty and undeveloped rocky peak, is this unusual museum for children. The Randall Museum, a museum of natural history, science, and the arts, has a menagerie of over 100 animals, including a raccoon, owls, snakes, tortoises, and various sea creatures. There are exhibitions on the Indigenous practice of basket-making, as well as earthquakes and ocean life. The emphasis of the museum is on participation. It also offers immersive and hands-on experiences with woodworking, ceramics, creative play, theater, model railroads, and much more.

Corona Heights was gouged out by brick-making operations in the 19th century. It was never planted with trees, so its bare red-rock peak offers a panoramic view over the city and East Bay, including the winding streets of Twin Peaks.

Lower Haight Neighborhood

K6 6, 7, 22 K, L, M, N, T

Halfway between City Hall and Haight-Ashbury, and marking the southern border of the Fillmore District, the Lower Haight neighborhood is an area in transition. New markers of gentrification line the streets, such as hip art galleries, salons, eclectic boutiques, and stores, including Rooky Ricardo's Records – which sells rare and unusual records. These sit alongside the inexpensive cafés, bars, and restaurants that were already in business in the area. The combination has created one of the most lively districts in San Francisco.

As in nearby Alamo Square *(p168)*, the Lower Haight neighbrhood is full of dozens of beautiful, old houses built from the 1850s to the early 1900s, in the beautiful and elaborate styles that are so famous in San Francisco *(p36)*. Highlights of the area's architecture include the Nightingale House at 201 Buchanan Street, which was built in the 1880s.

Did You Know?

The GLBT Historical Society hosts regular events, including readings, discussions, and screenings.

GLBT Historical Society Museum

K8 4127 18th St 24, 33, 35, 37 F, K, L, M, S, T 11am-6pm Wed-Mon, noon-5pm Sun Tue in fall and winter months glbthistory.org

This is the first full-scale, stand-alone museum devoted to the LGBTQ+ community in the United States. Though fairly small, the museum packs a punch, celebrating the city's vast LGBTQ+ past through dynamic and surprising exhibitions and programming. Discover treasures from the archives of the GLBT Historical Society that reflect the fascinating stories of this vibrant community.

Clarke's Folly

K8 250 Douglass St 33, 35, 37 To the public

This resplendent white manor house was surrounded by extensive grounds originally. It was built in 1892 by Alfred Clarke, known as Nobby, who worked in the San Francisco Police Department at the time of the Committee of Vigilance. The house is said to have cost $100,000, a huge sum in the 1890s. It was used as a hospital for a while. It is now divided into private apartments, and its turrets and other features make it a wonderfully evocative example of Victorian-era domestic architecture.

EAT

Loló

A family-owned spot with stylish decor and a menu that's equally bold. This is Mexico via the Mission District, with an array of tasty small plates.

L/M8 974 Valencia St lolosf.com

Dolores Street

L8 22, 33, 48 J

Lined by lovingly maintained late Victorian houses *(p36)* and divided by an island of palm trees, Dolores Street is one of the city's most attractive public spaces. The boulevard forms the western border of the Mission District. It starts at Market Street, where a statue in honor of Spanish–American War soldiers is overwhelmed by the hulking US Mint.

The Mission High School, with the characteristic white walls and red-tile roof of Mission-style architecture, is on Dolores Street, as is the historic Mission Dolores.

Mission Dolores

L7 16th St & Dolores St 22 J 8am-4pm daily missiondolores.org

Preserved intact since it was completed in 1791, Mission Dolores is the oldest building in the city and constitutes

The fascinating GLBT Historical Society Museum, the first of its kind in the US

Dolores Park, popular with sunbathers, tennis players, and dog walkers by day

the embodiment of the city's era as a Colonial-Spanish religious outpost. The mission was founded by a Franciscan friar, Father Junipero Serra, and formally known as the Mission of San Francisco de Asís. The name Dolores reflects its proximity to Laguna de los Dolores (Lake of Our Lady of Sorrows). The adobe building's 4-ft- (1.2-m-) thick walls have survived without serious decay. Paintings by Indigenous artists adorn the ceiling.

There is a fine Baroque altar and reredos, as well as a display of historical artifacts in the small museum. Most services are held in the basilica, which was built next to the original mission in 1918. The white-walled cemetery contains graves of prominent San Franciscans from the Gold Rush days. A statue honoring the graves of 5,000 Indigenous people, most of whom died in the great measles epidemics of 1806 and 1826, was stolen and then returned in 1993. It stands on a pedestal reading, "In Prayerful Memory of our Faithful Indians."

The adobe building's 4-ft- (1.2-m-) thick walls have survived without serious decay. Paintings by Indigenous artists adorn the ceiling.

12

Dolores Park

L8 22, 33 J

Originally the site of the city's main Jewish cemetery, Dolores Park was transformed in 1905 into one of the Mission District's few large open spaces. Bounded by Dolores, Church, 18th, and 20th streets, it is situated high on a hill with a good view of the city center.

The verdant Dolores Park is popular during the day with visitors and dog walkers who enjoy its ample paths and leisure spots. Above the park to the south and west, the streets rise so steeply that many turn into pedestrian-only stairways. Here are some of the city's finest Victorian houses, especially on Liberty Street.

LEVI STRAUSS & CO.

In 1853 Levi Strauss left New York to set up a branch of his family's cloth firm in San Francisco. In the 1860s he pioneered the use of durable blue canvas to make workpants for miners. In the 1870s his company began to use metal rivets to increase the strength of stress points in the garments, and demand increased. Levi's blue denim jeans are now produced and worn all over the world, and the company is still owned by Levi Strauss's descendants.

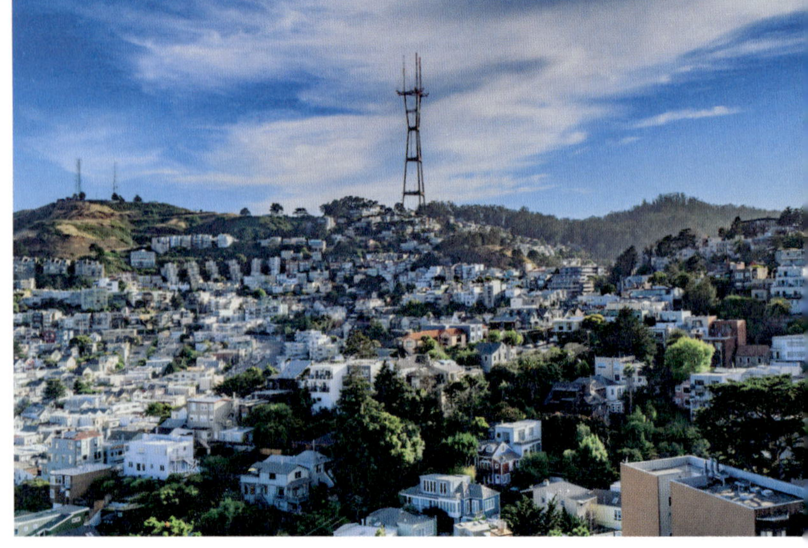

SHOP

The quirky characters of both Haight-Ashbury and the Mission extend to the locally owned stores scattered along their streets. Prepare for maze-like stores filled with vintage antiques, New Age curios, eccentric home design ideas, and even a few pirate treasures.

Relic Vintage
J7 1475 Haight St
relicvintagesf.com

Paxton Gate
L8 824 Valencia St
paxtongate.com

Wasteland
H7 1660 Haight St
shopwasteland.com

826 Valencia Pirate Supply Store
L8 826 Valencia St
shop.826valencia.org

Sutro Tower

G8 36, 37 To the public

Marking the skyline like an invading robot, Sutro Tower is 970 ft (290 m) high. It was named after local landowner and philanthropist Adolph Sutro, and it carries antennae for the signals of most of the city's TV and radio stations. Built in 1973, it is still much used, despite the rise of cable networks. The tower is visible from all over the Bay Area, and sometimes seems to float above the summer fogs that roll in from the sea. On the north side of the tower there are dense eucalyptus groves, first planted in the 1880s by Adolph Sutro. They drop down to the medical center campus of the University of California San Francisco (UCSF), one of the most highly rated teaching hospitals in the United States.

Twin Peaks

J9 36, 37

These two hills lie at the heart of San Francisco and reach a height of 900 ft (274 m) above sea level. At the top there is an area of parkland with steep and grassy slopes, from which you can enjoy incomparable views of the city.

Twin Peaks Boulevard circles both hills near their summits, and there is a parking and viewing point from which to look out over the city. Visitors who are prepared to climb up the steep footpath to the very top can leave the crowds behind and enjoy a 360-degree view. The residential districts on the lower slopes have streets that wind around the contours of the

↑ Fabulous view of downtown from the Twin Peaks

The Sutro Tower, a TV and radio mast and a prominent landmark on the city skyline

slopes, rather than following the formal grid that is more common in San Francisco.

Mission Cultural Center for Latino Arts

M9 2868 Mission St 12, 14, 27, 36, 49 J 24th St Mission 4–8pm Tue–Fri, 11am–3pm Sat missioncultural center.org

This dynamic arts center displays and promotes Latin American culture. It offers classes and workshops, including Argentine tango, Brazilian samba, and guitar, and stages theatrical events and temporary exhibitions in its gallery. One of the highlights of its calendar is the parade held in November to celebrate the Day of the Dead *(p51)*.

Noe Valley

K/L 10 24, 35, 48 J

Noe Valley is known as "Noewhere Valley" by its residents, who are intent on keeping it off the tourist map. It is a comfortable neighborhood mainly inhabited by young families. Named after its original land-grant owner, José Noe, the last *alcalde* (mayor) of Mexican Yerba Buena, the area was first developed in the 1880s following the completion of a cable-car line over the steep Castro Street hill. Like many other areas of San Francisco, this once working-class district underwent wholesale gentrification in the 1970s, resulting in today's engaging mix of boutiques, bars, and restaurants. The Noe Valley Ministry, at 1021 Sanchez Street, is a late-1880s Presbyterian church in the "Stick Style" *(p171)*, with an emphasis on vertical lines.

GREAT VIEW

Noe Valley Views

The neighborhood's eastern boundaries provide excellent vistas. There's a 30 per cent gradient on 24th Street between Grand View Avenue and Fountain Street, but the effort is rewarding.

Carnaval Mural

M9 24th St and South Van Ness Ave 12, 27, 48, 67 J 24th St Mission

One of the many brightly painted murals to be seen in the Mission District, the *Carnaval Mural* is painted above the House of Brakes and measures an impressive 24-ft- (7-m-) high and 75-ft- (23-m-) wide. It celebrates the diverse people who come together for the Carnaval festival. This event, held annually in late spring, is the high spot of the year.

Guided tours of other murals, some with political themes, are given by civic organizations. There is also an outdoor gallery with murals in Balmy Alley, near Treat and Harrison streets. Many of these murals are protests against government injustice.

Did You Know?

The *Carnaval Mural* was created in 1983 by muralist Daniel Galvez with the help of local artists.

The colorful *Carnaval Mural*, created in 1983 by Daniel Galvez and a group of local artists

A SHORT WALK
HAIGHT-ASHBURY

Distance 1 mile (1.5 km) **Time** 20 minutes
Nearest buses 7, 33

Stretching from the hilly Buena Vista Park to the flat expanses of Golden Gate Park, Haight-Ashbury *(p178)* was a place to escape to from the city center in the 1880s. It developed into a residential area, but between the 1930s and 1960s it changed dramatically to become the center of the "Flower Power" world. It is now one of the liveliest and most free-spirited places in San Francisco, with an eclectic mix of people, excellent book and record stores, and good cafés. This route takes you past some of the area's main highlights.

Wasteland, *at 1660 Haight Street, is an anarchic used-clothing, curio, and furniture emporium housed in a colorful painted Art Nouveau building. It is perfect for bargain hunters.*

The intersection of Ashbury Street and Haight Street is where this area gets its name.

The **Golden Gate Park Panhandle** *(p169) runs west into the heart of Golden Gate Park.*

Cha Cha Cha *(1801 Haight St) is one of the liveliest places to eat in San Francisco, serving Latin American food in a variety of small dishes.*

The Red Victorian Bed and Breakfast *(1665 Haight St) is a relic of the hippie 1960s. It caters to a New Age clientele with rooms with transcendental themes.*

Downtown San Francisco skyline seen from Buena Vista Park

Locator Map
For more detail see p174

Through its mass of twisting trees, the dramatic **Buena Vista Park** (p180) *offers magnificent views over the city.*

No. 1220 Masonic Avenue *is one of many ornate Victorian mansions built on a steep hill to the south of Haight Street.*

The grand home at No. 737 Buena Vista Avenue is **(Richard) Spreckels Mansion** (p180)*, built in 1897.*

Legs sticking out of the window of the Piedmont Boutique on Haight Street

The arched drumbridge int the Japanese Tea Garden

GOLDEN GATE PARK AND SUNSET

Lying to the south of the Presidio is the spectacular Golden Gate Park, a masterpiece of landscape gardening. Once a sandy wasteland, it was designed in 1871 by Park Commissioner William Hall in the style of Frederick Law Olmsted (the creator of New York City's Central Park), but completed in the 1890s by Scottish horticulturalist John McLaren. Little grows here by chance, and trees have deliberately been planted where they will best deflect the prevailing winds. All shrubs and bushes are carefully chosen to ensure there is color in every season. More parklands lie to the north and west of the Sunset district, linked by the Coastal Trail. This is where rugged Land's End, the scene of so many shipwrecks, meets the sea. Some of the park's buildings date from the 1894 California Midwinter Exposition, the first World's Fair held in California

GOLDEN GATE PARK AND SUNSET
Pacific Ocean
Land's End 21
17 Lincoln Park
Legion of Honor 3
Lincoln Park Municipal Golf Course
The Sutro Baths 20
15 Seal Rocks
18 Camera Obscura
Sutro Heights Park
13 Queen Wilhelmina Tulip Garden
19 The Beach Chalet
Ocean Beach 14
Golden Gate Park Golf Course
Buffalo Paddock 16
Polo Fields 12
Golden Gate Park
Spreckels Lake
Fly Casting Pool
Metson Lake
Mallard Lakes
Cabrillo Playground
Fulton Playground
Judah and La Playa
Judah and Sunset
Judah and 28th Ave
EL CAMINO DEL MAR
LEGION OF HONOR DRIVE
CLEMENT STREET
SEAL ROCK DRIVE
POINT LOBOS AVENUE
GEARY BOULEVARD
ANZA STREET
BALBOA STREET
CABRILLO STREET
FULTON STREET
LA PLAYA STREET
GREAT HIGHWAY
SUTRO HEIGHTS AVE
CHAIN OF LAKES DRIVE EAST
JOHN F. KENNEDY DRIVE
SPRECKELS LAKE DRIVE
MIDDLE DRIVE WEST
MARTIN LUTHER KING JUNIOR DRIVE
LINCOLN WAY
IRVING STREET
JUDAH STREET
KIRKHAM STREET
LAWTON
SUNSET BLVD
CALIFORNIA STREET
0 meters 800
0 yards 800
N

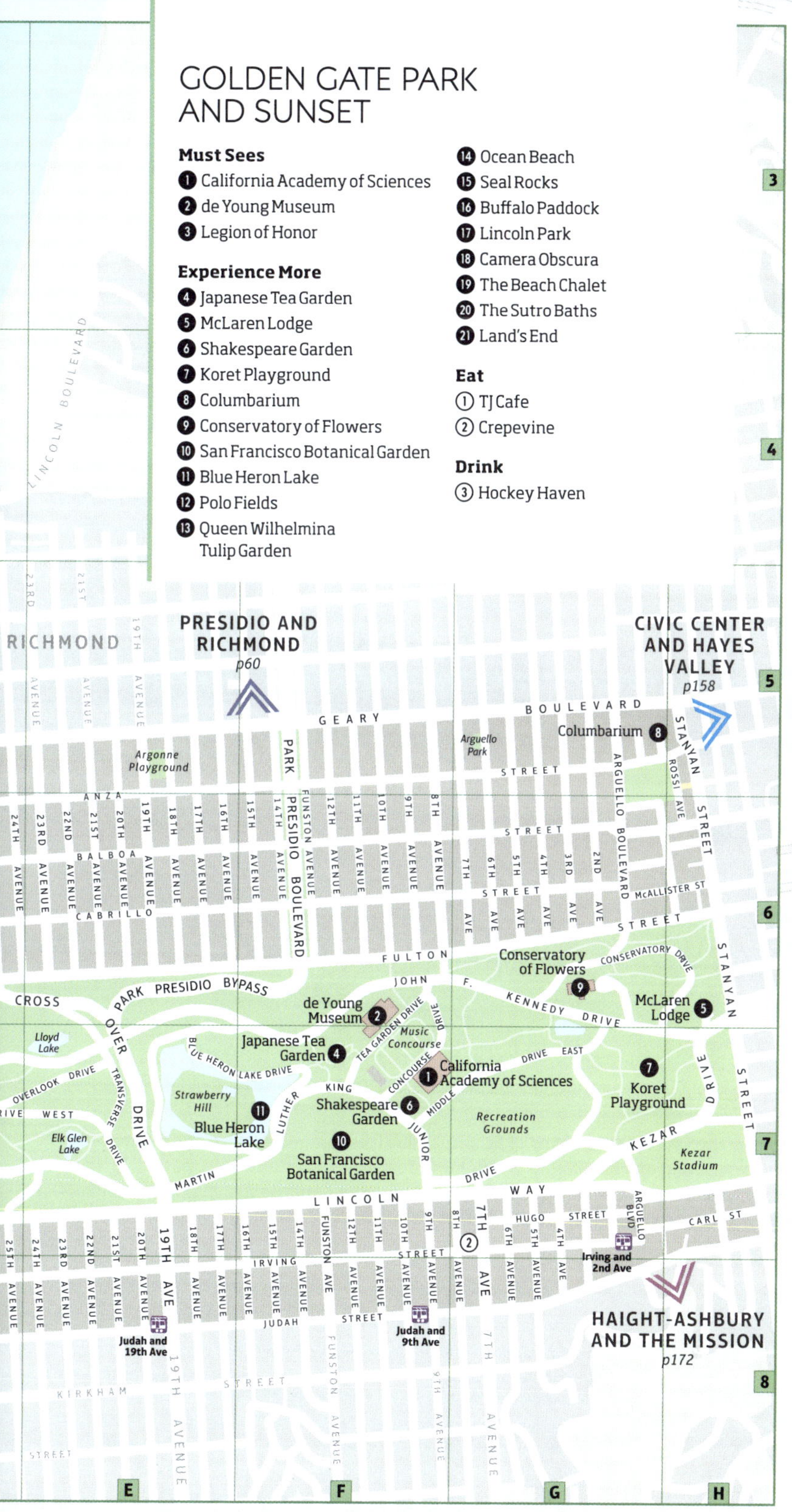

GOLDEN GATE PARK AND SUNSET
Must Sees
1 California Academy of Sciences
2 de Young Museum
3 Legion of Honor
Experience More
4 Japanese Tea Garden
5 McLaren Lodge
6 Shakespeare Garden
7 Koret Playground
8 Columbarium
9 Conservatory of Flowers
10 San Francisco Botanical Garden
11 Blue Heron Lake
12 Polo Fields
13 Queen Wilhelmina Tulip Garden
14 Ocean Beach
15 Seal Rocks
16 Buffalo Paddock
17 Lincoln Park
18 Camera Obscura
19 The Beach Chalet
20 The Sutro Baths
21 Land's End
Eat
1 TJ Cafe
2 Crepevine
Drink
3 Hockey Haven
PRESIDIO AND RICHMOND
p60
CIVIC CENTER AND HAYES VALLEY
p158
HAIGHT-ASHBURY AND THE MISSION
p172
RICHMOND
Argonne Playground
Arguello Park
Lloyd Lake
Elk Glen Lake
Strawberry Hill
Music Concourse
Recreation Grounds
Kezar Stadium
Judah and 19th Ave
Judah and 9th Ave
Irving and 2nd Ave

1

CALIFORNIA ACADEMY OF SCIENCES

Did You Know?

The museum's website has live video feeds for exhibits such as the penguin colony and coral reef.

F7 55 Music Concourse Dr 5, 44 N 9:30am-5pm Mon-Sat, 11am-5pm Sun
calacademy.org

The California Academy of Sciences lets curious minds get close to nature with exciting exhibits like an indoor rainforest, vast aquarium, and a natural history museum. The building itself blends in with the natural surroundings of Golden Gate Park, in an environmentally friendly structure with a beautiful roof of local plantlife.

The California Academy of Sciences has been located in Golden Gate Park since 1916, settling into a new building in late 2008. It houses the Steinhart Aquarium, Morrison Planetarium, and the Kimball Natural History Museum, and combines innovative green architecture with flexible exhibition spaces. A lovely piazza is at the heart of the building. The 2.5-acre (1-ha) living roof, which can be seen from the rooftop deck, is filled with native plant species, creating a beautiful oasis for birds, insects, and other creatures. Explore the fascinating exhibits at your own pace or flit between the many workshops and talks held throuhout the day. The museum's calendar is also full of lectures, weekly late-night events for adults of 21 and over, and sleepovers for children aged 5 to 17.

The exterior of the massive, cutting-edge, immersive, dome at Morrison Planetarium

Must See

Museum Highlights

Steinhart Aquarium

The amazing aquarium exhibit on the lower floor includes the world's largest indoor reef.

Living Roof

▼ An observation deck offers views of the park and allows visitors to see the green roof up close.

Morrison Planetarium

Visitors leave planet Earth behind as they enter one of the largest all-digital domes in the world.

T. rex

▶ Part of the Kimball Natural History Museum, the skeleton of a Tyrannosaurus rex sits at the museum entrance. This gigantic predator was the most powerful carnivore ever to walk the earth.

Osher Rainforest

◀ Set inside a large glass dome, this Neotropical rainforest has more than 1,600 live plants and animals.

Tusher African Hall

▶ Preserved animals from Africa are displayed here in lifelike dioramas. This area is also home to a colony of endangered African penguins *(right)*.

MUSEUM GUIDE

Steinhart Aquarium displays are spread throughout the museum, but most of the tanks are on the lower level beneath the piazza. The main floor is the gateway to all the other key exhibits, including the Kimball Natural History Museum, Morrison Planetarium, and Osher Rainforest, with some exhibits extending up several floors. An auditorium above the café hosts traveling exhibits as well as special performances and programs. The third floor houses the geology collection and Naturalist Center, and on the roof there is an observation deck.

2

DE YOUNG MUSEUM

F6 50 Hagiwara Tea Garden Dr 5, 44 N 9:30am-5:15pm Tue-Sun famsf.org

A bastion of American, Oceanian, and African art, the immense, copper-clad de Young Museum looms as a cultural and architectural landmark above a canopy of plane trees in the Golden Gate Park.

Founded in 1895, this stunning gallery suffered such bad damage in the Loma Prieta earthquake (1989) that the structure couldn't be saved. However, an exciting new facility opened in 2005 and has become as much a city landmark as its predecessor.

The museum contains a broad range of American art from the 17th century to contemporary works. With pieces by Indigenous people, early European immigrants, and enslaved people from Africa, the collection offers a look at the diversity of American experiences and cultures. Alongside displays of American origin are exhibits from the Department of Africa, Oceania, and the Americas, which owes its collection mainly to donations. These have developed into a broad and fascinating selection of exhibits from cultures around the world, and one of the most impressive textile and costume collections in the US.

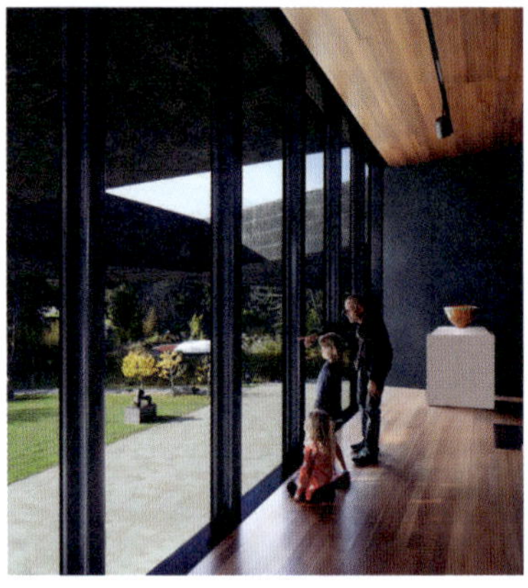

↑ Visitors admiring sculptures in the beautiful museum gardens

→ The Piazzoni Mural Room and *(inset)* sculpture of Diana from 1889

MUSEUM GUIDE

The lower-ground floor houses the special exhibitions. The main collection is divided into exhibits by geographical area spread out across the ground and upper floor. A sculpture garden can also be found on the ground floor.

14,000

The number of items in the museum's textile collection, from rugs to costumes.

The tower and observation deck on the north end of the de Young museum ↑

3

LEGION OF HONOR

B5 Lincoln Park, 100 34th Ave (at Clement St) 1, 18, 38 9:30am-5:15pm Tue-Sun famsf.org

Set in the gorgeous natural landscape of Land's End and housed in a replica of the Palais de la Légion d'Honneur in Paris, this museum features medieval to 20th-century European art, and is famous for hosting superb temporary exhibits.

Alma de Bretteville Spreckels (heiress to the Spreckels sugar fortune) commissioned the Legion of Honor in the 1920s to promote French art in California, and to commemorate the state's casualties in World War I. It contains mostly European art from the last eight centuries, with paintings by famous figures, including Monet, Rubens, and Rembrandt, as well as over 70 sculptures by Rodin. The gallery also houses collections of photography and ancient art covering 6,000 years of world history and cultures. The Achenbach Foundation, a famous collection of around 90,000 graphic works, is displayed in rotating exhibits.

GALLERY GUIDE

The museum's permanent collection is displayed in 19 galleries on the first floor. Beginning at the left of the entrance, works are arranged chronologically from the medieval period to the 20th century.

Gallery Highlights

1642

▲ *The Raising of Lazarus*, one of several hundred 5Rembrandt works in the Achenbach Foundation collection.

1880

▼ This Oval leaf molded plate was designed by the famous Wedgewood Factory.

1889

▲ Konstantin Makovsky's *The Russian Bride's Attire* depicts a Russian woman preparing for her wedding day.

1904

▼ The bronze cast of Rodin's *The Thinker* was made by Rodin's assistant, Henri Lebossé.

↑ A gallery of European sculptures, and *(inset)* the museum facade, inspired by a historic palace in Paris

1924

▼ The Skinner pipe organ was built by the Ernest M. Skinner Organ Company, and is used in organ concerts here throughout the year.

1914

▲ This version of *Water Lilies* is just one of around 250 paintings Monet created of the water lilies in his garden.

→ *A copy* of Rodin's *The Thinker* (1904), outside the gallery

EXPERIENCE MORE

Japanese Tea Garden

F7 75 Hagiwara Tea Garden Dr, Golden Gate Park 44 9am-5:30pm daily (Nov-Feb: to 4:30pm) gggp.org

This garden was established by the art dealer George Turner Marsh for the California Midwinter Fair of 1894. The steeply arched Moon Bridge forms a dramatic circular reflection in the pond below. The largest bronze Buddha to be found outside Asia, cast in Japan in 1790, is seated at the top of the garden stairs.

McLaren Lodge

H6 Near junction of Stanyan & Fell sts on the park's east side 7X, 21, 33 8am-5pm Mon-Fri sfrecpark.org

This sandstone villa, designed by Edward Swain, was built in 1896. As superintendent of the park, John McLaren lived here with his family until his death in 1943. Every December the cypress tree outside is lit in his memory.

Shakespeare Garden

F7 Music Concourse, Golden Gate Park 6, 7, 43, 44

Gardeners of this charming and romantic garden have

→ Looking onto the picturesque Japanese Tea Garden from the Tea House

200

The number of different flower and plant species in the Shakespeare Garden.

tried to cultivate all the plants, flowers, and herbs that have been mentioned in William Shakespeare's works. Along with the floral arrangements, there are relevant quotations written on bronze plaques that are set in a wall at the back of the garden.

Koret Playground

G7 Kezar Dr, near First Ave 5, 71 N Hours vary, check website sfrecpark.org

A great place for young visitors who need to let off some steam, this is the oldest public children's playground in the United States. In 1978 it was redesigned with sandboxes, swings, slides, and a fortress, and recent additions include a wave-inspired climbing wall. On the Herschell-Spillman merry-go-round, housed in a Greek-inspired structure that dates from 1892, children ride on brightly painted beasts (additional fee required).

↑ Stunning cherry trees blossoming in the Shakespeare Garden

THE CREATION OF GOLDEN GATE PARK

As San Francisco prospered in the 1860s, its citizens demanded the same amenities as other great cities. Prominent among these was a large city park, so city planners turned to a surveyor and engineer named William Hammond Hall. Hall started work at the east end, laying out meandering roads and trying to create a seemingly natural landscape. The developing park soon proved popular: families came to picnic and young dandies raced their carriages.

Despite the popularity of the park, it was nearly prevented from reaching maturity by budget cuts and public corruption, with city officials siphoning off funds. Hall was falsely accused of corruption and resigned in protest. The park fell into a period of decline, but after a decade of decay, Hall was asked to resume the task of managing it, which he agreed to do with the help of John McLaren, who shared his passion and vision for the park.

Columbarium

G5 1 Loraine Court 771-0717 33, 38 9am-5pm Mon-Fri, 10am-3pm Sat & Sun

The San Francisco Columbarium is the sole survivor of the old Lone Mountain Cemetery, which once covered sizable tracts of the Richmond District. Most of the remains were disinterred and moved to Colma in 1914. This Neo-Classical rotunda houses the remains of 6,000 people in elaborate decorated urns. Unused for several decades, it was rescued and restored by the Neptune Society in 1979. The ornate, bright interior under the dome has lovely stained-glass windows. The narrow passages encircling the dome are remarkable for their acoustics.

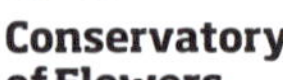

Conservatory of Flowers

G6 100 John F. Kennedy Dr, Golden Gate Park 5, 21, 33, 44 N 10am-4:30pm Thu-Tue gggp.org

This beautiful, ornate, Victorian-style glasshouse is full of flowers and plants from around the world, especially from tropical zones. There are five distinct galleries, each focusing on a different ecosystem. The original building, opened in 1879, was largely destroyed by a storm in 1995. A campaign for its repair was launched, and it reopened in 2003.

PICTURE PERFECT
Light Shows

The Conservatory of Flowers is illuminated with light projections every night from dusk to midnight. The installation can be viewed from JFK Drive and in Conservatory Valley - no admission is necessary.

San Francisco Botanical Garden

F7 9th Ave at Lincoln Way, Golden Gate Park 5, 7, 44 N Mar-Sep: 7:30am-6pm daily (Oct: to 5pm; Nov-Jan: to 4pm) sfbotanicalgarden.org

On display at the Botanical Garden are 8,000 species of plants, trees, and shrubs from around the world. There are Mexican, African, South American, and Australian gardens, and one devoted to native California plants.

Well worth a visit is the enchanting Moon-Viewing Garden. It exhibits East Asian plants in a setting that, unlike that of the Japanese Tea Garden *(p198)*, is naturalistic rather than formal. Both medicinal and culinary plants are grown in the Garden of Fragrance, which is designed for the visually impaired. Here the emphasis is on taste, touch, and smell, and the plants are identified in Braille. Another area is planted with Indigenous California redwood trees, with a stream winding through. This recreates the flora and atmosphere of a northern Californian coastal forest. There is also a New World Cloud Forest, with flora from the mountains of Central America. Surprisingly, all these gardens thrive in the coastal fog. The garden has a store, selling seeds and books, and also houses the Helen Crocker Russell Library of Horticulture, open to the public. The store

Well worth a visit is the enchanting Moon-Viewing Garden. It exhibits East Asian plants in a setting that is naturalistic rather than formal.

is the starting point for free guided tours on weekdays at 1:30pm, and from 10:30am to 1:30pm on weekends.

Blue Heron Lake

F7 50 Blue Heron Lake Dr, Golden Gate Park 28, 29, 44 Daily sfrecpark.org

This artificial lake, created in 1895, encircles Strawberry Hill such that the summit of the hill now forms an island, linked to the mainland by two stone-clad bridges.

Formerly known as Stow Lake, Blue Heron Lake's pretty, circular stream is ideal for rowing laps on a boat rented from the boathouse, though leisurely drifting feels more appropriate in this tranquil setting.

The Chinese moon-watching pavilion on the island's shore was a gift from San Francisco's sister city Taipei, in Taiwan. The red and green pavilion was shipped to San Francisco in 6,000 pieces, then assembled on the island.

The millionaire Collis P. Huntington donated the money to create the reservoir and the waterfall that cascades into Blue Heron Lake and is one of the park's most attractive features.

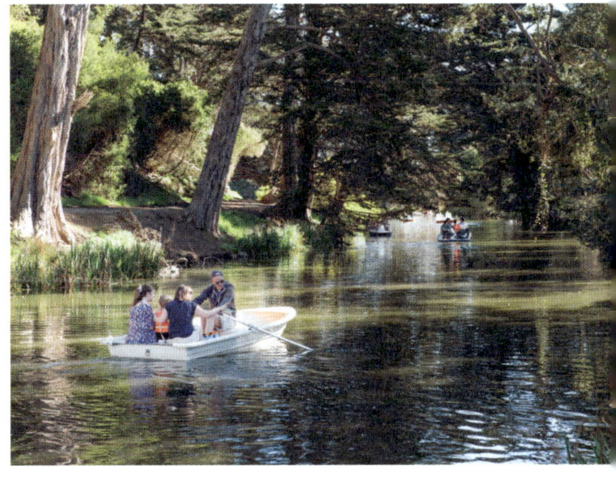

↑ Boating on Blue Heron, one of the park's main attractions

EAT

TJ Cafe

This simple, counter service café is popular for its hearty breakfast platters, big burgers and sandwiches, as well as its fish and chips. Order to-go and enjoy your meal at nearby Ocean Beach.

B6 724 La Playa St
tjcafesf.com

Crepevine

With an exhaustive menu of sweet and savory crêpes and other breakfast and lunch options, this is a great place to fill up before setting out to explore Golden Gate Park.

G7 624 Irving St
crepevine.com

Tropical plants fill the magnificent Conservatory of Flowers

Did You Know?

A velodrome was built around the Polo Fields in 1906 and is still used by cyclists to this day.

12 Polo Fields

C7 John F. Kennedy Dr, Golden Gate Park 5, 29

You are far more likely to see joggers and soccer teams than polo ponies using the Polo Fields stadium in the western half of Golden Gate Park. Once home to equestrian matches, the fields now hosts weekend soccer games and cyclists. The park's equestrian trails and the Bercut Equitation Field can be explored on horseback, with horses available by the hour at the adjacent riding stables. For anglers, there are several fly-casting pools nearby.

To the east of the stadium, in the green expanse of Old Speedway Meadows, many celebrations were held during the late 1960s, including some notable rock concerts. The Grateful Dead and Jefferson Airplane, among others, played here. Here, in the spring of 1967, thousands attended a huge "Be-in," one of many events that led to the "Summer of Love."

13 Queen Wilhelmina Tulip Garden

B7 5, 18, 31, 31AX

The Dutch windmill was built near the northwest corner of Golden Gate Park in 1903. Its original purpose was to pump water from an underground source to irrigate the park, but it is no longer in use. Its companion, the Murphy Windmill, was erected in the park's southwest corner in 1905. The garden was named after the Dutch Queen Wilhelmina, and tulip bulbs are donated each year by the Dutch Bulb Growers' Association; early spring is the best time to see the colorful display of tulips in full bloom.

14 Ocean Beach

A7 5, 7X, 18, 31, 31AX, 48 L, N

Most of San Francisco's western boundary is defined by this sandy beach. Though sublime when viewed from Cliff House or Sutro Heights, the sea here is dangerous for swimming because of its icy waters and a strong undertow. Surfers in wet suits are a

← The Queen Wilhelmina Tulip Garden with its windmill and glorious flower beds

common sight, but there is often a stiff wind, or fog. On rare hot days, it is also a popular spot for sun-bathers and picnickers; and locals come for barbecues and to watch the sun go down.

Walking along the Ocean Beach, and *(inset)* Seal Rocks, a haven for sea lions.

15 Seal Rocks

A6 18, 38

Seal Rocks is a collection of rocky islands (not accessible to visitors) in the Lands End area, popular with basking sea lions and sea birds. They are best viewed from Ocean Beach (at low tide) or Sutro Heights Park. Bring binoculars to watch them in their natural setting. At night, the barking of the sea lions is somehow both reassuring and eerie, especially when it is foggy. On a clear day you can see the Farallon Islands, which lie 32 miles (51 km) off the coast. This group of islands and sea stacks are also inhabited by sea lions and contain a rookery that has been protected by the state since 1907.

16 Buffalo Paddock

C7 John F. Kennedy Dr, Golden Gate Park 5, 29

The shaggy buffalo that graze in this paddock are the largest North American land animals. With its short horns and humped back, the buffalo (or "American bison") is the symbol of the American plains. This paddock was opened in 1892. In 1902 William Cody, alias "Buffalo Bill," traded one of his bulls for one from the Golden Gate Park herd. Both parties thought that they had rid themselves of an aggressive beast, but Cody's newly purchased bull jumped a high fence once back at his encampment and escaped. Apparently, it took a total of 80 men to recapture it.

DRINK

Hockey Haven

Operating since 1949, what this vibrant pub lacks in fanciness it makes up for in fun. Pool tables, a thumping jukebox, friendly service, and a relaxed vibe draw in the local clientele on a nightly basis.

C6 3625 Balboa St 752-4413

Lincoln Park

B4 1, 1AX, 18, 38

This splendid park, located above the Golden Gate Park, is the setting for the Legion of Honor *(p196)*. The land was originally allocated to Golden Gate Cemetery, where graves were segregated according to the nationality of their occupants. When these graves were cleared in the first decade of the 20th century, the park was established and landscaped by John McLaren, who served as superintendent of the Golden Gate Park for many years *(p199)*.

The park now has an 18-hole golf course and scenic walks. City views from the hilltop course are, as you might expect, superb.

Camera Obscura

A6 1096 Point Lobos Ave 38AX Daily

One of San Francisco's quirky hidden gems, Camera Obscura is located at Land's End, right next to the former Cliff House restaurant that closed in 2021. Owned and managed by the National Park Service (NPS), this observatory was added to the National Register of Historic Places in 2001, 24 years after the NPS acquired the property. It projects an image onto a horizontal viewing table by way of a reflected image from a viewpoint at the top of the building. A metal hood in the dome at the top of the building then slowly rotates, taking about five minutes to finish, presenting a 360-degree panorama of what can be seen around the building.

→ The evocative ruins of the Sutro Baths, a great lookout point over the Pacific Ocean

19   

The Beach Chalet

A7 1000 Great Hwy 5, 5R, 31, 31AX, 38 9am-8pm Mon-Fri, 10am-8pm Sat & Sun beachchalet.com

Where the Golden Gate Park meets the ocean, you'll find this charming historic building. Noteworthy architect Willis Polk *(p47)* designed the chalet in 1925, while other artisans have added their touches over the years, creating a distinctly "only-in-San Francisco" establishment. Elaborate murals by famed artist Lucien Labaudt were commissioned by the Works Progress Administration in 1936 and depict famous places and people in San Francisco. Intricate wood carvings by Michael von Meyer show seaside imagery such as mermaids, octopuses, and vintage ships,

← The Camera Obscura *(inset)* and Holograph Gallery, perched atop a cliff

underscoring the sweeping views of the Pacific Ocean right outside the Beach Chalet windows. You can browse historic artifacts housed on the first floor, view a three-dimensional model of Golden Gate Park, sample seasonal beers from the brewery, and enjoy live entertainment and good food in the restaurant.

20

The Sutro Baths

A5 1004 Point Lobos 38, 38AX, 38R Sunrise-sunset daily

Today, all that remains of the Sutro Baths are atmospheric ruins in a wild and rocky setting. Developed in 1890 by Adolph Sutro, an entrepreneur and former city mayor, the baths housed the largest indoor pools in the country. The incoming tide would fill and refresh the water of the pools every five days. The pools were a popular destination for visitors and locals in the first half of the 20th century, but they eventually fell out of favor. In the 1960s, a mysterious fire laid waste to the once iconic buildings. Set within the craggy cliffside near the famed Cliff House and close to the wide expanse of the ocean, these brooding ruins afford striking views.

Set within the craggy cliffside near the famed Cliff House and close to the wide expanse of the ocean, these brooding ruins afford striking views.

21

Land's End

B4 1, 1AX, 18, 38

A rugged seascape of rock, cliff, and matted cypress woods, Land's End is the wildest part of San Francisco. It is reached on foot along the Coastal Trail, which can be accessed by stairs from the Legion of Honor, or from a parking area at Point Lobos. The Coastal Trail ends in a spectacular viewing point overlooking the Golden Gate Bridge *(p64)*. It is inadvisable to leave the trail, as there is a risk of being stranded by incoming tides; call the National Park Service for tide information (415-561-4700). Mile Rocks Lighthouse can be seen offshore from here, or at least what is left of it. The tower was removed in 1966 and the top converted into a helicopter pad.

↑ The Coastal Trail at Land's End, offering city and ocean views

A SHORT WALK
GOLDEN GATE PARK

Distance half a mile (1 km) **Time** 15 minutes
Nearest buses 5, 44

Golden Gate Park is one of the largest urban parks in the world. It stretches from the Pacific Ocean to the center of San Francisco, forming an oasis of greenery and calm in which to escape from the bustle of city life. Within the park an amazing number of activities are possible, both sporting and cultural. The landscaped area around the Music Concourse, with its fountains, plane trees, and benches, is the most popular and developed section. Here you can enjoy free Sunday concerts at the Spreckels Temple of Music. Two museums stand on either side of the Concourse, and the Japanese and Shakespeare gardens are within walking distance of each other.

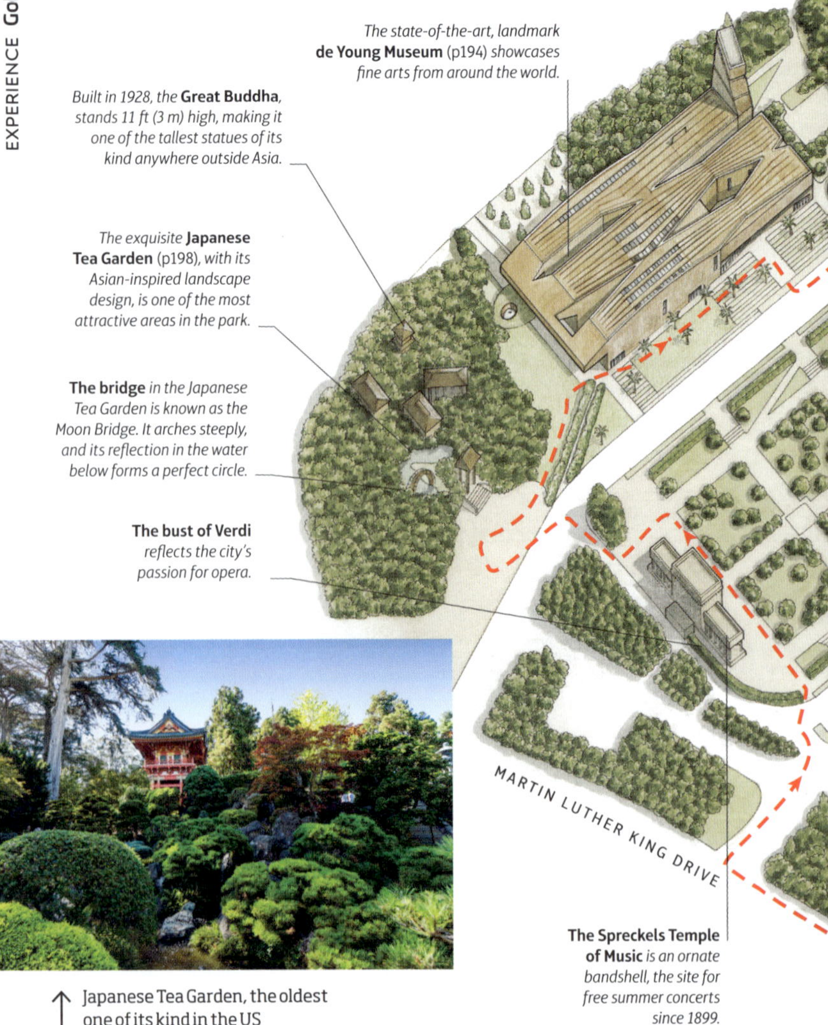

The state-of-the-art, landmark **de Young Museum** (p194) *showcases fine arts from around the world.*

Built in 1928, the **Great Buddha**, *stands 11 ft (3 m) high, making it one of the tallest statues of its kind anywhere outside Asia.*

The exquisite **Japanese Tea Garden** (p198), *with its Asian-inspired landscape design, is one of the most attractive areas in the park.*

The bridge *in the Japanese Tea Garden is known as the Moon Bridge. It arches steeply, and its reflection in the water below forms a perfect circle.*

The bust of Verdi *reflects the city's passion for opera.*

The Spreckels Temple of Music *is an ornate bandshell, the site for free summer concerts since 1899.*

↑ Japanese Tea Garden, the oldest one of its kind in the US

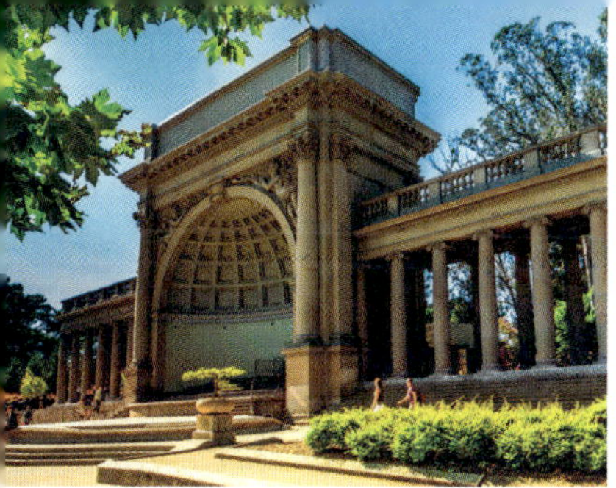

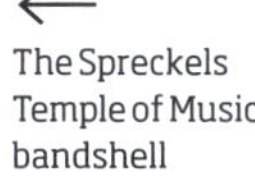

The Spreckels Temple of Music bandshell

GOLDEN GATE PARK AND SUNSET
Golden Gate Park

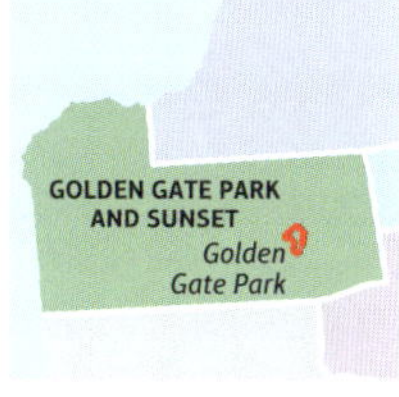

Locator Map
For more detail see p190

The statue of the Apple Cider Press, *by sculptor Thomas Shields-Clarke, is one of the few monuments to survive from the California Midwinter Fair of 1894.*

The bust of Miguel de Cervantes, *the Spanish author, was sculpted by Jo Mora. He is depicted with his two fictional creations, Don Quixote and Sancho Panza.*

The John McLaren Rhododendron Dell *is planted in memory of the first superintendent of Golden Gate Park.*

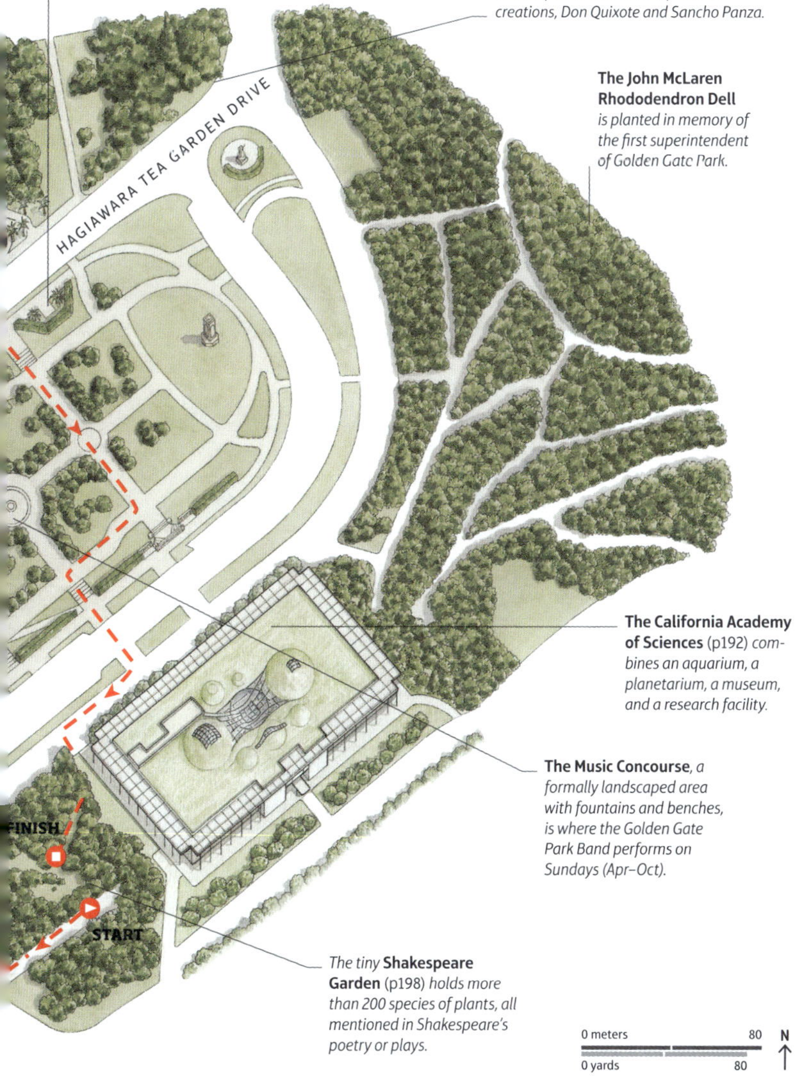

HAGIAWARA TEA GARDEN DRIVE
FINISH
START
0 meters 80
0 yards 80
N

The California Academy of Sciences (p192) *combines an aquarium, a planetarium, a museum, and a research facility.*

The Music Concourse, *a formally landscaped area with fountains and benches, is where the Golden Gate Park Band performs on Sundays (Apr–Oct).*

The tiny **Shakespeare Garden** (p198) *holds more than 200 species of plants, all mentioned in Shakespeare's poetry or plays.*

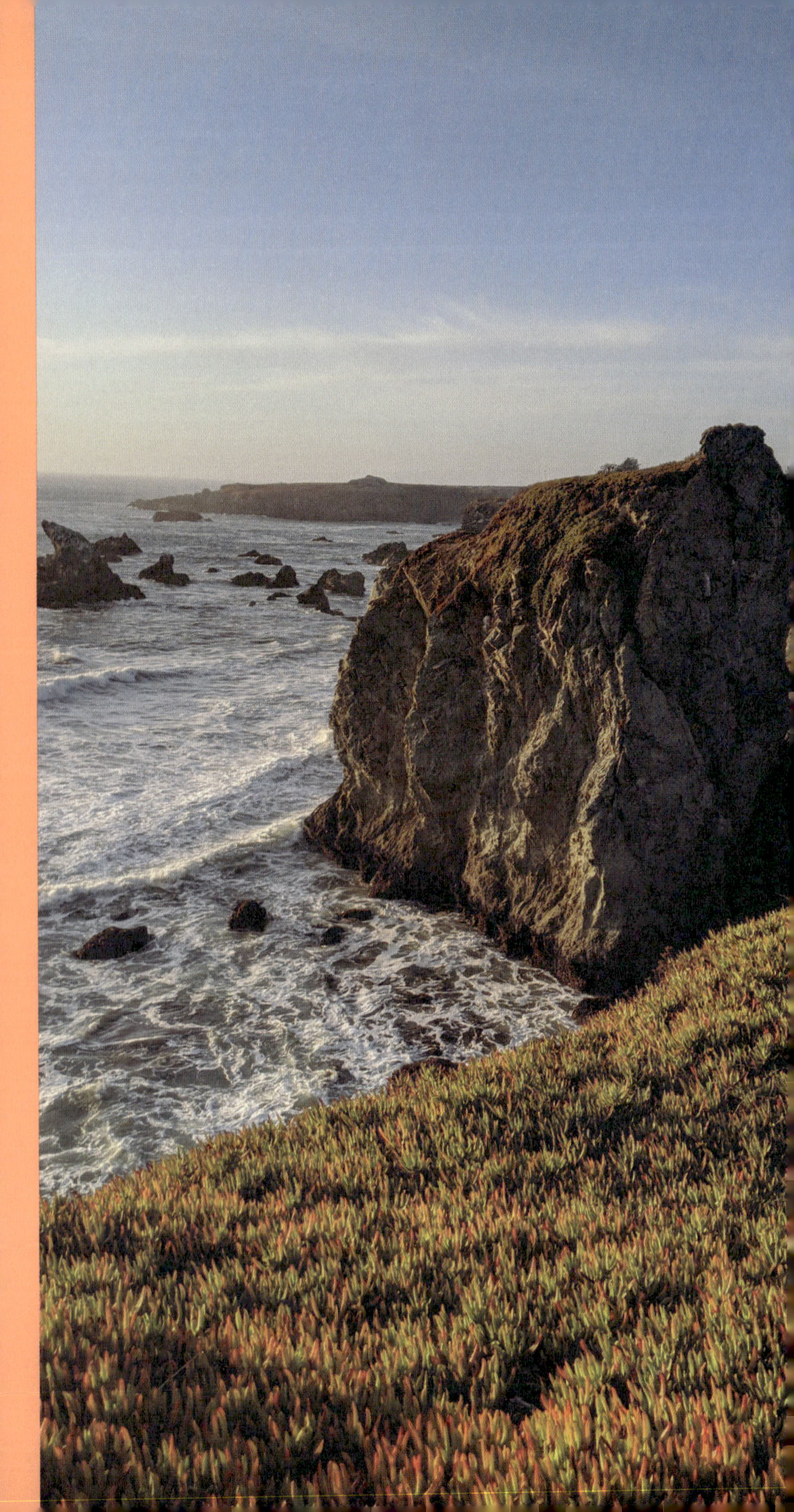

The gorgeous, rugged Sonoma County coastline

THE BAY AREA

San Francisco is the smallest of the nine counties that encircle the San Francisco Bay. To the north of Golden Gate Bridge, the wild, windswept coastline and redwood forests of Marin County were once home to the Miwok people. During the Mexican–American war (1846–8), these areas of Marin County were seized by Americans as part of the invasion of California (1846–7). Oakland, meanwhile, in the East Bay, is highly developed. Constructed in 1868, Oakland Long Wharf became the genesis of today's massive Port of Oakland, and the city flourished as a major shipping and transportation hub. Manufacturing also boomed from the 1920s, attracting thousands of African Americans from the South; later in 1966, it was here that Huey Newton and Bobby Seale founded the Black Panther Party. Since the 1970s, the city has seen much regeneration, though gentrification remains a controversial issue. Neighboring Oakland is Berkeley, a city most associated with its iconic University of California campus, which was established here in 1868.

The Peninsula area to the south of San Francisco is home to Silicon Valley, which began with Hewlett and Packard's efforts in 1938 around Stanford University. Everything from Intel's silicon transistors in the 1960s to 21st-century internet giants Google and Facebook has started here. Farther south, San Jose was founded by the Spanish in 1777. The city was largely an agricultural hub until World War II, but it has since seen phenomenal growth, and its population surpassed San Francisco's in the 1990s.

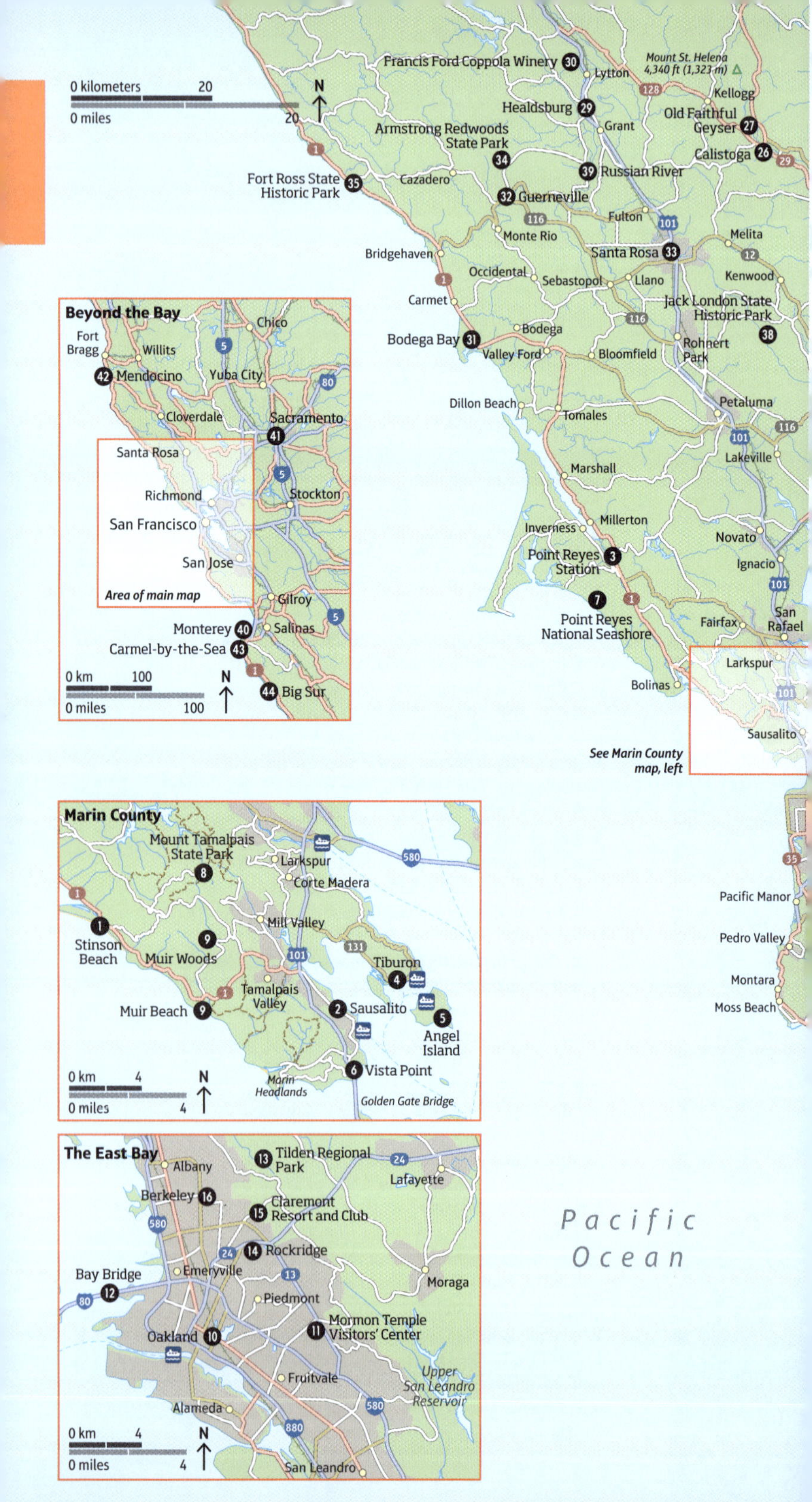

0 kilometers 20
0 miles 20
N
Francis Ford Coppola Winery 30
Lytton
Mount St. Helena
4,340 ft (1,323 m)
128
Kellogg
Healdsburg 29
Grant
Old Faithful Geyser 27
Armstrong Redwoods State Park 34
Calistoga 26
29
1
Fort Ross State Historic Park 35
Cazadero
39 Russian River
32 Guerneville
116
Fulton
101
Monte Rio
Melita
Bridgehaven
Santa Rosa 33
12
Occidental
Sebastopol
Llano
Kenwood
1
Carmet
Jack London State Historic Park
116
38
Bodega
Bodega Bay 31
Valley Ford
Bloomfield
Rohnert Park
Dillon Beach
Tomales
Petaluma
116
101
Lakeville
Marshall
Millerton
Inverness
Novato
Point Reyes Station 3
Ignacio
101
7
1
Point Reyes National Seashore
Fairfax
San Rafael
Larkspur
Bolinas
101
Sausalito
See Marin County map, left
35
Pacific Manor
Pedro Valley
Montara
Moss Beach
Pacific Ocean
Beyond the Bay
Fort Bragg
Willits
Chico
5
42 Mendocino
Yuba City
80
Cloverdale
Sacramento
41
Santa Rosa
5
Richmond
Stockton
San Francisco
San Jose
Area of main map
Gilroy
5
Monterey 40
Salinas
Carmel-by-the-Sea 43
1
0 km 100
0 miles 100
N
44 Big Sur
Marin County
Mount Tamalpais State Park
8
Larkspur
580
Corte Madera
1
1
Mill Valley
Stinson Beach
9
Muir Woods
131
101
Tiburon
4
1
Tamalpais Valley
Muir Beach 9
2 Sausalito
5
Angel Island
0 km 4
0 miles 4
N
Marin Headlands
6 Vista Point
Golden Gate Bridge
The East Bay
Albany
13 Tilden Regional Park
24
Lafayette
Berkeley 16
15 Claremont Resort and Club
580
24
14 Rockridge
Emeryville
Bay Bridge
12
13
Moraga
80
Piedmont
Mormon Temple Visitors' Center 11
Oakland 10
Fruitvale
Upper San Leandro Reservoir
Alameda
580
880
0 km 4
0 miles 4
N
San Leandro

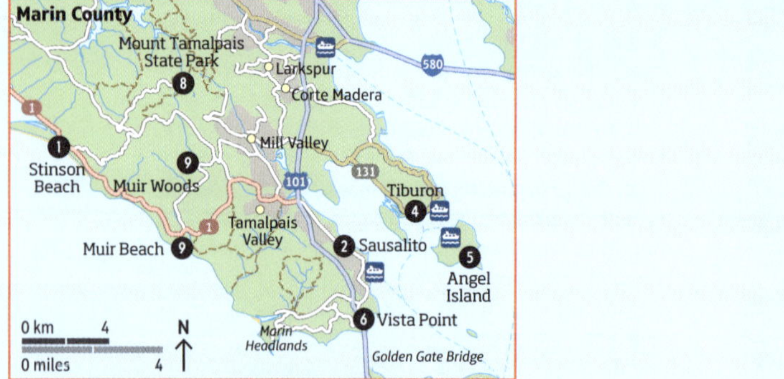

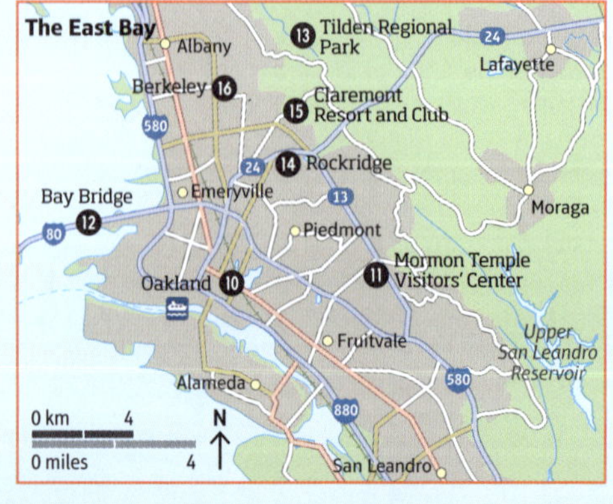

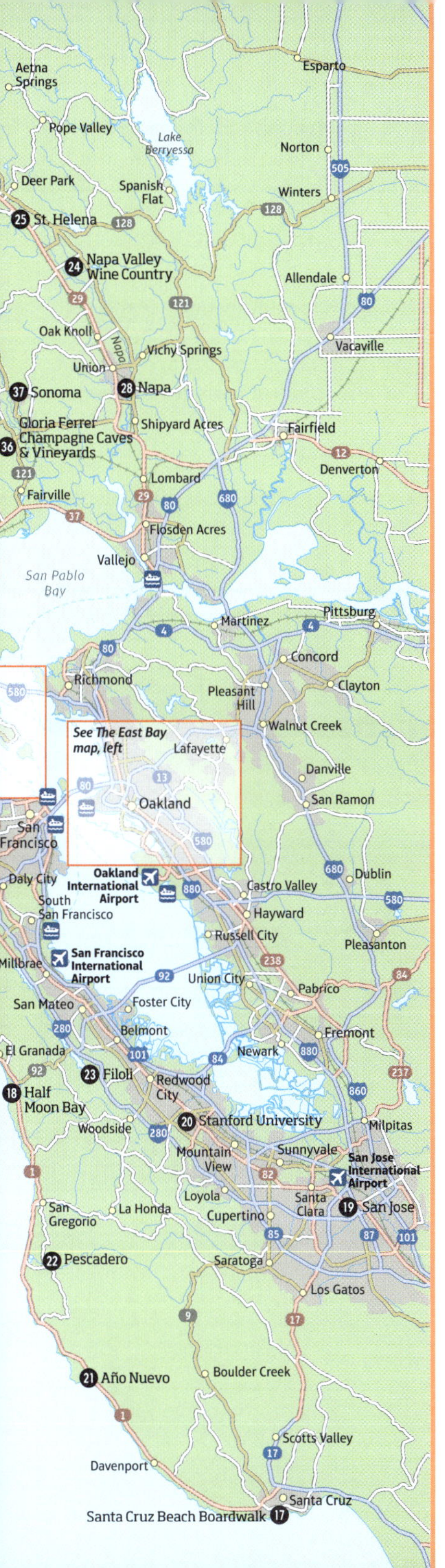

THE BAY AREA

Marin County

1. Stinson Beach
2. Sausalito
3. Point Reyes Station
4. Tiburon
5. Angel Island
6. Vista Point
7. Point Reyes National Seashore
8. Mount Tamalpais State Park
9. Muir Woods and Beach

The East Bay

10. Oakland
11. Mormon Temple Visitors' Center
12. Bay Bridge
13. Tilden Regional Park
14. Rockridge
15. Claremont Resort and Club
16. Berkeley

The Peninsula

17. **Must See:** Santa Cruz Beach Boardwalk
18. **Must See:** Half Moon Bay
19. San Jose
20. Stanford University
21. Año Nuevo
22. Pescadero
23. Filoli

Napa Valley

24. **Must See:** Napa Valley Wine Country
25. St. Helena
26. Calistoga
27. Old Faithful Geyser
28. Napa

Sonoma County

29. **Must See:** Healdsburg
30. Francis Ford Coppola Winery
31. Bodega Bay
32. Guerneville
33. Santa Rosa
34. Armstrong Redwoods State Park
35. Fort Ross State Historic Park
36. Gloria Ferrer Caves & Vineyards
37. Sonoma
38. Jack London State Historic Park
39. Russian River

Beyond the Bay

40. **Must See:** Monterey
41. Sacramento
42. Mendocino
43. Carmel-by-the-Sea
44. Big Sur

GETTING TO KNOW THE BAY AREA

The Bay Area has no official boundaries, but is roughly made up of the nine counties that border the San Francisco Bay. San Francisco itself is only a small part of this region, so rent a car or take a taxi-cab and head out to explore the beautiful, varied, and historic region of northern California.

PAGE 216

MARIN COUNTY

A wild, windswept coastline, redwood forests, and seaside villages are all just a few minutes north from the Golden Gate Bridge. Accessible by ferry, Sausalito and Tiburon are charming bayside hamlets loaded with boutique stores, galleries, and scenic cafés and restaurants. Hugging the Pacific, a wide bay, and a wildlife-rich estuary, Point Reyes National Seashore is for hikers, bikers, and wilderness lovers.

Best for
Hiking and nature

Home to
Vista Point and Mount Tamalpais State Park

Experience
A ferry ride to Angel Island for an afternoon of hiking

PAGE 222

THE EAST BAY

The cities in the East Bay have enough highlights of their own to lure people across the Bay from San Francisco. Just 20 minutes by car over the Bay Bridge you'll find museums, galleries, waterfront walks, and historic sights abound in Oakland, while Berkeley has a verdant university campus and is the capital of California cuisine.

Best for
City life and museums

Home to
Oakland and Berekely

Experience
Exploring trendy shopping districts like Fourth Street in Berkeley

PAGE 230

THE PENINSULA

South of San Francisco are coastal sights from the lively Santa Cruz Beach Boardwalk to the natural beauty of Half Moon Bay. Some of this area is also known as Silicon Valley, home of Apple, Google, and a plethora of other tech-centric companies. Families will love The Tech Interactive and the spooky Winchester Mystery House in San Jose, while others can enjoy some time in quiet, picturesque towns like Pescadero.

Best for
Families, beaches, and cool towns

Home to
Santa Cruz Beach Boardwalk and Half Moon Bay

Experience
A day at California's oldest amusement park by the ocean in Santa Cruz

PAGE 238

NAPA VALLEY

Hundreds of world-famous wineries have celebrity status in this region, making it the perfect place for a luxury break. But the pleasures of Napa Valley aren't restricted to wine connoisseurs. Hot-air balloons float over the hills and vineyards, while passengers on the Napa Valley Wine Train enjoy a fine-dining experience as they ride the rails through beautiful rolling hills.

Best for
Wine tasting and upscale resorts

Home to
Napa Valley Wine Country

Experience
The ultimate indulgence in food and drink at The French Laundry

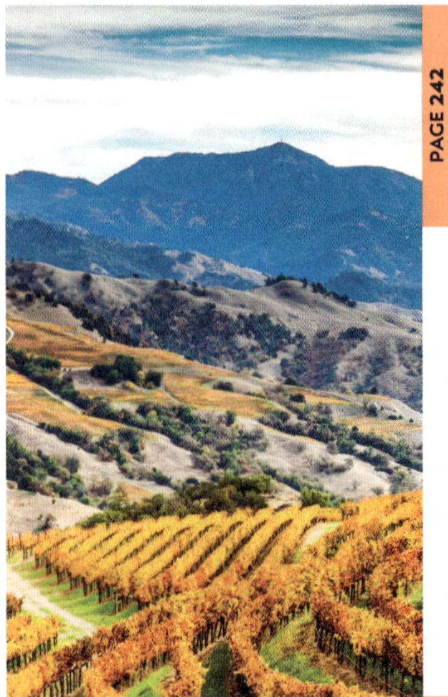

PAGE 242

SONOMA COUNTY

From early California history in the small town of Sonoma, to exquisite drinking and dining in verdant wine valleys, Sonoma County is another must-see stop on any good tour of the Bay Area. Along winding country roads, hundreds of premium wineries welcome visitors, offering tastes of the grape, plus music festivals and cuisine-focused events. For families and nature lovers, there's a gorgeous, rugged coastline and beautiful national parks.

Best for
Wine and national parks

Home to
Healdsburg

Experience
Taking the family for a day of sun and outdoor fun at the Russian River

PAGE 248

BEYOND THE BAY

Head out for a day trip from San Francisco and you'll find all kinds of adventures to remind you of the irresistible pull of the Pacific Coast that has drawn settlers and inspired writers and artists for centuries. Explore Sacramento and Mendocino to the north, and the lovely town of Monterey in the south – but make sure to take time out to drive down Highway 1 and enjoy the breathtaking coastline of Big Sur.

Best for
History, beaches, and old towns

Home to
Monterey

Experience
Visiting the historic Old Town in Sacramento, the capital of California

Hanging out on the waterfront and enjoying the views at Sausalito

MARIN COUNTY

Did You Know?

Over 400 floating homes can be seen in Sausalito, including one inspired by the Taj Mahal.

Stinson Beach

US 101 N to Hwy 1 9am to 1 hour after sunset daily nps.gov/goga/stbe.htm

Since the early days of the 20th century this has been a popular vacation spot; the first visitors came on ferries from San Francisco and were met by horse-drawn carriages. Stinson remains the preferred swimming beach for the whole area, with shallow water making it very safe for children, and an expansive stretch of soft white sand, where surfers mingle with swimmers and sunbathers. The village nearby (also named Stinson Beach) has a few cafés and restaurants, and some good bookstores.

Sausalito

US 101 N, first exit after Golden Gate Bridge, to Bridgeway From Ferry Building

In this attractive small town that was once a fishing community, Victorian bungalows cling to steep hills rising from the bay. Parallel to the waterfront, Bridgeway serves as a promenade for the weekend crowds that come to patronize the popular waterfront restaurants, gift stores, art studios, food markets, and boutiques.

The **US Army Corps of Engineers Bay Model Visitor Center** is well worth a look to see a working hydraulic scale model, which simulates the movement of the tides and currents of San Francisco Bay.

US Army Corps of Engineers Bay Model Visitor Center

2100 Bridgeway Hours vary, check website spn.usace.army.mil

Point Reyes Station

1 Bear Valley Rd; pointreyes.org

A delightful hamlet (population 350) built along the now defunct railroad at the southern end of Tomales Bay, this is the Marin Coast's main commercial and social hub. Its red-brick, vaguely Italianate architecture reflects its founding by settlers who

Stinson remains the preferred beach for the whole area, with shallow water making it very safe for children, and an expansive stretch of soft white sand.

Boats docked at Ayala Cove, the only ferry terminal on Angel Island

came here from northern Italy. Many original buildings still stand on Main Street, including the Old Creamery, Livery Stable, and original rail depot (today the post office). This charming hamlet is a great place to stay while exploring the beautiful Point Reyes National Seashore *(p218)* and surrounding coastal area on hiking or horse-riding trips.

4

Tiburon

US 101 N, Tiburon Blvd exit Golden Gate Transit bus 8 From Ferry Building or Pier 43

The waterfront of this chic town is fringed with lovely parks, and the main street is lined with stores and restaurants housed in "arks." These are houseboats dating from the turn of the 20th century that were pulled ashore when the lagoon was filled in, and refurbished. They now stand in what is called "Ark Row."

Angel Island

From San Francisco Ferry Terminal & Tiburon angelisland.org

Angel Island is reached by ferry from Tiburon and San Francisco. Boats dock at Ayala Cove. Hiking trails loop the wooded island, rising to 776 ft (237 m) above sea level, and past an old military garrison where immigrants from Asia were interrogated before being allowed to enter the US. During World War II, prisoners of war were held here. No motor vehicles are allowed, so it's a great place for walking or cycling.

EAT

Curled around the edge of Richardson Bay, Sausalito has plenty of options for dining with a waterfront view.

The Spinnaker
100 Spinnaker Dr
spinnakersausalito.us

$$$

The Trident
558 Bridgeway
thetrident.net

$$$

Barrel House Tavern
660 Bridgeway
barrelhousetavern.com

$$$

Fish.
350 Harbor Dr
331fish.com

$$$

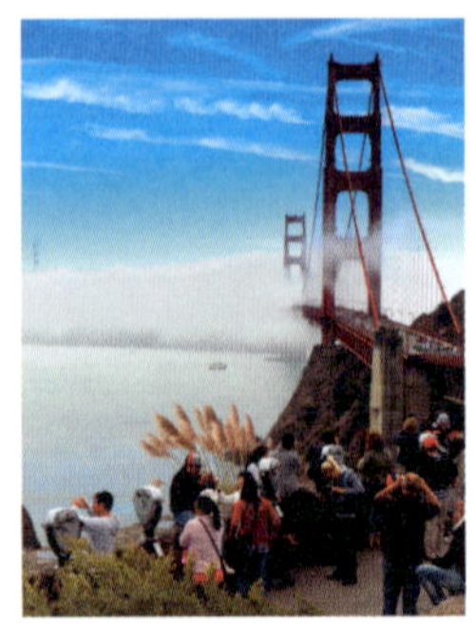

The Golden Gate Bridge shrouded in fog, seen from Vista Point

Vista Point

US 101 N, then take Conzelman Rd Golden Gate Transit bus 30, 70 goldengate.org

This famous viewpoint, immediately northeast of the Golden Gate Bridge *(p64)*, offers an iconic vista of San Francisco and the Bay from atop Fort Baker. If you are coming by car, be aware that the parking lot often fills up quickly in summer, especially on weekends, so get there early or take public transport.

More spectacular vistas can be enjoyed from the Marin Headlands, on the northwest side of the bridge. A path from Fort Baker leads under the bridge, then via Conzelman Road (accessible off southbound US 101) up to the first viewpoint at Battery Spencer, a World War II gun emplacement. The road snakes uphill to two other viewpoints. The most spectacular view awaits at the top, at Hawk Hill.

The **Bay Area Discovery Museum** close to Fort Baker is a wonderful, hands-on children's museum that is worth a visit once you're done admiring the scenery. With a focus on STEM subjects, it allows children to test their creative problem-solving skills with its interactive exhibits.

Bay Area Discovery Museum

557 McReynolds Rd 10am-4pm Wed-Mon bayareadiscoverymuseum.org

Point Reyes National Seashore

US Hwy 1 to Olema; then follow signs for Point Reyes National Seashore Golden Gate Transit buses 70 & 101 to San Rafael Center, then West Marin Stage 68

Point Reyes peninsula is wild and windswept, and a haven for wildlife, including a herd of tule elk. There are cattle and dairy ranches, and three small towns: Olema, Point Reyes Station *(p216)*, and Inverness. The peninsula is due west of the San Andreas Fault, which caused the devastating 1906 earthquake. A displaced fence on the Earthquake Trail near Bear Valley Visitor Center shows how the Fault caused the peninsula to move a full 20 ft (6 m) north of the mainland.

Point Reyes Lighthouse, built in 1870 and located at the peninsula's tip, may be the windiest and foggiest place on the Pacific Coast. The lighthouse is now automated;

Visitors taking the 307 steps to reach the Point Reyes Lighthouse

→ Walking amid the giant redwoods in Muir Woods National Monument

the original Fresnel lens is only for show. It's reached via a 307-step staircase from the clifftop **Lighthouse Visitor Center** – a great place to spot migrating whales.

Lighthouse Visitor Center
27000 Sir Francis Drake Blvd 10am-4pm Thu-Mon nps.gov/pore/planyourvisit/lighthouse.htm

Mount Tamalpais State Park

3801 Panoramic Hwy 7am-sunset parks.ca.gov

Mount Tamalpais State Park is a wilderness nature preserve with trails that wind through redwoods and alongside creeks. There are picnic areas, campsites, and meadows for kite-flying. Mount Tamalpais, at 2,571 ft (784 m), is one of the highest peaks in the Bay Area; the rough tracks gave rise to the invention of the mountain bike. Near the summit is the **Mountain Theater**, a natural amphitheater where musicals and plays are performed.

Mountain Theater
East Ridgecrest mountainplay.org

Muir Woods and Beach

US 101 N, then Hwy 1 to Muir Beach turnoff nps.gov/muwo

Nestling at the foot of Mount Tamalpais is Muir Woods National Monument, one of the few remaining stands of first-growth coast redwoods. These giant trees (the oldest is at least 1,000 years old) once covered the coastal area of California. The woods were named in honor of John Muir, a 19th-century naturalist who was one of the first to persuade Americans of the need for conservation.

Redwood Creek bubbles out of Muir Woods and makes its way down to the sea at Muir Beach, a wide expanse of sand popular with beachcombers and picnickers. The road to the beach passes the Pelican Inn. This 16th-century style inn is extremely proud of its English menu, and its welcoming hospitality.

The beach is likely to be crowded on weekends, but if you are prepared to walk a mile or so farther you will probably find that you have the place to yourself.

STAY

Cavallo Point Lodge
Some rooms at this former military base are in impeccably restored officers' quarters.

601 Murray Circle, Sausalito cavallopoint.com

$$$

The Inn Above Tide
A romantic destination with views over the San Francisco Bay.

30 El Portal, Sausalito innabovetide.com

$$$

A LONG WALK

THE MARIN HEADLANDS

Distance 2 miles (3 km) **Time** 45 minutes **Terrain** Hilly; some paved roads; the Coastal Trail is a woodland track **Nearest transportation** Bus 76X to Bunker Rd & Field Rd

At its northern end, the Golden Gate Bridge is anchored in the rolling green hills of the Marin Headlands. This is an unspoiled wild area of windswept ridges, sheltered valleys, and deserted beaches, once used as a military defense post and now part of the vast Golden Gate National Recreation Area. From several vantage points there are spectacular views of San Francisco and the sea and, in fall, you can see migrating eagles and ospreys gliding past Hawk Hill.

Locator Map

***Barracks** house various offices, among them the Headlands District Office, the Golden Gate Raptor Observatory, and an energy and resources center.*

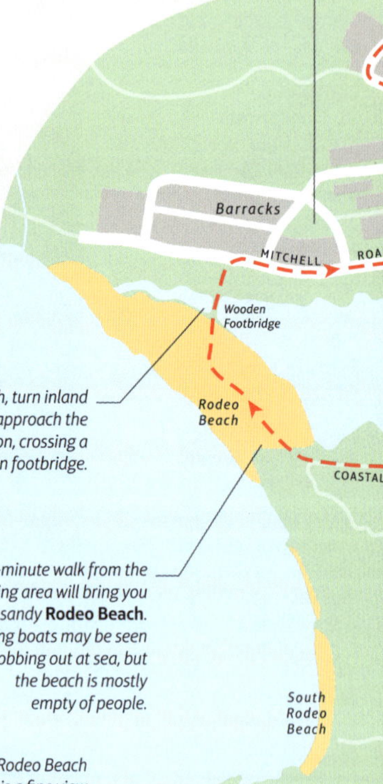

From the beach, turn inland again as you approach the tip of the lagoon, crossing a wooden footbridge.

*A 15-minute walk from the parking area will bring you to the sandy **Rodeo Beach**. Fishing boats may be seen bobbing out at sea, but the beach is mostly empty of people.*

*From Rodeo Beach there is a fine view of **Bird Island** lying to the south.*

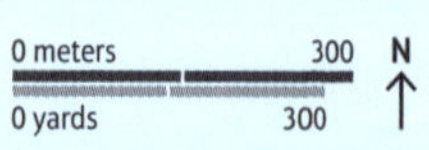

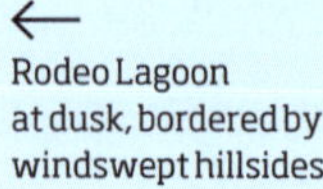

Rodeo Lagoon at dusk, bordered by windswept hillsides

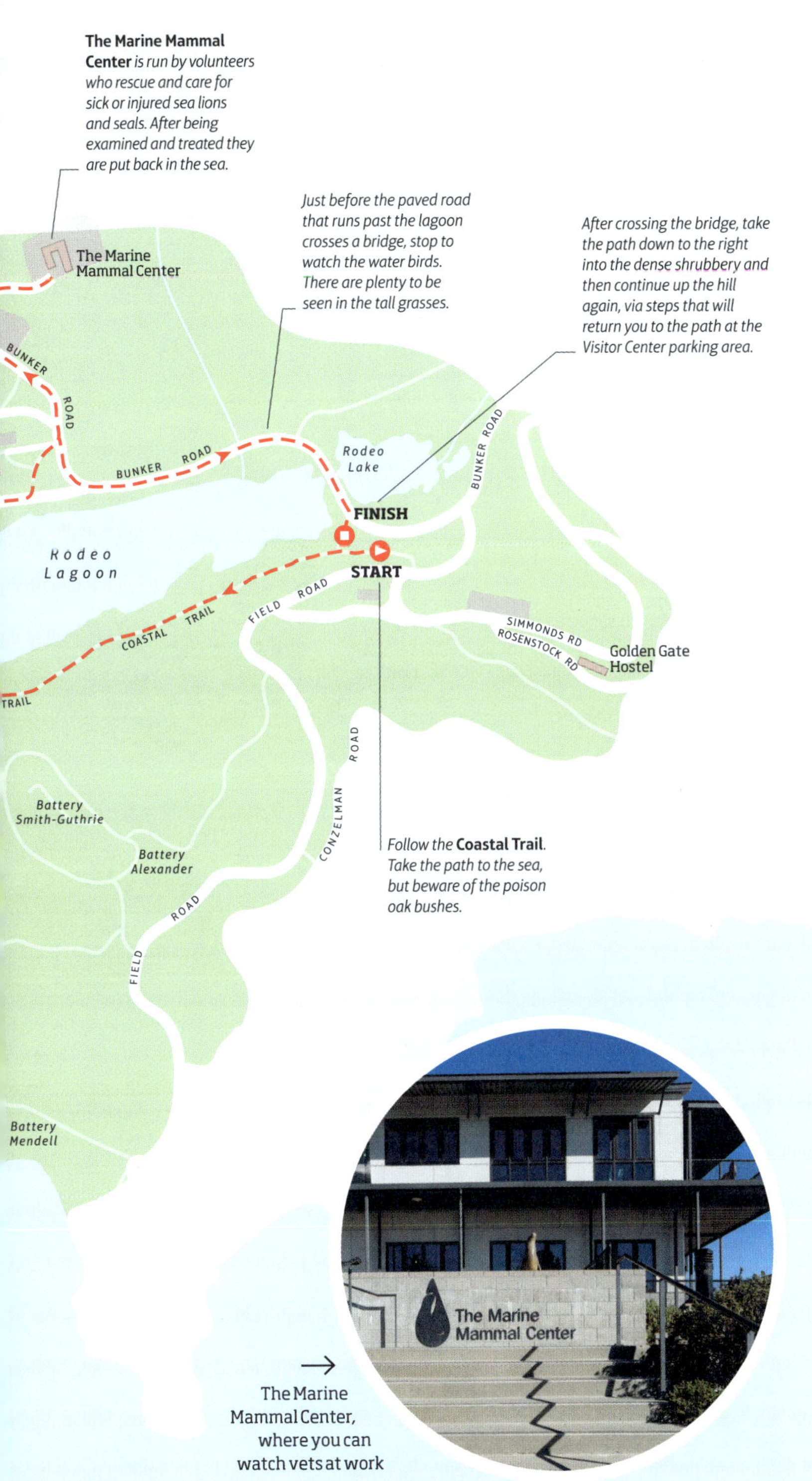

The Marine Mammal Center *is run by volunteers who rescue and care for sick or injured sea lions and seals. After being examined and treated they are put back in the sea.*

Just before the paved road that runs past the lagoon crosses a bridge, stop to watch the water birds. There are plenty to be seen in the tall grasses.

After crossing the bridge, take the path down to the right into the dense shrubbery and then continue up the hill again, via steps that will return you to the path at the Visitor Center parking area.

Follow the **Coastal Trail**. *Take the path to the sea, but beware of the poison oak bushes.*

→ The Marine Mammal Center, where you can watch vets at work

THE EAST BAY

Oakland

482 Water St; visitoakland.com

Many visitors to Oakland arrive by ferry and dock at **Jack London Square**. Jack London, author of *The Call of the Wild* (1903) and *White Fang* (1906), grew up in Oakland in the 1880s, and was a frequent visitor to the Oakland Estuary waterfront. It is a bright and busy promenade, lined with stores and restaurants, which have outdoor tables in fine weather. There are also pleasure boats offering trips along the estuary. Little of the waterfront that London knew remains, but the writer's footsteps can be traced to Heinold's First and Last Chance Saloon, which is located in Jack London Square and has been around since 1883.

Dating from the same era is **Old Oakland**, also known as Victorian Row: two square blocks of attractive wood-and-brick commercial buildings erected between the 1860s and 1880s, and thoroughly renovated in the 1980s. They now contain an appealing array of stores, restaurants, and art galleries. Friday mornings bring crowds of shoppers to the popular **Old Oakland Farmers' Market**, where stalls sell fresh produce and prepared foods. By night, the crowds move on to The Trappist on 8th Street. Don't miss Ratto's, located at 827 Washington Street, an Italian delicatessen which opened in 1897 and was once famed for its "Pasta Operas," in which singers serenaded the diners. The musical tradition carries on: every Saturday after-noon you can hear live jazz here.

Oakland is home to the Bay Area's second-largest **Chinatown** – or perhaps it should be called "Asiatown," as its Cantonese majority is augmented by communities of Korean, Vietnamese, and Southeast Asian descent. The neighbor-hood receives far fewer tourists than San Francisco's Chinatown but its restaurants have good food at reasonable prices, and the area is full of interesting and colorful murals.

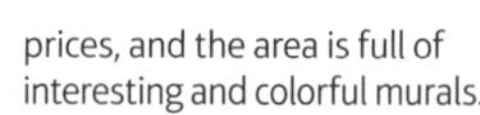

At the center of Oakland lies **Lake Merritt**, formed when a saltwater tidal estuary was dredged, embanked, and partly dammed. The lake is off-limits for swimmers, but, coupled with the surrounding park, it makes for a lovely oasis of rich blue and green. Designated in 1870 as the first state game refuge in the United States, Lake Merritt still attracts migrating flocks of birds. Rowers can rent boats from two boathouses on the west and north shores, and joggers and cyclists can circle the lake on a 3-mile (5-km) path. The north shore at Lakeside Park has flower gardens, an aviary,

A contemporary art exhibit at the Oakland Museum of California

←
A busy street in Chinatown, and *(inset)* a restaurant here serving tasty duck noodles

and **Children's Fairyland**: a whimsical storybook theme park for youngsters. The park has been a Lake Merritt fixture since 1948, and has dozens of storybook sets – such as Peter Rabbit's Garden and The Alice in Wonderland Tunnel – and a carousel, a miniature Ferris Wheel, and live entertainment.

The **Oakland Museum of California** is California's only museum exclusively dedicated to documenting the state's art, history, and natural sciences. The building and the handsomely terraced gardens are features that mark this museum as an important architectural icon. The Gallery of California Natural Sciences showcases more than 2,000 native species across 7 habitats.

3.4 miles

The circumference of Lake Merritt (5.5 km).

The Gallery of California History has a large collection of artifacts from across the state, while the Gallery of California Art houses early oil paintings of Yosemite and San Francisco. Check the museum website for details of the latest exhibitions.

The history and culture of African Americans in Northern California and the Bay Area are thoughtfully conserved at the **African American Museum and Library**. Changing exhibitions are hosted in the second-floor museum. The huge reference library, which includes a microfilm collection, is a significant resource on African American experiences. The invaluable collection consists of more than 12,000 volumes by or about African Americans, including Martin Luther King, Jr., Malcolm X, the Black Panther Party, religion, and California history.

Jack London Square
12th St, then AC Transit 12, 72, 72M, 72R bus
Oakland

Old Oakland
12th St old-oakland.com

Old Oakland Farmers' Market
Clay St & 9th St 8am-2pm Fri uvfm.org

Chinatown
Lake Merritt

Lake Merritt
Lake Merritt, 19th St
lakemerritt.org

Children's Fairyland
699 Bellevue Ave AC Transit 12 Summer: 10am-4pm daily (winter: Fri-Sun)
fairyland.org

Oakland Museum of California
1000 Oak St
Lake Merritt Hours vary, check website
museumca.org

African American Museum and Library
659 14th St
10am-5:30pm Mon-Thu, noon-5:50pm Fri
oaklandlibrary.org/aamlo

EAT

Commis
Perch at the counter in this Michelin-starred restaurant to watch the chefs work each seasonally led dish to perfection. The tasting menu changes daily, but favorites - including slow-poached egg yolk with onion cream - remain constant.
3859 Piedmont Ave, Oakland commis restaurant.com

$$$

Stunning facade of Oakland's Church of Jesus Christ of Latter-day Saints

Mormon Temple Visitors' Center

4766 Lincoln Ave, Oakland Fruitvale, then AC Transit 39 bus 9am-9pm daily templehill.org

Designed in 1963 and built on a hilltop, Oakland's Church of Jesus Christ of Latter-day Saints is one of only two Mormon temples in northern California. The stunning building's central ziggurat is surrounded by four shorter towers, all terraced and clad with white granite and capped by gold pyramids.

Those eager to see the temple up close should first head to the Visitors' Center, which offers guided tours by missionaries, who explain the tenets of the faith with multimedia presentations.

Bay Bridge

baybridgeinfo.org

The San Francisco–Oakland Bay Bridge (known simply as the "Bay Bridge") was built from 1933–6. It consists of two distinct structures joining at Yerba Buena Island in the middle of the Bay, and reaches 4.5 miles (7.2 km) from shore to shore. Its completion heralded the end of the age of ferryboats on San Francisco Bay, by linking the peninsular city at Rincon Hill to the mainland at Oakland.

The bridge has two levels, originally housing road vehicles on the upper deck and trains and trucks below. However, the rail tracks were removed in the 1950s, leaving the bridge for use by more than 250,000 vehicles a day. Five traffic lanes wide, westbound traffic into San Francisco now uses the top deck; eastbound traffic to Oakland, the lower.

The eastern cantilever section is raised on more than 20 piers. It climbs up from the toll plaza causeway in Oakland to 191 ft (58 m) above the bay at Yerba Buena Island. In 1989 a 50 ft (15 m) segment of the bridge collapsed during the Loma Prieta earthquake. The East Bay crossing was rebuilt between 2002 and 2013 in order to make it more earthquake resistant. The current suspension bridge features a single tower across the shipping channel, which gives way to a graceful sky-way. Boring through the island in a tunnel 76 ft (23 m) high and 58 ft (17 m) wide, the roadway emerges at the West Bay section of the bridge. Two suspension spans join at the concrete central anchorage, which is deeper in the water than that of any other bridge.

Tilden Regional Park

2501 Grizzly Peak Blvd, Orinda Downtown Berkeley, then AC Transit 67 bus 5am-10pm daily ebparks.org/parks/tilden

Though preserved for the most part in a natural, wild condition, Tilden Park offers a variety of attractions. It is noted for the enchantingly landscaped **Botanic Garden**, specializing in California plants. Visitors can enjoy a leisurely stroll from alpine meadows to desert cactus gardens by way of a lovely redwood glen, and there are also guided nature walks. If you have children, make sure you don't miss the carousel, the miniature farmyard, and the model **steam train**.

Botanic Garden
(510) 544-3169
8:30am-5pm daily (Jun-Sep: to 5:30pm)

Steam train
(510) 548-6100
11am-6pm Sat-Mon

14

Rockridge

Rockridge

A leafy residential area with large houses and flower gardens, Rockridge also attracts shoppers to College Avenue. The streets are lined with posh markets, boutiques, and al fresco restaurants.

15  

Claremont Resort and Club

41 Tunnel Rd, Berkeley Rockridge, then AC Transit 79 bus claremontresortandclub.com

The Berkeley Hills form a backdrop to this chic, palatial hotel built in 1915. When Prohibition ended in 1933, the hotel failed to prosper like other similar establishments, due partly to a law that forbade the sale of alcohol within a 1-mile (1.6-km) radius of the Berkeley campus. After a change in the law in 1937, an enterprising student actually measured the distance, and found that the radius line passed through the center of the building, and so a hotel bar was built just beyond it.

As well as being one of the Bay Area's plushest hotels, this is a good place to have a drink and enjoy the views.

DRINK

The East Bay has a lively craft beer scene, with plenty of microbreweries and warehouse spaces with gardens.

Triple Rock Brewery
1920 Shattuck Ave, Berkeley triplerock.com

Jupiter
2181 Shattuck Ave, Berkeley jupiterbeer.com

Westbrae Biergarten
1280 Gilman St, Berkeley
(510) 647-9079

←
Bay Bridge at night with the stunning San Francisco skyline in the background

Shops and cafés on Telegraph Avenue, popular with students

16 Berkeley

 2030 Addison St; visitberkeley.com

Berkeley is renowned for its university, **UC Berkeley**, though some would argue that its reputation for counter-cultural movements sometimes eclipses its reputation for academic excellence. For all that, it remains one of the most prestigious universities in the world.

Founded as a utopian "Athens of the Pacific" in 1868, Berkeley has more than ten Nobel Laureates among its fellows and staff.

The campus *(p228)* was laid out by landscape architect Frederick Law Olmsted on the twin forks of Strawberry Creek; changes by San Francisco architect David Farquharson were later adopted. Today there are over 41,000 students and a wide range of museums, cultural amenities, and a number of buildings of note. These include the **Phoebe A. Hearst Museum of Anthropology**, the **Berkeley Art Museum and Pacific Film Archive**, and Sather Tower, which is also known as the Campanile.

At Berkeley's Strawberry Canyon lies the **University Botanical Garden**, where more than 10,000 species of plant from all over the world thrive. Collections are arranged in thematic gardens linked by paths. Particularly noteworthy are the Asian, African, South American, European, and Californian gardens. The Chinese medicinal herb garden and the carnivorous plants are also well worth a visit.

Running from Downtown Oakland to UC Berkeley is arguably the most stimulating street in the East Bay: **Telegraph Avenue**. The blocks near UC Berkeley have one of the highest concentrations of bookstores in the country, in addition to which there are plenty of coffee houses and restaurants. This district was the center of student protest in the 1960s. Today it swarms with students from dawn to dusk, along with numerous street vendors, musicians, artists, protesters, and eccentrics.

If you are traveling with children, don't miss **The Lawrence Hall of Science**, UC Berkeley's museum, which makes science great fun for all the family. The changing interactive exhibits encourage visitors of all ages to explore, investigate, discover, and invent, from plotting the stars in the planetarium to learning about animals, such as pythons, geckos, lizards, and rabbits, in the Animal Discovery Room. You can design your own rocket and build a city with Lego bricks. And in the National Geographic 3D Theater you can experience science on the big screen.

One of California's largest collections of historical artifacts pertaining to Jewish culture, from ancient times to today, is housed at the **Magnes Collection of Jewish Art and Life**. Among them are art treasures from Europe and

INSIDER TIP
Take the Train

Berkeley can be easily reached in around 30 minutes from downtown San Francisco. The Downtown Berkeley BART station on Shattuck Avenue is within walking distance of the campus.

The striking Cubist-style Berkeley Art Museum and Pacific Film Archive

India, paintings by Marc Chagall and Max Liebermann, and poignant reminders of the devastation people suffered during Nazi-era Germany, such as a burned Torah scroll rescued from a synagogue. Lectures, films, and traveling exhibits enliven the halls.

When you are ready for something to eat, head for **North Shattuck**, a north Berkeley neighborhood formerly nicknamed "Gourmet Ghetto," which acquired fame as something of a foodie destination when American chef Alice Waters opened Chez Panisse here in 1971. The restaurant on 1517 Shattuck Ave is acclaimed for its use of fresh local ingredients in a French-inspired style that gave rise to what is known as California cuisine. In its original house on Shattuck Avenue, Chez Panisse has influenced many worthy imitators. There is also an abundance of specialty markets and coffee houses in the neighborhood.

Another rewarding neighborhood is **Fourth Street**, a gentrified enclave north of University Avenue, characteristic of Berkeley's climate of fine craftsmanship and exquisite taste. Here you can buy everything from handmade paper and stained-glass windows to organically grown lettuce and designer garden tools. It is also known for its restaurants.

UC Berkeley
2227 Piedmont Ave
Downtown Berkeley

Phoebe A. Hearst Museum of Anthropology
103 Kroeber Hall
11am–5pm Wed–Sun (Thu: to 8pm) hearstmuseum.berkeley.edu

Berkeley Art Museum and Pacific Film Archive
2155 Center St
Downtown Berkeley
11am–7pm Wed–Sun
bampfa.org

University Botanical Garden
200 Centennial Dr
H 9am–5pm Wed–Mon botanicalgarden.berkeley.edu

Telegraph Avenue
AC Transit 800
Downtown Berkeley

The Lawrence Hall of Science
Centennial Dr From Mining Circle, UC Berkeley
Downtown Berkeley, then AC Transit 65 bus
10am–5pm daily
lawrencehallofscience.org

Magnes Collection of Jewish Art and Life
Bancroft Library, UC Berkeley, 2121 Allston Way
AC Transit 6, 7, 18, 51B, 52, 65, 67, 79, 88, F Downtown Berkeley 11am–4pm Tue–Fri (during the academic year only) magnes.berkeley.edu

North Shattuck
Upper Shattuck Ave
Downtown Berkeley, then AC Transit 7, 18, 67 bus
northshattuck.org

Fourth Street
AC Transit Z
Ashby, then AC Transit 51B, Z bus fourthstreet.com

A LONG WALK

THE UNIVERSITY OF CALIFORNIA CAMPUS IN BERKELEY

Distance 2.5 miles (4 km) **Time** 50 minutes **Terrain** Some sloping paths and hills, which provide beautiful views **Nearest BART station** Downtown Berkeley

This walk concentrates on a distinct area of Berkeley: the campus of the distinguished University of California *(p226)*. A stroll around the area offers a stimulating glimpse into the intellectual, cultural, and social life of this vibrant university town. Its days as "Berzerkeley" – when student protestors and tear-gas clouds filled the streets in the 1960s – are only a fading memory now, and the campus is a lovely place for a walk, full of natural spaces, interesting architecture to admire, and museums to explore.

Follow University Drive past the **Valley Life Sciences Building**, *which contains natural history, zoology, and paleontology museums.*

Head into campus via **The Crescent**.

Cross over Strawberry Creek at Bay Tree Bridge, and bear left for the nature area, with its eucalyptus trees, some of the tallest in the world.

HEARST AVENUE
SHATTUCK AVENUE
UNIVERSITY AVENUE
START
OXFORD STREET
THE CRESCENT
UNIVERSITY DRIVE
West Gate
FINISH
Wellman Hall
Valley Life Sciences Building
HEARST
ADDISON STREET
CENTER STREET
Strawberry Creek
FRANK SCHLESSINGER WAY
Downtown Berkeley
Evans Diamond at Stu Gordon Stadium
Edwards Stadium
Zellerbach Hall
KITTREDGE STREET
BANCROFT WAY
ELLSWORTH STREET
DANA ST
FULTON STREET
DURANT AVENUE
CHANNING WAY

0 meters 300
0 yards 300
N

Sather Gate, an entryway to the campus at the north end of Sproul Plaza

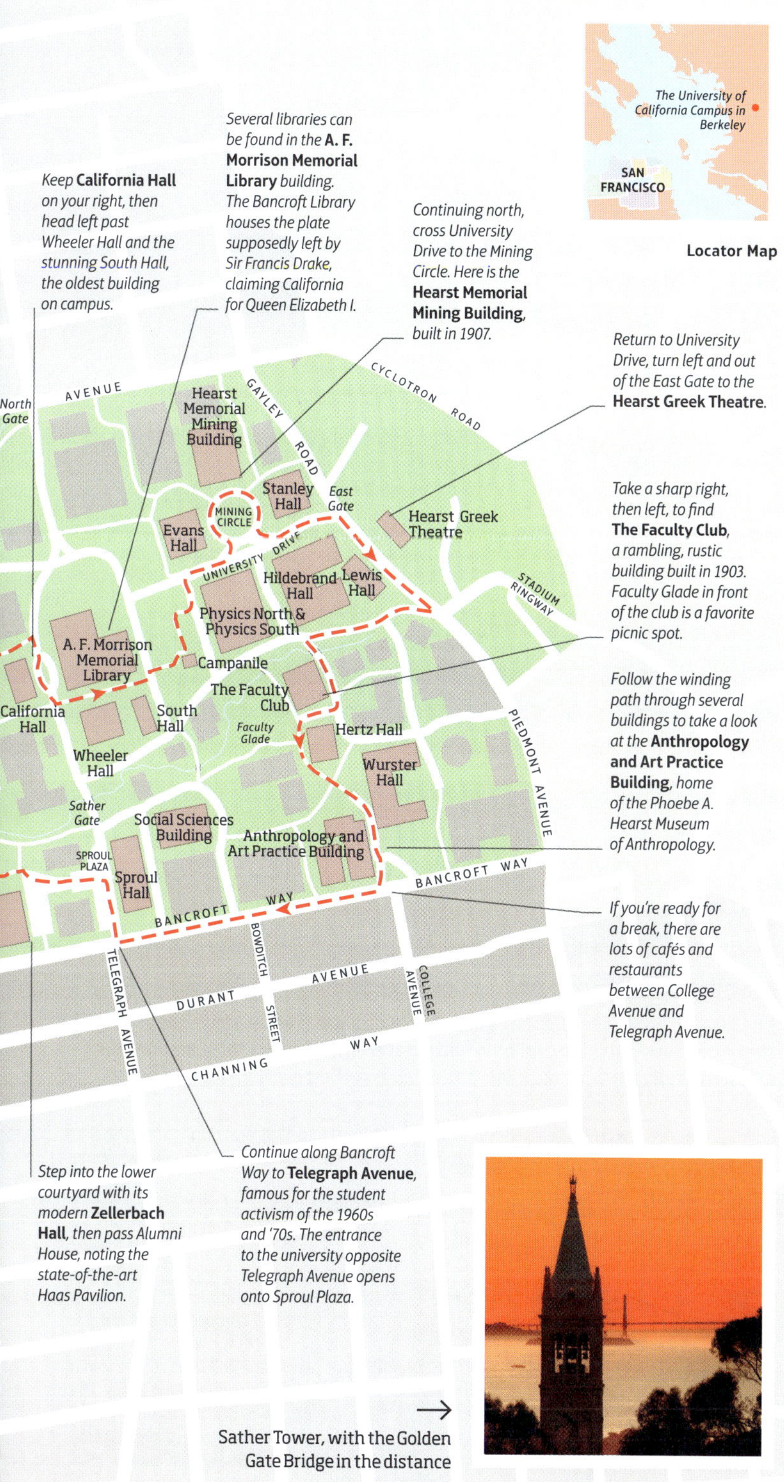

→ Sather Tower, with the Golden Gate Bridge in the distance

Did You Know?

The Giant Dipper reaches a height of 70 ft (21 m) and speeds of 55 mph (89 km/h).

17

SANTA CRUZ BEACH BOARDWALK

400 Beach St, Santa Cruz 10am–11pm daily beachboardwalk.com

The historic Santa Cruz Beach Boardwalk is a classic seaside amusement park that's both eye-catching and busy with foot traffic. Hosting thrilling rides and family-friendly attractions, it has an enviable setting overlooking the beach.

↑ Visitors swarming between the brightly colored rides along the Boardwalk

Dating from 1907 and dominating the Santa Cruz waterfront, the Boardwalk is the oldest amusement park on the West Coast. The entire Boardwalk is a California Historic Landmark, and although most of the original amusements have been replaced by modern rides, two still-functioning centenary rides are National Historic Landmarks. The first of these is the classic Looff carousel; one of only five remaining in the USA, it was built in 1911 and features hand-carved horses, which spin to music from a 19th-century pipe organ. But the main attraction is undoubtedly the Giant Dipper roller coaster, whose wave-like tracks soar up above the Boardwalk. Built in 1924, this

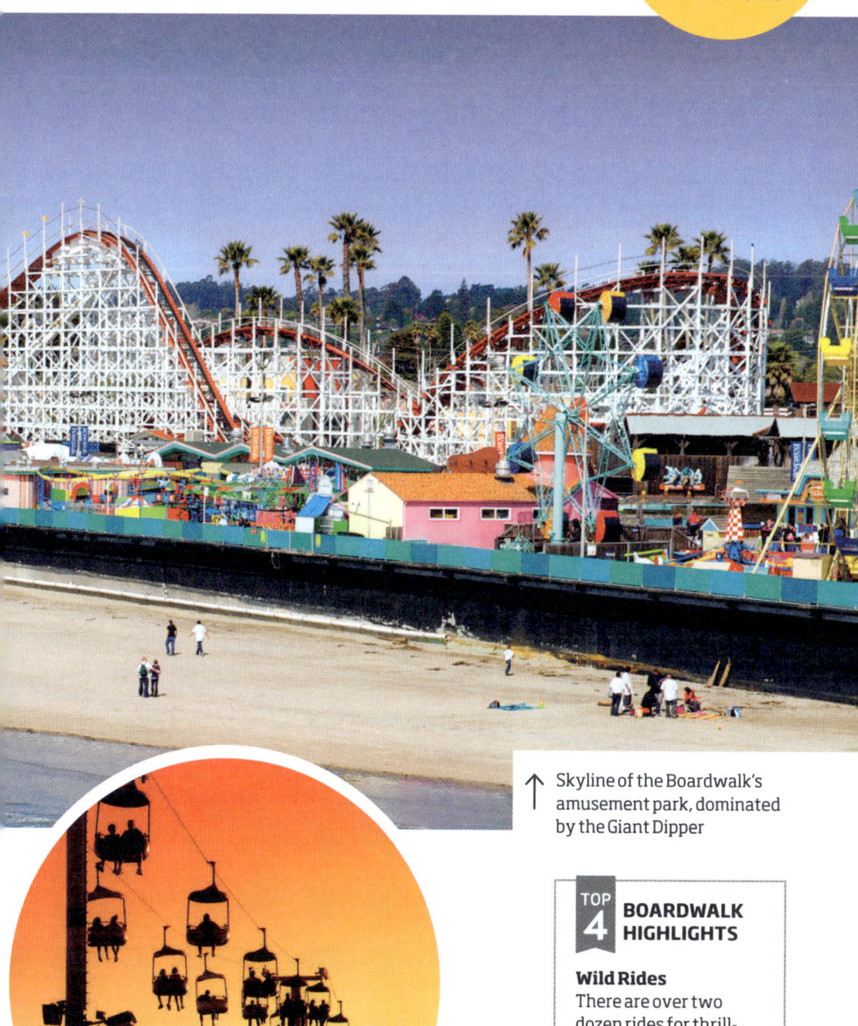

↑ Skyline of the Boardwalk's amusement park, dominated by the Giant Dipper

← Enjoying a sunset ride on the Sky Glider

red-and-white landmark still provides riders with a swooping, heart-pounding adrenaline rush. The apogee of the Giant Dipper, as well as those of other thrilling rides along the Boardwalk, offers a postcard view of sand, sea, and the Santa Cruz Pier. Slightly more low-key attractions in the area include a video arcade, a laser tag arena and laser maze challenge, and even an ice-skating rink in winter. There are also plenty of gentler rides that aim to delight toddlers. If the crowds become too much, head to the Santa Cruz Wharf for a leisurely stroll or a quiet coffee break, and stunning views from the pier.

TOP 4 BOARDWALK HIGHLIGHTS

Wild Rides
There are over two dozen rides for thrill-seekers to enjoy.

Sweet Snacks
From cotton candy and churros to fish and chips, you'll be spoilt for choice come snack time.

Sea Lions
Head to the Santa Cruz Wharf to watch the sea lions relax in the sun.

Main Beach
A sandy stretch with volleyball nets and gentle waves, and movies screened in summer.

18

HALF MOON BAY

637 Main St; visithalfmoonbay.org

A perfect weekend getaway, the small town of Half Moon Bay – located between San Francisco and Santa Cruz – is home to great beaches and some of the world's most epic waves and surfing contests. It also falls along the gray whale coastal migration path, offering front-row seats to this magnificent spectacle.

Founded in the 1840s as a small fishing and agricultural community, Half Moon Bay later developed as a beach resort. Its Main Street still displays renovated Victorian buildings that house quaint art galleries, stores, and restaurants. Inland, the Pilarcitos Creek watershed protects many rare wildlife species.

Half Moon Bay's State Beach is comprised of four contiguous beaches (Francis, Venice, Dunes, and Roosevelt) that unfurl for 4 miles (6 km). While it's ideal for long, leisurely walks, swimming is not advised due to rip currents. At the north end of the bay is Mirada Surf Beach, at the lively resort of El Granada. Sheltered within its harbor – once a whaling station – are three lovely beaches that are safe for swimming, including Princeton Beach and Pillar Point Harbor Beach. Outside the harbor, white-sand Mavericks Beach has panoramic bay views and is a great place for experienced surfers to tackle the region's legendary waves.

Another good spot in the Half Moon Bay area is the photogenic Montara Lighthouse. It was transferred from Cape Cod in 1928, and from

1 2 3

here gray whales may be glimpsed migrating close to shore during winter. To its south, scimitar-shaped Moss Beach is popular for the Fitzgerald Marine Reserve; its tidepools teem with starfish, anemones, and crabs at low tide.

Pumpkins are a major crop around Half Moon Bay, and the annual Art & Pumpkin Festival is a highlight of the local calendar. In late October, 250,000 visitors pour in for the weekend-long festival featuring costume and pie-eating contests, and a parade of gargantuan gourds (which often exceed 1,000 kg/2,200 lbs in weight). The festival also includes arts and crafts, music concerts, and tasty pumpkin-based treats.

1 The patio at the Half Moon Bay Brewing Company is a popular spot in summer.

2 Many species of wildlife may be found in the region, including pelicans.

3 The gentle curve of the bay's coastline is also home to a links golf course.

←

Stretches of beach in Half Moon Bay, which may offer either gentle surf or *(inset)* giant waves

EAT

Sam's Chowder House

A waterfront favorite known for its signature New England-style chowder. Head outside for firepits on the patio.

4210 N. Cabrillo Hwy
samschowderhouse.com

Half Moon Bay Brewing Company

Hearty dishes such as fish and chips washed down by choice brews, from a light pilsner to a creamy dark stout.

390 Capistrano Rd
hmbbrewingco.com

THE PENINSULA

San Jose

408 S Almaden Blvd; sanjose.org

The original capital city of California, San Jose is now the nation's capital for innovation and industry, home to major companies like Adobe, eBay, and Samsung, with headquarters for Apple Inc, Facebook, and Google also located nearby. As the tenth largest city in the US and with many residents being professionals in high-tech industries, San Jose citizens enjoy a high disposable income, although this is slightly offset by its astronomical rents.

In contrast to the modern atmosphere of downtown San Jose, **The Winchester Mystery House®** is one of the city's oldest and most unique attractions. In 1884 Sarah Winchester, heiress of the rifle fortune, was grieving over the loss of her child and husband. She consulted a medium who advised her to build a house that would never be completed, in order to silence the evil spirits that haunted her. She employed carpenters for 38 years and built 160 rooms set amid beautiful gardens. The stairways that lead nowhere and windows set into the floor are just a few of the oddities within. Book a Flashlight Tour to see the house at its creepiest.

For more standard – but no less fascinating – attractions, San Jose also has its fair share of museums. Inspired by the Temple of Amon at Karnak, Egypt, the **Rosicrucian Egyptian Museum** houses ancient Egyptian, Babylonian, Assyrian, and Sumerian artifacts. Funerary boats, mummies, Coptic textiles, pottery, jewelry, and a full-size tomb are on display. The museum's accompanying planetarium – one of the oldest in the country – also has daily and special weekend shows. **The Tech Interactive** is a colorful technological museum divided into several themed galleries, including exploration, biodesign, and virtual reality. Many of the exhibits have a "hands-on" element, such as designing robots or measuring your moods with wearable technology; The Body Worlds Decoded exhibition uses augmented reality to examine what is going on inside the human body. The **Children's Discovery Museum** is great for families and kids of all ages. Children can play in a real red fire engine or in an ambulance with flashing

INSIDER TIP
Cosplay Days

Over Memorial Day weekend, visitors to downtown San Jose will probably find the streets full of people in elaborate costumes. The sudden influx of robots and super heroes is due to 30,000 people descending on the city every year to enjoy FanimeCon, one of the country's largest anime and comics conventions.

The weird and wonderful Winchester Mystery House® set in beautiful gardens

The front facade of The Tech Interactive in downtown San Jose

lights, and the more adventurous can climb trees connected by sky bridges in the outdoor Tree Climber. At the Waterways exhibit, kids will enjoy discovering the special properties of water by creating unique fountains from magnetic half-pipes. There's even a hands-on, early-learning exhibit for children aged 0–4.

For a museum with a twist, **History Park** is a charming attraction in Kelley Park that recreates San Jose as it was in the early 20th century. More than 21 original houses and businesses have been restored and set around a town square. They include a fire station, an ice-cream parlor with a working soda fountain, a gas station, and a vintage trolley that travels around the grounds.

The Winchester Mystery House®
201 South... 525 South Winchester Blvd 10am-4pm daily (to 5pm Sat & Sun); May-Aug: 10am-4pm daily (to 7pm Sat & Sun) winchestermystery house.com

Rosicrucian Egyptian Museum
1660 Park Ave Hours vary, check website egyptianmuseum.org

The Tech Interactive
201 South Market St (at Park Ave) 10am-5pm Tue-Sun Mon thetech.org

Children's Discovery Museum
180 Woz Way 9:30am-4:30pm Tue-Sun cdm.org

History Park
635 Phelan Ave 9am-4pm Mon-Fri, noon-4pm Sat & Sun historysanjose.org

EAT

Outdoor dining is a way of life in sunny California, and San Jose offers lots of options for it.

SP2 Communal Bar + Restaurant
72 N Almaden Ave Mon & Tue sp2sanjose.com
$$

Scott's Seafood
200 S 1st St scottsseafoodsj.com
$$$

Siena Bistro
1359 Lincoln Ave Sun & Mon sienabistro.com
$$

Families exploring a fire engine at the Children's Discovery Museum

The Romanesque-style arches of the Memorial Church, Stanford University

Stanford University

Palo Alto Caltrain to Palo Alto station stanford.edu

One of the country's most prestigious private universities, with over 16,000 students, Stanford was built by railroad mogul Leland Stanford in memory of his son, and opened in 1891. The heart of the campus is the Main Quad, designed mainly in Romanesque style. The main landmarks are the Hoover Tower, the Memorial Church, and the Stanford University Museum of Art, where you can see the Golden Spike that completed the transcontinental railroad in 1869. The Cantor Arts Center owns an impressive collection of Rodin sculptures. For guided tours of the college phone 650-723-2560.

Año Nuevo

Take Cabrillo Hwy, then New Years Creek Rd 8am-6pm daily parks.ca.gov

In the 19th century, northern elephant seals were hunted almost to extinction for their oil-rich blubber. They disappeared from many traditional habitats along the Pacific Coast, including Año Nuevo. Descendants of the survivors began showing up here in the 1950s. Today, a year-round population is protected within this State Park, 20 miles (32 km) north of Santa Cruz. The site is a traditional breeding ground for the world's largest seals, which leave the sea to mate, give birth, and laze in the sun. In winter months, males (which are typically five times bigger than females) engage in bloody battles for harem dominance. Visits are limited to guided naturalist walks during mating season. Stellar sea lions also breed here, and sea otters can be seen foraging in the kelp. In addition, Año Nuevo Point is a great birding spot. Viewing the seals requires a 3-mile (5-km) hike along sandy trails.

STAY

Stanford Park Hotel

This stunning building oozes grandeur, from the antiques in the lobby to the elegant grounds.

100 El Camino Real, Menlo Park stanfordpark hotel.com

$$$

Pescadero Creek Inn

A quiet and charming spot for those who want to get out of the busy cities of the Bay Area and back to nature.

393 Stage Rd, Pescadero pescadero creekinn.com

Did You Know?

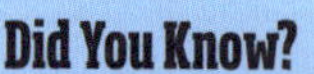

The Pescadero State Beach is a long swath of sand backed by rocky cliffs.

Remote and beautiful Pigeon Point Lighthouse near Pescadero

Pescadero

Daly City, then SamTrans 118 to Linda Mar park and ride, then 17 bus

Only an hour's drive from San Francisco to the north and Silicon Valley to the east, the picturesque town of Pescadero is a pleasant escape from the fast-paced world around it. Although it contains little more than a white-washed church (the oldest in the county), a general store, a post office, and the popular Duarte's Tavern along its two main streets, the town has the charming and photogenic appearance of an old movie set. Its many white-washed buildings follow a tradition that goes back to the 19th century, when a cargo of white paint was rescued from a nearby shipwreck.

Eight miles (12 km) south is **Pigeon Point Light Station State Historic Park**, where visitors can enjoy the scenery and views. Tours are offered at 1pm from Thursday through Monday (call 650-879-2120 to check availability or book).

About 20 minutes south, families can enjoy Swanton Berry Farm's **Coastways Ranch U-Pick** for an afternoon of fruit-picking.

Pigeon Point Light Station State Historic Park

210 Pigeon Point Rd 8am-sunset daily parks.ca.gov

Coastways Ranch U-Pick

640 Hwy 1 Hours vary, check website swantonberryfarm.com

Filoli

86 Cañada Rd, near Edgewood Rd, Woodside 10am-5pm daily filoli.org

The lavish 43-room Filoli mansion was built in 1915 for William Bourne II, owner of the Empire Gold Mine. Gold from the mine was used in its opulent decoration. The elegant house is surrounded by a large, enchanting garden, with many English garden-style features, and an estate where guided nature walks, as well as tours of the orchard can be arranged. "Filoli" stands for "Fight, love, live," which refers to Bourne's love for the Irish and their struggle. You can either visit the house on your own or take a guided tour, which costs a little extra.

24

NAPA VALLEY WINE COUNTRY

600 Main St, Napa; visitnapavalley.com

Since the legendary Judgment of Paris in 1976 – when the Napa Valley wines beat Burgundy to top honors in both the red and white categories – this region has been firmly on every wine lover's radar. People also come for the experience: to tour grand chateaux, dine at world-renowned restaurants, and sip small-batch wines in tiny, boutique tasting rooms.

1   

Charles Krug Winery

2800 Main St, St. Helena 10:30am-5pm daily charleskrug.com

Many firsts can be attributed to Napa Valley's oldest winery. Charles Krug, who founded the estate in 1861, was a pioneer of varietal labeling. He was also the first to import French oak barrels for wine aging. The tasting room, yet another first in California when it opened to the public in 1882, is the crowning glory, with a soft peach, Tuscan-style exterior leading to a sleek space with daily tastings of limited-release wines.

2 

V. Sattui

1111 White Lane, St. Helena 9am-6pm daily (winter: to 5pm) vsattui.com

With tasting room staff pouring everything from estate cabernet to champagne-method bubbles, you can't really go wrong at V. Sattui. Even those who aren't wine lovers can delight in exploring the vast grounds, with vine-combed slopes and shaded picnic areas. Book in advance to take a tour through the cellars and listen to the fascinating history of this family-run winery, which was started in San Francisco in the 19th century, destroyed by Prohibition, and, finally, resurrected here in 1976.

3 

The French Laundry

6640 Washington St, Yountville 10 4-8pm daily thomaskeller.com/tfl

Possibly the most coveted tables in Napa Valley are those that fill the chic dining room of Thomas Keller's venerable

↑ Facade of the Michelin-star restaurant, The French Laundry

↑ The rolling hills and stunning golden vineyards of Napa Valley

restaurant. Its unlikely location in the small rural town of Yountville, and the cozy atmosphere inside, belie the intense work that goes into the ever-changing daily menu. Each of the nine courses is underpinned by classical French cooking and Keller's formidable imagination, which has earned his restaurant the top Michelin rating of three stars.

Robert Mondavi Arch and Tower

930 3rd St, Napa 10 11am-4pm daily robertmondavi winery.com

The flagship estate of one of Napa's pioneering vineyard owners is styled to resemble California's Spanish missions, with graceful arches and a vast, elegant courtyard. A passionate ambassador for Napa Valley wines until his death in 2008, Robert Mondavi is credited with helping to elevate the area to one of the world's most recognized wine regions. Still family-run, the winery continues to pour its renowned cabernets and signature fumé blanc, fermented with sauvignon blanc grapes. Visitors can join tasting flights, cellar tastings with reserve wines, and barrel room tours.

Chandon

1 California Dr, Yountville 29 10am-5pm daily chandon.com

From classic brut to blushing rosé, it's all about the bubbles at Chandon, a lavish estate founded by Moët & Chandon in 1973. While it exudes a certain French elegance, there's nothing stuffy about the atmosphere. As befits a spot specializing in fizz, a visit here is all about having a good time.

Experiences range from tasting flights, including the estate's still varieties, to weekend mixology classes, when participants can make and sip cocktails using the signature sparkling wine.

Opus One Winery

7900 St. Helena Hwy, Oakville 10 10am-4pm daily opusone winery.com

Opus One was founded in 1979 as an unprecedented joint venture between two wine legends – Napa Valley's Robert Mondavi and Baron Philippe de Rothschild, founder of Château Mouton Rothschild in Bordeaux, France. Their plan was to create a single, world-class Bordeaux blend based on California cabernet, and their legacy is a wine that is consistently considered one of Napa's best.

The striking stone building of the winery, tucked low against the hillside, hosts intimate, appointment-only tastings of the current vintage, or you can book a tour to explore the vast grounds and production areas.

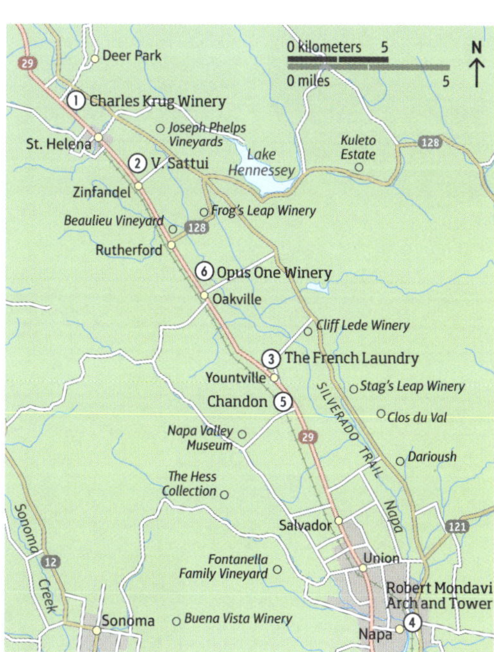

NAPA VALLEY

St. Helena

1154 Main St; sthelena.com

Perhaps the most polished of Napa Valley's towns, St. Helena overflows with the temptation to shop, sip, and eat. The charming and quaint Main Street is packed with cocktail bars and restaurants firmly focused on vibrant local and seasonal ingredients. You can delve deeper into the scene at the **Culinary Institute of America at Greystone**; responsible for training many a star chef, the institute also offers cooking classes, demonstrations, and tastings. Or you can enjoy a more leisurely experience with a meal cooked by the next generation of cooking talent at the on-site restaurant. You'll discover some of the area's most revered wine estates, including Charles Krug *(p238)* and **Beringer**, in the surrounding vine-clad hillsides.

Culinary Institute of America at Greystone
2555 Main St, St. Helena ciachef.edu

Beringer
10am–5:30pm daily beringer.com

Calistoga

1133 Washington St; visitcalistoga.com

At the northern tip of the Napa Valley, the laid-back town of Calistoga is renowned for its geothermal waters and mud baths. The resorts here take full advantage of both, offering indulgent spa treatments and pools fed by hot springs. Typical of the town's retro-cool vibe is **Calistoga Motor Lodge & Spa**, with its tucked-away garden, where guests can slather on mud before drying out in the sun. The main drag of Lincoln Avenue is dotted with quirky gift stores, bookshops, and galleries. The hillsides are dominated by grand wineries, including **Castello di**

TOP 3 LUXURY EXPERIENCES IN NAPA VALLEY

Napa Valley Aloft
nvaloft.com
Hot-air balloons launch daily at sunrise for peaceful voyages over the vineyards, with distant views of San Francisco's skyline.

Spa Terra at Meritage Resort
meritageresort.com/wellness
Nestled in a wine cave, this resort offers treatments, mineral pools, and heat rooms.

Napa Valley Wine Train
winetrain.com
Pullman carriages chug through the landscape for tasting tours or fine-dining experiences.

→ The Napa Valley Wine Train passing by a vineyard

Amorosa, housed in a medieval-style castle. And, with access to the famed routes of Highway 29 and the Silverado Trail, there are plenty more wine-tasting opportunities nearby.

Calistoga Motor Lodge & Spa
1880 Lincoln Ave
calistogamotorlodgeandspa.com

Castello di Amorosa
4045 St. Helena Hwy castellodiamorosa.com

27 Old Faithful Geyser

1299 Tubbs Ln, Calistoga
10, 29 9am-6pm daily (to 7pm Sat)
oldfaithfulgeyser.com

Though not as famous as the bigger "Old Faithful" in Wyoming, California's smaller version is still one of the few geysers in the world erupting at predictable intervals (every 20–30 minutes). Its occasional failure to erupt has been linked to imminent earthquakes. Casting a light mist through the air and often creating a hazy rainbow, the eruptions make for a particularly picturesque picnic backdrop. The grounds around the geyser contain a geology museum, gardens, and a farm. Try not to frighten the goats here: these black-and-white creatures are Tennessee Fainting Goats, which stiffen and topple over when they sense danger. Other weird and wonderful animals occupying a section of the site's grounds include four-horn sheep and guard llamas.

An eruption of boiling water and steam at Old Faithful Geyser

28 Napa

 **1330 1st St, Napa; visitnapavalley.com**

There's an undeniable air of sophistication to downtown Napa, from Michelin-starred dining to the excellent **Blue Note** jazz club and First Street Napa – an open-air shopping mall with boutiques and galleries – all clustered within a few blocks. There are plenty of opportunities for wine sampling at tasting rooms and bonded wineries; at **Vintner's Collective** you can try small-batch wines not available anywhere else.

Blue Note
1030 Main St
Hours vary, check website
bluenotenapa.com

Vintner's Collective
1245 Main St
11am-7pm daily
vintnerscollective.com

INSIDER TIP
Microclimate

Napa Valley has several microclimates that can cause the temperature to vary considerably from north to south, and by as much as 30°F (15°C) from morning to night. Pack carefully so you don't get caught out by a sudden chill.

Did You Know?

Healdsburg was named after one of its early entrepreneurs, Harmon Heald, who settled here in the early 1800s.

HEALDSBURG

219A Healdsburg Ave; healdsburg.com

Nestled in the Alexander Valley and surrounded by the nation's top wine regions, Healdsburg is a beautiful town with a small-village feel. Its tree-shaded streets are lined with Victorian mansions that house boutiques, restaurants, and wine-tasting rooms.

Today this lively and progressive riverfront town combines old-fashioned charm with hip restaurants. At its heart is a classic 19th-century Spanish plaza, shaded by soaring coast redwoods and surrounded by excellent antiques stores. The Russian River runs through town, and visitors can enjoy canoeing and kayaking at various points along its length. On one bend of the river in the south side of town lies Veterans Memorial Beach, a silvery swath of sand beside the historic steel-truss Memorial Bridge. This popular stretch is staffed with lifeguards, and offers calm swimming in summer.

Healdsburg Museum

This regional museum is a hidden gem housed in the Neo-Classical Healdsburg Library, which is located on Matheson Street. Entry is free, and inside it profiles the history of Sonoma County with fascinating exhibits that include Indigenous Pomo and Wapo basketry, and an eclectic miscellany of historical artifacts. A touch-screen computer station also offers an animated 3D tour of the plaza.

Wineries

Located at the junction of three major wine-growing regions, Healdsburg is surrounded by dozens of wineries, most of which are open to visit. South of town, Rodney Strong Vineyards offers complimentary tours and year-round events, many hosted in an outdoor amphitheater. Nearby, the ruggedly beautiful Chalk Hill Estate has a renowned culinary program. And at Ferrari-Carano, a gorgeous Italianate winery in Dry Creek Valley, paths meander through a 5-acre (2-ha) garden that offers a kaleidoscope of color throughout the year.

The meticulously tended vines and *(inset)* fruit of a vineyard in Healdsburg

Diners sitting beneath wide canopies at one of Healdsburg's many restaurants

EAT & DRINK

SingleThread
The 11-course tasting menu uses ingredients fresh from the restaurant's own farm. Book well in advance to enjoy this popular Michelin-starred spot.

131 North St **singlethreadfarms.com**

$$$

Dry Creek Kitchen
Sleek fine dining spot offering locally sourced ingredients, deftly prepared, and a superb list of Sonoma wines.

317 Healdsburg Ave
drycreekkitchen.com

$$$

Lo & Behold
A contemporary bar and kitchen serving international comfort food paired with seasonal cocktails.

214 Healdsburg Ave
loandbeholdca.com

$$$

SONOMA COUNTY

Francis Ford Coppola Winery

300 Via Archimedes, Geyserville 60 11am-5pm Thu-Mon francisfordcoppolawinery.com

This resort winery produces award-winning wines and is famous as the quasi Hollywood of Wine Country estates. Movie director (and winery owner) Francis Ford Coppola has stamped his legacy throughout the French-style stone château. Sampling wines here is secondary to admiring the displays of iconic memorabilia from Coppola's movies, including Don Corleone's desk from *The Godfather* and Colonel Kurtz's uniform from *Apocalypse Now*. Scenes from the movies are screened and Coppola's Oscars are on display. Don't miss the Bottling Ballet Mécanique Tour, a behind-the-scenes tour of the bottling plant. Coppola's personal passion for fine food is reflected in a gourmet restaurant with gorgeous views from the terrace over the Alexander Valley. Plus, there are Bocce ball courts, a swimming pool, and a Performing Arts Pavilion, the venue for free live entertainment every weekend from April through October.

Bodega Bay

913 Hwy 1; bodegabay.com

In 1963 the coastal town of Bodega Bay appeared in Alfred Hitchcock's *The Birds*. In the tiny neighboring town of Boedga, visitors can still see the Potter Schoolhouse, which was used in the movie. The area is now a very popular resort destination known for its sea-weathered clapboard homes, golf courses, and nearby beaches. It is also home to a thriving deep-sea fishing community, and visitors can watch the fishing fleets unload their day's catch at Tides Wharf dock on Hwy 1.

Bodega Head, the rugged, hook-like peninsula that shelters Bodega Bay, is one of California's best whale-watching points. The northern end of the bay marks the start of **Sonoma Coast State Park**, which is scalloped with miles of sandy coves separated by surging headlands and rocky bluffs. Swimming is generally not safe owing to strong waves and undertows, but the area offers fabulous clifftop hiking and sublime vistas.

10 miles

The length of coast designated as Sonoma Coast State Park (16 km).

Sonoma Coast State Park
parks.ca.gov

Guerneville

16209 First St; russianriver.com

Surrounded by towering redwoods, this charmingly rustic town spans the wide, lazy Russian River in the heart of the Russian River Valley Wine Region. It's known for its famously laid-back attitudes, its riverside resorts, and its bevy of LGBTQ+-owned businesses. Main Street is lined with trendy art galleries, boutiques, and cafés, many housed in quaint Victorian buildings, brightly colored as

↑ Patrons enjoying food on the terrace at Francis Ford Coppola Winery

One of the sandy coves that characterizes Sonoma Coast State Park, near Bodega Bay

if by Crayola. In summer, you can rent a chair and umbrella and spend a few hours lazing on the riverside gray-sand Johnson's Beach; float in a rented inner-tube; or get some exercise on a paddleboat or kayak. The beach has a roped-off "kiddy pool" and is open on weekends from May through September. Camping in nearby Armstrong Redwoods State Park is serenely satisfying any time of year. And you'll want to visit some of the more than 50 local wineries, such as **Korbel Champagne Cellars**, famous for its California Champagnes.

Korbel Champagne Cellars
 13250 River Rd, Guerneville korbel.com

33

Santa Rosa

9 Fourth St; visit santarosa.com

At the northern end of the Sonoma Valley, Santa Rosa is the largest city in wine country. This peaceful town is a lively center for the arts and has many sites of interest. A good place to start is Railroad Square Historic District, a trendy enclave of fine-dining, galleries, and boutiques, built in the early 20th century by Italian stonemasons. Don't miss the Church of the One Tree, built in 1873 from the wood of a single redwood tree; and the Sonoma County Museum, dedicated to the arts and history of the Wine Region. Cartoon-lovers will appreciate the Charles M. Schultz Museum, honoring Snoopy and his creator. On the edge of downtown, the Luther Burbank Home & Gardens preserves a modest Greek Revival house where horticulturalist Luther Burbank lived and conducted plant-breeding experiments. For a bucolic escape, Shiloh Ranch Regional Park is laced with trails and rich in wildlife.

34 

Armstrong Redwoods State Park

17000 Armstrong Woods Rd, Guerneville
20, 28 8am to 1 hour after sunset daily
parks.ca.gov

Only a five-minute drive from Guerneville, but a whole world away from urbanity, this 1.3-sq-mile (3.3-sq-km) grove of majestic coast redwoods provides a cool summer escape amid the world's tallest living things. The tallest tree in the grove, Parson's Tree, soars to 310 ft (95 m). Hiking beneath the soaring canopy – or better still, camping – is a sublime experience. Several interlinked self-guided nature trails total 6 miles (9 km).

STAY

Farmhouse Inn
Wine on arrival, a Michelin-starred restaurant, and suites with enormous double-sided fireplaces all contribute to the sense of understated luxury at this secluded hotel. Rooms are arranged around the outdoor pool and surrounded by quiet woodlands.

7871 River Rd, Forestville
farmhouseinn.com

$$$

Fort Ross State Historic Park

19005 Coast Hwy 1 95 10am–4:30pm daily fortross.org

Occupying a breezy ocean-front perch, Fort Ross State Historic Park preserves a wooden stockade com-munity that flourished as the southernmost Russian settlement in North America from 1821 to 1841. Named for *Rossia* (Russia), it was established by the Russian American Company as an agricultural colony and base for hunting sea otters.

The reconstructed and restored buildings offer a fascinating insight into life for Russians in the contested world of early 19th-century California. A scenic trail leads from the Visitor Center and Museum to the wooden stockade. The only original Russian structure is Rotcher House, which belonged to the company manager, decorated with homely furnishings. The Kuskov House displays weapons and agricultural tools, while another building is devoted to the crafts – including tanning, carpentry, and blacksmithing – which sustained the Russians. A tiny Russian Orthodox chapel is adorned with religious icons. Don't miss the nearby Russian Cemetery, with its weather-beaten wooden crosses.

Gloria Ferrer Caves & Vineyards

23555 Arnold Dr, Sonoma 32 10am–5pm daily gloriaferrer.com

This beautiful Spanish Mission-style winery and large estate, 5 miles (8 km) south of Sonoma, is renowned for its distinctive sparkling wines using Méthode Champenoise blends. Located in the Los Carneros AVA (American Viticultural Area) at the southern end of the Sonoma Valley, the winery's distinct *terroir* is influenced by the cool air and creeping fogs of the Pacific Ocean: perfect conditions for growing Chardonnay and Pinot Noir grapes that are used for Gloria Ferrer's famous "blanc de noirs" – sparkling wine made from red grape varieties. The tasting room is open for tours for a fee. You can sit on the outside terrace to enjoy picnics and specialty culinary experiences, such as Spanish tapas pairings. Chocoholics might like to sample the chocolate-covered Blanc de Noirs – a bottle of sparkling wine dipped in melted chocolate, then chilled; you break the "zip tab" to nibble on bite-size chunks of chocolate between sips. Each summer, the winery hosts the Catalan Festival of Food, Wine & Music.

GREAT VIEW
Mission Trail

The Mission San Francisco Solano is the last of the 21 missions on the Historic Mission Trail that you come to, traveling north from San Diego. All are located on or near Hwy 101 and most still operate as Catholic parishes.

Sonoma

453 1st St East; sonomacity.org

One of California's most picturesque towns, Sonoma is graced with quaint buildings recalling its Spanish–Mexican heritage. The compact town dates back to 1823 and is of immense historic importance. It was here on June 14, 1846, that American farmers seized the Mexican governor, General Mariano Vallejo, and declared an independent republic. Twenty-five days later, the United States annexed California. The bronze monument at the northeast corner of grassy Sonoma Plaza, recalls the "Bear Flag Rebellion." Sites of historic significance surround the plaza, including the 1823 Mission San Francisco Solano. It's flanked by the Sonoma Barracks, headquarters of the Mexican Army, and La Casa Grande, an adobe

The alluring Russian River lazily winding its way past lushly forested banks

building that was Vallejo's first home. A ten-minute stroll brings you to Vallejo's later home, the Gothic Revival Lachryma Montis. Other treats include the former Toscano Hotel, furnished in turn-of-the-20th-century decor and, next door, the Sonoma Cheese Factory. Sonoma is bursting with trendy art galleries, boutiques, restaurants, and wine-tasting rooms, tempting you wisely to linger.

East of Sonoma's plaza is the restored **Mission San Francisco Solano de Sonoma**, the last of California's 21 historic Franciscan missions. Father José Altimira of Spain founded the mission in 1823 at a time when California was under Mexican rule. Today, all that survives of the original building is the corridor of Father Altimira's quarters.

Mission San Francisco Solano de Sonoma
 114 E Spain St
10am–5pm daily
parks.ca.gov

Fine historic buildings in Sonoma, recalling its Spanish-Mexican past

38 

Jack London State Historic Park

2400 London Ranch Rd, Glen Ellen 9am–5pm daily jacklondonpark.com

A short drive north of Sonoma leads to the Jack London State Historic Park. In the early 1900s, London, author of *The Call of the Wild* (1903) and *The Sea-Wolf* (1904), abandoned his hectic lifestyle to live in this 1-sq-mile (3-sq-km) expanse of oaks, madrones, and redwoods. The park retains eerie ruins of London's dream home, the Wolf House, which was mysteriously destroyed by fire just before completion.

After London's death in 1916, his widow, Charmian Kittredge, built a magnificent home on the ranch, called the House of Happy Walls. Today it is a museum, well worth a visit for its display of Jack London memorabilia, including his writing desk and early copies of his works.

39

Russian River

16200 First St, Guerneville; russianriver.com

The second largest river in the Bay Area – after the Sacramento River – Russian River starts in the Laughlin Range in Mendocino County and flows south for 110 miles (177 km). All along the river are campgrounds, beaches, redwood forests, wineries, day spas, and charming towns, making it a great trip whether you're after action and adventure or simply some peace and tranquility. The river spills into the Pacific Ocean near the hamlet of Jenner. Here hundreds of harbour seals bask in the sun on Goat Rock Beach, which was used as a location in the movie *The Goonies*.

> **The park retains eerie ruins of London's dream home, the Wolf House, which was mysteriously destroyed by fire just before completion.**

↑ Monterey's historic Cannery Row, a six-block street on the harbor

MONTEREY

401 Camino El Estero; seemonterey.com

Monterey was established by the Spanish in 1770, and served as the capital of northern California under Spanish and later Mexican rule. During the Mexican–American War (1846–8), the US flag was raised over the town and northern California became part of the United States. Today Monterey has several prestigious universities and is a popular resort town renowned for its spectacular setting, world-class aquarium, historic attractions, and great seafood.

Monterey Bay Aquarium

886 Cannery Row MST Trolley 10am-5pm daily montereybay aquarium.org

This venue is one of the world's best aquariums. It exhibits more than 550 species and some 35,000 live specimens. Highlights include the peaceful Kelp Forest and the Open Sea Gallery, full of sea creatures such as giant tuna, sharks, green sea turtles, and shoaling sardines. Daily feedings and educational shows are must-sees, as are the playful sea otters (the aquarium's mascot) and interactive exhibits such as the Splash Zone and touch pool.

Cannery Row

Cannery Row MST Trolley canneryrow.com

This popular waterfront street spanning four blocks was formerly occupied by sardine canning factories. It was the setting for John Steinbeck's novel, *Cannery Row* (1945); the title came from the nickname for Ocean View Avenue, as the name "Cannery Row" was formalized in 1958. The last cannery closed in 1973 following the collapse of the industry due to overfishing, and the area fell into decay. Today the canneries have been converted into hotels, eclectic stores, wine-tasting rooms, and restaurants, including the Sardine Factory, which opened in 1968 and signaled the renaissance of Cannery Row.

Old Fisherman's Wharf

1 Old Fisherman's Wharf MST Trolley monterey wharf.com

This historic wharf in Monterey harbor was an active fishing pier into the 1970s. Today

Did You Know?

The Monterey Jazz Festival is a major annual event that dates back to 1958.

it's a lively commercial venue with a medley of candy and souvenir stores, and seafood restaurants with wonderful views. As you explore, keep an eye out for sea otters drifting on the surface and sea lions frolicking in the harbor. For close-ups with the local marine life, Old Fisherman's Wharf offers glass-bottom boats, whale-watching tours, and deep-sea fishing trips.

National Steinbeck Center

1 Main St, Salinas Buses to Salinas Transit Center 10am-5pm Wed-Sun steinbeck.org

Monterey and neighboring Salinas are synonymous with novelist John Steinbeck (1902–68), who set many of his stories here. The Nobel Prize-winning author's life, literature, and legacy are the theme of the National Steinbeck Center, two blocks from his birthplace in downtown Salinas. The museum brings Steinbeck's works to life with movie clips and dioramas that recreate scenes from his novels.

An adjoining section celebrates the heritage of the local Japanese community (the first of whom immigrated in the 1890s). Another section explores the history of farming in Salinas Valley.

Del Monte Beach

123 Tide Ave 12, 20, 67

This gorgeous curve of dune-backed, golden-white sand curls north from Old Fisherman's Wharf and merges into other beaches that run unbroken for almost 20 miles (32 km). The lovely Monterey Bay Recreational Trail snakes alongside the beach, and is a delight for walking, skating, or cycling. There are firepits for chilly evenings, and picnic benches at the west end.

The waters are usually calm enough to make for a pleasant kayak ride, and to allow waders to spy sand dollars in the shallows. Offshore, a large reef encrusted with clams tempts divers with its large population of octopuses, sponges, and fish. Spawning halibut can even be seen close to shore in spring.

Monterey State Historic Park

20 Custom House Plaza MST Trolley Hours vary, check website parks.ca.gov

Monterey's well-preserved historic core features many notable 19th-century buildings. You can explore the area and a few museums on a self-guided walk, but those wishing to get a better look inside the historic buildings should book a tour.

EAT

Monterey's Fish House

A seafood restaurant with a casual yet lively atmosphere. The huge range of dishes - from ahi tuna to cioppino - use fish and shellfish fresh from the bay.

2114 Del Monte Ave montereyfishhouse.com

$$$

Ghirardelli's

This gourmet ice cream and chocolate store also serves classic American drinks such as malts and shakes. The terrace overlooking the bay is the perfect place to enjoy a sundae.

660 Cannery Row ghirardelli.com

BEYOND THE BAY

41

Sacramento

 1002 2nd St; visit sacramento.com

Founded by John Sutter in 1839, California's capital city has many historic buildings along the waterfront in Old Sacramento. Some of the structures here were built to serve the gold miners of 1849, but most date from 1860–70, when Sacramento sealed its positon as the link between rural California and the commercial centers along the coast. The Pony Express and transcontintental railroad both had their western terminus here, with paddle-wheel riverboats providing the connection to San Francisco. A handful of museums trace the area's historic importance, including the **California State Railroad Museum**, which houses some fine old locomotives and operates excursions on an old steam train from April through September.

A short distance from the old town is the **California State Capitol**, Sacramento's primary landmark and one of the handsomest buildings in the state. It was designed in 1860 by Reuben Clark and Miner F. Butler in grand Greek Revival style, with Corinthian porticos and a tall central dome. Along with the chambers of the state legislature, which are open to visitors even when they are in session, the Capital houses a museum of the state's history.

California State Railroad Museum
125 I St 10am-5pm daily csrmf.org

California State Capitol
1315 10th St Hours vary, check website capitolmuseum.ca.gov

42

Mendocino

 345 N Franklin St, Fort Bragg; visitmendocino.com

The settlers of this village came to California from New England in 1852, and built their new homes to resemble those they had left behind on the East Coast. Perched on a rocky promontory high above the Pacific Ocean, Mendocino has retained the picturesque charm of its days as a major fishing and logging center, and has been declared an historical monument. While tourism is now its main industry, the town remains

→ Elegant Bixby Bridge, part of the stunning Pacific Coast Highway

Fine historic buildings on the waterfront in Old Sacramento

virtually untarnished by commercialism. Visitors can stroll around the many boutiques, bookshops, galleries, and cafés, while those who prefer the attractions of nature can look out for migrating gray whales and admire the stunning ocean vistas.

Carmel-by-the-Sea

Ocean Ave; carmelcalifornia.com

The charming seaside town of Carmel-by-the-Sea ("Carmel," for short) has been a haven for artists and writers since the early 20th century. Ocean Avenue is lined with art galleries, boutiques, and cafés, and beautiful homes border the steep hillsides down to the ocean, where Carmel Beach provides a 1-mile (1.5-km) stretch of white sand.

Big Sur

47555 CA-1, Big Sur; bigsurcalifornia.org

California's coastal beauty is nowhere more awe-inspiring than along Big Sur: the rugged shoreline south of Monterey *(p248)*. The Pacific Coast Highway snakes past surging headlands, leaps across plunging canyons, and weaves above remote beaches pounded by crashing surf. The 65-mile (105-km) route between Carmel and San Simeon is one of the world's most magnificent coastal drives – but make sure to drive carefully, as the route has many clifftop switchbacks and is often fog-bound, especially in summer.

Make sure to stop to photograph Bixby Bridge, a classic landmark and single-arch engineering marvel with a stunning setting. It's also worth taking the time to explore the **Pfeiffer Big Sur State Park**, which has a well-marked network of scenic trails and a large campground.

Pfeiffer Big Sur State Park
Near mile marker 47.2 on Hwy 1 8am-sunset daily parks.ca.gov

STAY

Pine Inn

Just a few blocks from the beach, this iconic inn - the oldest in town - offers elegant rooms and a great on-site restaurant that's popular with locals.

Ocean Ave & Monte Verde, Carmel
pineinn.com

$$

Did You Know?

Bixby Bridge was constructed using concrete partly due to its aesthetic similarity to sea cliffs.

NEED TO KNOW

A traditional cable car at Union Square

BEFORE YOU GO

Things change, so plan ahead to make the most of your trip. Be prepared for all eventualities by considering the following points before you travel.

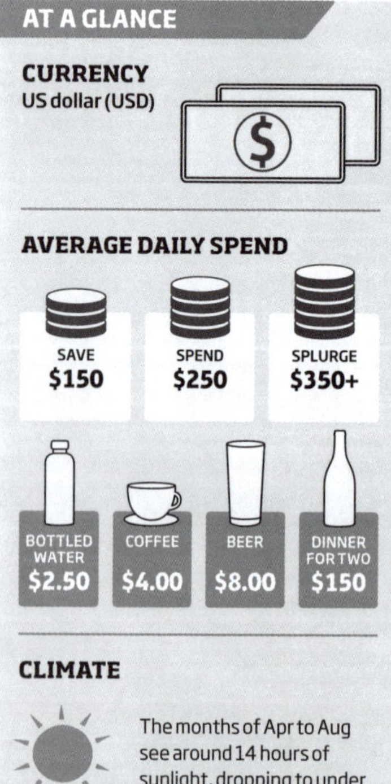

The months of Apr to Aug see around 14 hours of sunlight, dropping to under 10 hours from Nov to Feb.

Temperatures can change by the hour, averaging 65°F/18°C in summer and 50°F/10°C in winter.

Rain rarely occurs from Feb to Nov, while fog can roll in any day.

ELECTRICITY SUPPLY

Plug sockets are type A and B, fitting two- and three-pronged plugs. Standard voltage is 100–120 volts AC.

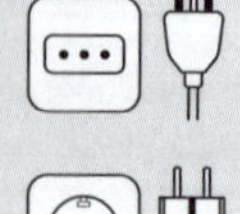

Passports and Visas

For entry requirements, consult your nearest US embassy or check the **US Department of State** website. Canadians typically do not require visas to enter the US. Holders of a UK, European Union, Australian, or New Zealand passport with a return ticket do not require visas if staying in the US for 90 days or less, but must apply for an Electronic System for Travel Authorization (**ESTA**) at least 72 hours before travel. All other visitors need to secure a visa before traveling.

ESTA
W esta.cbp.dhs.gov/esta
US Department of State
W travel.state.gov

Government Advice

Now more than ever, it is important to consult both your and the US government's advice before traveling. The US Department of State, the **UK Foreign & Commonwealth Office**, and the **Australian Department of Foreign Affairs and Trade** offer the latest information on security, health, and local regulations.

Australian Department of Foreign Affairs and Trade
W smartraveller.gov.au
UK Foreign & Commonwealth Office
W gov.uk/foreign-travel-advice

Customs Information

You can find information on the laws relating to goods and currency taken in or out of the United States on the **US Customs and Border Protection** website.

US Customs and Border Protection
W cbp.gov

Insurance

We recommend taking out a comprehensive insurance policy covering theft, loss of belongings, medical care, cancellations and delays,

and read the small print carefully. The US healthcare system is predominantly private – and costly – so medical cover is essential.

Vaccinations

No inoculations are needed to visit the US.

Booking Accommodations

Booking a package deal, including airfares and hotels (and sometimes car rentals), is often the most inexpensive way of visiting San Francisco. Make sure to book in advance to get the best deals, especially if visiting from June through August. Prices also spike around holidays and local festivals, so check your dates before you book. As well as luxury hotels, you can also find a range of good-value hostels and B&Bs. **San Francisco Travel** has a range of suggestions.

San Francisco Travel
W sftravel.com

Money

Most retailers will accept cash or card, including contactless payments. You're never far from an ATM in the city, though you may be charged $2.50 to $3.50 per transaction in addition to any ATM withdrawal fees. Currency can be exchanged at larger bank branches, as well as at bureaux de change.

Tax (around 10 per cent), service charge (around 20 per cent), and an SF mandate charge are often added to a restaurant bill. A useful trick to figure out a restaurant tip is to double the tax. In hotels, it is customary to tip porters $1.50 per bag and housekeeping $2 per night.

Travelers with Specific Requirements

Disabled access is extensive throughout San Francisco, from ramped curbs to telecommunication devices for hearing-impaired travelers. However, the city is famous for its steep hills, particularly around Russian Hill and Nob Hill, which may prove challenging for those with mobility issues. Public transportation is largely accessible for those with specific requirements, and prices are usually discounted. The free Muni Access Guide for public transportation is available on the SFMTA website *(p257)* and **Access Northern California** provides information on accessible travel and recreation.

Access Northern California
W accessnca.org

Language

The official language of San Francisco is English, although more than a hundred languages are spoken across this cosmopolitan city. Spanish and Chinese are well established as second and third languages.

Opening Hours

Situations can change quickly and unexpectedly. Always check before visiting attractions and hospitality venues for up-to-date opening hours and booking requirements.

Businesses, restaurants, museums, and stores close earlier during the winter season, from November to March. Most banks are closed on Sundays. Some museums close on Mondays or Tuesdays, and on federal holidays.

PUBLIC HOLIDAYS

Jan 1	New Year's Day
Jan 15	Martin Luther King, Jr. Day
Feb 19	Presidents' Day
May 27	Memorial Day
Jun 19	Juneteenth
Jul 4	Independence Day
Sep 2	Labor Day
Oct 14	Columbus Day
Nov 11	Veterans Day
Nov 28	Thanksgiving Day
Dec 25	Christmas Day

GETTING AROUND

Whether navigating the hills by cable car, or taking a ferry across the bay, San Francisco's public transportation options are well worth exploring.

AT A GLANCE

PUBLIC TRANSPORT FARES

SINGLE TICKET

$2.85

120 minutes of travel on Muni-operated transport

1-DAY PASSPORT

$15.00

Unlimited travel on Muni-operated transport

7-DAY PASSPORT

$44.00

Unlimited travel on Muni-operated transport

TOP TIP

Download the MuniMobile app for routes and times.

SPEED LIMIT

RURAL FREEWAYS	URBAN FREEWAYS
65 mph (105 km/h)	**65** mph (105 km/h)

NEIGHBORHOOD SLOW ZONE	URBAN AREAS
20 mph (32 km/h)	**35** mph (55 km/h)

Arriving by Air

San Francisco International Airport (SFO) is one of the world's busiest airports, receiving flights from all major international airlines, but is very user-friendly. Nearby airports include San Jose International Airport (SJC), about an hour away from San Francisco, and Oakland International Airport (OAK), which is 30 minutes away.

SFO is 14 miles (23 km) south of the city center. The airport offers international connections to and from the Pacific Rim, Latin America, and Europe. For a list of transportation options, approximate journey times, and travel costs for transportation between San Francisco International Airport and downtown San Francisco, see the table opposite. The Bay Area Rapid Transport (BART) station is connected to the terminal by a light-rail shuttle.

Visitors will arrive at the airport on the lower level. The top level provides services for those departing the city. All car rentals, parking shuttles, public buses, and door-to-door shuttle minibuses deliver and pick up passengers at this level.

Train Travel

Amtrak trains link most major US cities and are a great way to see parts of the country you would not otherwise experience. Advance booking is recommended for travel during peak periods. Those visiting San Francisco by train will arrive at the Amtrak station in Emeryville, to the north of Oakland. From here, take a free 45-minute shuttle to the Ferry Building in the city center.

Alternatively, you can arrive by Amtrak to Oakland, then take the **San Francisco Bay Ferry** to Downtown San Francisco. Or travel to San Jose, then transfer on to the **Caltrain** to San Francisco. Separate tickets are required for the ferry and Caltrain.

Amtrak
W amtrak.com
CalTrain
W caltrain.com
San Francisco Bay Ferry
W sanfranciscobayferry.com

GETTING TO AND FROM THE AIRPORT

Transportation	Journey time	Fare
Taxi	25–45 minutes	$45–65
SuperShuttle shared ride	40–60 minutes	$20–$85
American Airporter Shuttle	60–75 minutes	$19
Bay Area Rapid Transit (BART)	30 minutes	$11.15

Long-Distance Bus Travel

For travelers on a budget, buses are a great way to travel. **Greyhound** buses take passengers from Los Angeles to San Francisco in around seven hours from $43. The **Green Tortoise** bus company offers a friendly and adventurous way to see California, often stopping at tourist sights.

Green Tortoise
W greentortoise.com
Greyhound
W greyhound.com

Public Transportation

The San Francisco Peninsula and the East Bay are linked by the Bay Area Rapid Transit (**BART**) network – an efficient way to get to and from SFO and Oakland International airports.

The city of San Francisco has a reliable public transportation system run by the San Francisco Municipal Transportation Agency (**SFMTA**). The city's bus and Metro network is known as the **Muni** and covers buses, light-rail Metro trains, streetcars (electric trams), and cable cars. Timetables, ticket information, transport maps, and more can be obtained from the SFMTA website.

BART
W bart.gov
SFMTA
W sfmta.com
Muni
W sfmta.com/muni-transit

Planning Your Journey

Public transportation is busiest at 7am–9am and 4pm–7pm from Monday through Friday. This may be the best time to explore the city by foot. The cable cars are a popular tourist activity, so are busy during the summer months.

The Muni Metro runs from around 5am to 1am on weekdays, from 7am on Saturdays, and 8am on Sundays. There are ten Muni Owl services that run 24 hours a day, 7 days a week. Schedules are modified for public holidays, so check the SFMTA website before traveling.

Tickets

Clipper is the Bay Area's transport pass. It can be used to pay for BART, Caltrain, ferries, and Muni services. Plastic Clipper cards can be bought and topped up at station machines and at Walgreens stores. Smartphone versions can be loaded onto Apple or Google Wallets.

MuniMobile is the city's transport app. It can be used to buy single tickets (for 120 minutes) and Muni Passports (for one, three, or seven consecutive days). These allow unlimited travel on Muni Metro, buses, historic streetcars, and cable cars, but not BART or other services. Paper Muni Passports are available from ticket kiosks.

You can also pay in cash on buses and at Muni Metro ticket machines. This costs slightly more, for example a Muni single costs $3 cash or $2.85 via Clipper or MuniMobile. You must have the exact change. Request a receipt if you wish to use other Muni services within your ticket's 120 minutes.

Clipper
W clippercard.com

Buses

There are bus stops every two or three blocks. Bus shelters list the route number of the buses that stop there, as well as maps and service frequency information. Most have digital signs showing when the next bus will arrive. Route numbers followed by a letter are either express services or make limited stops.

Metro

The Metro light-rail system operates both above and below ground. Lines J (Church), K (Ingleside), L (Taraval), M (Ocean View), N (Judah), and T (Third) share the same tracks, so check the letter and name of the vehicle when boarding from Market Street. To go west, follow signs indicating "Outbound"; to go east, chooose "Downtown."

Streetcars

The F line streetcar runs along Market Street only, and features vintage streetcars from all over the world. While these streetcars are scenic, they're not the best option to take if you're in a rush. They stop frequently for riders to take in views and snap pictures. These streetcars are also wheelchair accessible at most stops, but not all of them.

Cable Cars

San Francisco's cable cars are world-famous, and even classed as a "moving national monument." Service runs every ten minutes from 6am to midnight daily. If you don't have a Muni Passport, the fare is $9 per journey, with no free transfers. There are three routes: the Powell-Hyde line, which passes Union Square and climbs Nob Hill, providing good views of Chinatown. The Powell-Mason line begins in the same place and branches off to pass North Beach, ending at Bay Street. Sit facing east on the Powell lines for the best views. The California line runs from the base of Market Street at the Embarcadero, through the Financial District and Chinatown, over Nob Hill, ending at Van Ness Avenue.

BART

BART trains run from 4am on weekdays, from 6am on Saturdays, and from 8am on Sundays, until around midnight. Tickets are issued by machines in BART stations, which take cards or cash. You must present your ticket at the turnstile both when you board and leave the train. You can also use a Clipper card. The final destination of the train will be displayed on the front of the train itself, and the direction of travel will be marked on the platform.

BART
W bart.gov

Taxis

Taxis in San Francisco operate 24 hours a day. They are licensed and regulated, so expect efficient service, expert local knowledge, and a set price. A taxi will have its rooftop sign illuminated if vacant. It will also display the company name and telephone number, plus the cab number. Make a note of this, and if you leave anything in the cab, call the company and quote the cab number.

To catch a cab, wait at a taxi stand, call and request a pick-up, or hail a vacant cab. Tell your driver your exact destination. The meter will be on the dashboard; expect to add a 15 to 20 per cent tip to the final amount. Fares are often posted inside the cab. The minimum fare is $4.15, plus $0.65 per fifth-mile or per minute waiting or in stationary traffic. Typical fares from the city center include $36 to Sausalito, $49 to Berkeley and $250 to Napa. The driver will write you a receipt on request. If you travel 15 miles (24 km) or more beyond the city limits, the fare will be 150 per cent of the metered rate.

All taxi-cabs are non-smoking. If you have a complaint about a taxi driver, call the **Police Department Taxicab Complaint Line**.

The taxi companies **Uber** and **Lyft** are very cost-effective and reliable in San Francisco. Download the apps on your smartphone. Payment is handled through the apps and you can track your journey, split fares with other users, and report complaints through the app.

The newest way to get around – driverless taxis (or robotaxis) – are available via **Waymo**.

Lyft
W lyft.com
Police Department Taxicab Complaint Line
T 415-701-4400
Uber
W uber.com
Waymo
W waymo.com

Driving

Congestion, a shortage of parking spaces, and strictly enforced laws discourage many visitors from driving in San Francisco, but possibly the best way to experience the twists and turns of Lombard Street is on four wheels.

Car Rental

To rent a car, you must be at least 25 years old with a valid driving license. Most agencies require a large deposit. Always return the car with a full tank of gas to avoid inflated gas prices charged by the agency. It is slightly cheaper to rent a car from San Francisco airport. Additional rental taxes can drive up the price, especially if you hire from within the city. It is also more cost-effective to do a round trip, to avoid large drop-off costs. Check your existing insurance policy before signing up to car insurance, as you may already be partially covered.

Rules of the Road

The maximum speed limit is 35 mph (55 km/h) in the city. Many streets are one-way, with traffic lights at most corners. In the US, if there is no oncoming traffic, drivers may turn right at a red light, always giving pedestrians the right of way. Otherwise, a red light means stop, and an amber light means proceed with caution.

Parking

Parking meters operate 9am to 6pm Monday through Saturday, except on national holidays, when parking is free. Meters in some tourist areas operate on Sundays, including at Fisherman's Wharf and the Embarcadero. Most meters have two-hour time limits, some have four-hour limits, and others no time limit at all. You can prepay from 4:30am online. Costs range from $2 to $6 per hour. City-center parking garages are also available from $16 per day.

Curbs here are color-coded. A red curb means no stopping; yellow denotes a commercial loading zone; green allows 10 to 30 minutes of parking; and white allows you to park for five minutes during business hours, with the driver remaining in the vehicle. Blue curb areas are reserved for the disabled. By law, you must curb your wheels when parking on steep hills. Turn your wheels into the road when your car is parked facing uphill, and toward the curb when facing downhill. Check signs for tow warnings and follow all instructions.

Penalties

If you park your car at an out-of-order meter, expect to get a parking ticket. Blocking bus stops, fire hydrants, driveways, garages, and wheelchair ramps will also incur a fine, as will running a red light or a stop sign, or driving while texting. Traffic fines in San Francisco can exceed $100. If your car has been towed away, contact the **City and County of San Francisco Impound**. Expect to pay a towing and storage fee when retrieving your car.

City and County of San Francisco Impound
T 415-865-8200

Driving Outside the City

No toll payment is required to leave the city, but you will need to pay $9.50 to re-enter. During rush hour, cars with three or more occupants can use the carpool lane, avoiding both traffic and tolls. In other parts of the Bay Area, only two occupants are required. It is legal to drive in the carpool lane when it's not rush hour, but not to avoid the bridge tolls. Those caught using the carpool lane illegally face steep fines.

Cycling

Cycling is popular in San Francisco. There are many bicycle lanes and all Muni buses are equipped to carry bikes on the outside. Bikes can also be taken on the light-rail Muni cars and on BART, although not at rush hour. There are two marked scenic bicycle routes. One goes from Golden Gate park south to Lake Merced; the other starts at the southern end of Golden Gate Bridge and crosses to Marin County.

Bicycles, e-bikes, equipment, and tours are available from **Bay City Bike** and **Blazing Saddles**. They rent out bikes from $32 per day, or $135 for seven days. Bay Area Bike Share stations, which are spread across the city, also hire bikes, with charges starting at $4 for 30 minutes.

Bay City Bike
W baycitybike.com
Blazing Saddles
W blazingsaddles.com

Walking

Compact and gridded, San Francisco is entirely walkable. Downtown and the Mission, in particular, are forgivingly flat, while Nob Hill and Russian Hill reward steep climbs with spectacular views. Distances get a little more arduous once you're out on the avenues of the Richmond and Sunset, but walking is a good way to get a feel for each neighborhood.

Boats and Ferries

Ferries are a great way to explore the Bay Area. They shuttle to and from San Francisco, Oakland, and Larkspur, as well as the smaller towns of Tiburon and Sausalito, and nearby Angel Island. Viewing the coastline from the ferry is less expensive than a sightseeing cruise. The trip from San Francisco to Sausalito is $14 each way and food and drink are available on board. These ferries only carry foot passengers and bicycles, not motor vehicles. **Golden Gate Ferry** and San Francisco Bay Ferry *(p256)* services depart from the Ferry Building, and the **Blue and Gold Fleet** and **Red and White Fleet** dock at Fisherman's Wharf.

Several companies also offer sightseeing cruises of the Bay. Many of these boat trips pass near Alcatraz, but only **Alcatraz Cruises** stops there. **Hornblower** dining yachts offer weekend brunches and dinners from Thursday to Sunday. **Oceanic Society Expeditions** arranges nautical environmental safaris to the Farallon Islands, where whales, sea lions, seals, and dolphins are often spotted. Shorter whale-watching expeditions run by **San Francisco Whale Tours** also depart from PIER 39 from March to October.

Alcatraz Cruises
W alcatrazcruises.com
Blue and Gold Fleet
W blueandgoldfleet.com
Golden Gate Ferry
W goldengate.org
Hornblower
W hornblower.com
Oceanic Society Expeditions
W oceanicsociety.org/expeditions
Red and White Fleet
W redandwhite.com
San Francisco Whale Tours
W sanfranciscowhaletours.com

PRACTICAL INFORMATION

Forward planning is essential for any successful trip. Prepare yourself for any eventuality by brushing up on the following points.

AT A GLANCE

EMERGENCY NUMBERS

GENERAL EMERGENCY

911

TIME ZONE

PST/DST. Daylight Saving Time (DST) from the second Sunday in March till the first Sunday in Nov.

TAP WATER

Safe to drink, but bottled water is widely available.

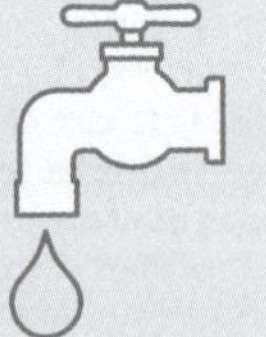

WEBSITES AND APPS

sfchronicle.com
Search under "Datebook" for listings and events.

sftravel.com
Full of information and ideas for trips and activities throughout the city.

Moovit, Transit
These apps tell you the best way to your destination via public transportation.

ParkMobile
Book parking spaces in advance, or find open parking spaces in the city.

Personal Security

San Francisco is one of the safest large cities in the US. Police patrol tourist areas frequently, and few visitors are victims of street crime. That said, it is always advisable to take the usual precautions against petty crime. The city is experiencing a housing crisis, and thousands of people are living in encampments, which has unfortunately led to a rise in petty crime. Tackling this issue is a priority for the local government, but it may take some years before things visibly improve.

San Francisco is at risk of earthquakes and wildfires. Should you experience a quake, there are simple safety guidelines to follow. If indoors, stand under a doorway or table, away from windows and wall hangings and hold on until the shaking stops. If outdoors, stay away from power cables and trees. If driving, pull over, away from power lines and bridges, and remain in the car. If on the beach, move to higher ground. The Federal Emergency Management Agency (**FEMA**) has a website for safety precautions and you can also access a California-wide early warning system through the free **MyShake** app, which alerts users to earthquakes. The **Department of Forestry and Fire Protection** website has maps showing the locations of any wildfires. The peak wildfire season is from July to October when hot, dry winds are most frequent.

As a rule, San Franciscans are very accepting of all people, regardless of their race, gender, or sexuality. California recognized the rights of those wanting to legally change their gender in the mid-1980s and same-sex marriage was legalized in 2008. San Francisco has a hugely diverse LGBTQ+ community, with a history stretching back to the Gold Rush. If you do feel unsafe, the **Safe Space Alliance** pinpoints your nearest place of refuge.

Department of Forestry and Fire Protection
W fire.ca.gov

FEMA
W fema.gov

MyShake
W myshake.berkeley.edu

Safe Space Alliance
W safespacealliance.com

Health

Healthcare in the US is high quality but costly. Ensure you have full medical cover prior to your visit, and keep receipts to claim on your insurance.

Walgreens pharmacies can be found all over the city, and branches at 498 Castro Street, 135 Powell Street, 459 Powell Street, Divisadero Street, and Westborough Square are open 24 hours. Certain medications available over the counter in the UK require a prescription in the US. There are several emergency rooms open 24 hours, including the following:

California Pacific Medical Center
W cpmc.org

Saint Francis Memorial Hospital
W saintfrancismemorial.org

Smoking, Alcohol, and Drugs

You must be over 21 to buy and drink alcohol, and to buy tobacco products. It is legal for over 21s to smoke marijuana in the home or in a building licensed for its consumption. Drinking alcohol is not allowed in most public areas. Driving while under the influence of alcohol or any drug is prohibited. It is illegal to smoke in public buildings, workplaces, restaurants, bars, and anywhere that exposes others to secondhand smoke.

ID

Take some form of photo identification when buying alcohol, tobacco, or marijuana, as businesses are required by law to check it.

Local Customs

San Francisco is a very laid-back city. Casual clothing is quite acceptable for all but the most upmarket restaurants and nightclubs.

Responsible Travel

The **Visit California** website has responsible travel tips. Respect wildlife in and around the city, avoid wasting water, be alert to the possibility of wildfires, dispose of any trash responsibly, and try to use local businesses when possible.

Visit California
W visitcalifornia.com/things-to-do/travel-california-respect-california

Cell Phones and Wi-Fi

Cell phone service in San Francisco is excellent. The main US network providers are AT&T, Sprint, T-Mobile US, and Verizon. Most of these offer prepaid, pay-as-you-go phones and US SIM cards, starting at around $30 (plus tax), which you can purchase upon arrival. Alternatively, buy an eSIM from an independent provider such as Airalo, Alosim, or Saily. Calls within the US are cheap, but making international calls may be pricey.

Free Wi-Fi is widely available throughout the city and the Bay Area. Service can be accessed on trains, in the subway tunnel linking San Francisco and Oakland, and in many cafes and hotels.

Post

Stamps can be purchased at post offices, hotel reception desks, and some grocery stores. Check current postal rates at post offices or online at the **US Postal Services** website. Letters can be mailed from post offices, your hotel, and street mailboxes. Express mail can also be arranged through private delivery companies, such as DHL, FedEx, and UPS.

US Postal Services
W usps.com

Taxes

Sales tax in San Francisco is 8.5 per cent. As a general rule, tax is charged on everything except groceries, plants used for food, and prescription drugs.

Discount Cards

Several websites, including **City Pass**, offer discounts and passes, often grouping together attractions and public transportation. Visitors with proof of student status receive discounts at many museums and theaters. You can apply for an International Student Identity Card (ISIC) prior to traveling.

City Pass
W citypass.com

INDEX

Page numbers in **bold** refer to main entries.

G

H

I

J

K

L

M

ACKNOWLEDGMENTS

This edition is updated by
Contributor Emma Gregg
Senior Editor Dipika Dasgupta
Senior Designer Stuti Tiwari
Project Editors Anuroop Sanwalia, Tijana Todorinović
Editors Ekta Chada, Abhidha Lakhera, Manjari Thakur
Assistant Picture Research Administrator Manpreet Kaur
Rights and Permissions Specialist Vagisha Pushp
Deputy Picture Research Manager Virien Chopra
Publishing Assistant Simona Velikova
Jacket Designer Katie Cavanagh
Jacket Picture Researcher Cristina Antequera
Senior Cartographer Mohammad Hassan
Cartography Manager Suresh Kumar
Pre-production Coordinator Tanveer Zaidi
Pre-Production Designer Rohit Rojal
Pre-Production Manager Balwant Singh
Production Controller Kariss Ainsworth
Deputy Managing Editor Dharini Ganesh
Managing Editor Beverly Smart
Managing Art Editor Gemma Doyle
Senior Managing Art Editor Priyanka Thakur
Editorial Director Hollie Teague
Art Director Maxine Pedliham
Publishing Director Georgina Dee

DK would like to thank the following for their contribution to the previous edition: Kat Rosa, Karen Misuraca, Matt Charnock, Nick Edwards, Ella Buchan, Christopher P. Baker, Gabrielle Innes, Sophie Blackman, Jamie Jensen, Barry Parr, Dawn Douglas, Shirley Streshinsky, Rachel Everett

The publisher would like to thank the following for their kind permission to reproduce their photographs:

Key: a-above; b-below/bottom; c-centre; f-far; l-left; r-right; t-top

123RF.com: Mariusz Blach 14-5b; Maciej Błędowski 8clb; Coralimages 162bl; Murry Dalton 224tl; Filip Fuxa 14clb,; Nick Kontostavlakis 64-5t; Pius Lee 17t; Wasin Pummarin 94-5t.

Alamy Stock Photo: Aflo Co. Ltd. 79cr; AGE Fotostock 86-7t, 118crb, 178-9t; Allen Brown 177tl; Arcaid Images 148-9bl; Archive PL 83tl; Gonzalo Azumendi 179cl, 183t; Sergio Torres Baus 106bl; Bildagentur-online / Schickert 123t; Jon Bilous 180-1b; Bob Masters 109br; Phillip Bond 37tr, 221br; Kanwarjit Singh Boparai 192cb; Dembinsky Photo Associates / Dominique Braud 24br; Paul Brown 151b; Jan Butchofsky 198-9t; California Dreamin 101tr, 41cla, 238br; Cannon Photography LLC 34-5bl, 112bl, 139cb, 242-43t; Cavan Images 66bl; Sunny Celeste 53tl; Scott Chernis 43t; Felix Choo 47br, 88bl, 102tr, 170cr, 171cl; Chronicle 64crb; Ronnie Chua 40-1b, 152b; Citizen of the Planet 235br; Patrick Civello 36t; Classic Image 94cb, 118cb; Robert Clay 39cl; Directphoto Collection 106crb; Ian G Dagnall 42bl, 126-7b, 226t, 240clb; Ethan Daniels 37cl; Danita Delimont Creative 233tr; David Sanger Photography 203cr; Joe Decker 232-3b; Danita Delimont 41crb, 45bl, 118-9t; Don Douglas 205br; Randy Duchaine 118c; Daniel Duenser 50br; Everett Collection Inc 55br, 65crb; Eye35 Stock 171cr; F8grapher 198bl; Michele Falzone 78-9c, 130bl; Stephen Finn 187tl; Tim Fleming 185br; Zachary Frank 205t; Neil Fraser 156bl; Robert Fried 56t, 244bl, 246b; Gado Images 99tr / Smith Collection 80t; GL Archive 95bc, 97ca, 97br; Paul Christian Gordon 194bl; Granger Historical Picture Archive 55cra, 118clb; Susie Hedberg 176-177b; Yuval Helfman 202bl, 220bl; Bill Helsel 18cb, 132-3; Hemis 104b; Hero Images Inc. 42tl; Heyengel 26tl; Historic Images 52bl; Hi-Story 53cb; History and Art Collection 162bc; The History Collection 118fclb; Peter Horree 81b, 125cr; Dave G. Houser 243bl, 247t; Della Huff 78bl, 155br, 229br, 243cla; imageBROKER 206bl, 241tr; Imago / Wu Xiaoling 162cr; Interfoto 97tr / History 53br; Anton Ivanov 193crb; Rich Iwasaki 79cra; Jejim120 170br; Joerg Hackemann 22cra; Mark A. Johnson 111br; Roy Johnson 144br; Mariusz Jurgielewicz 51tl; Matthew Kiernan 113br; Art Kowalsky 18tl, 36bl, 114-5; Kimberly Kradel 202-3tl; Bob Kreisel 48-49b, 70b; Chris LaBasco 153cra; Michael Lingberg 177cra; Andrew Lloyd 37crb; Jon Lord 217b Lucky-Photographer 236-7b; Patti McConville 49cla; Ilene MacDonald 166-7b; Stefano Politi Markovina 22t, 24clb, 105tl, 149tr, 123cra; Mauritius Images Gmbh 27cla; Brian McGuire 94bc; Panther Media GmbH 84-85b; Mike Kipling Photography 65bc; Geoffrey Morgan 76-7t; Luciano Mortula 22bl; MShieldsPhotos 22cl; Ilpo Musto 104cl; Naeblys 146t; Jonathan Nguyen 82b, 150tl, 165tl; Ron Niebrugge 152-3t; Nikreates 110cra, 162cra, / *Shaking Man statue* © Terry Allen/VAGA at ARS, NY and DACS, London 2018 142bl; 1NiKreative 129tl; North Wind Picture Archives 52cb, 53cla; Novarc Images 131br; Oldtime 94clb; Efrain Padro 12-3b, 119br; @Painet Inc. 51tr; David Parker 95crb; Susan Pease 130-1t, 123tl; Photo.zoommer.ru 218tl; Aurora Photos 233tl; Pictorial Press Ltd 55tr, 179br; The Picture Pantry 13br; Chuck Place 233cra; Prisma by Dukas Presseagentur GmbH 79crb; Oleksandr Prokopenko 26cra; Ed Rhodes 184br, 248t; Cheryl Rinzler 228bl; Robertharding / Richard Cummins 29br; Robertharding / Toms Auzins 40-41t; Clive Sawyer 84t; R Scapinello 186-7b; Searagen 96-97t; Ian Shaw 136crb; SiliconValleyStock 98-9b, 235tl; Jo Ann Snover 216-7t; Stars and Stripes 51bl, 51br, 164b; Stephen Saks Photography 38-9b, 250t; Stockimo / Leelocke 21tl, 188-9; Rebecca Stunell 230-1t; SvetlanaSF 49cr; Jeff Tangen 12c; Travelpix 56cr; Rohan Van Twest 201tr; UPI / Kevin Dietsch 57cb; Michael Urmann 207tl; Martin Valigursky 236tl; Victor Volta 38tl; David Wall 128bl; Scott Wilson 66-67, 89br; World History Archive 94crb; Zoonar GmbH 113tr; ZUMA Press, Inc. 165br, 167tl, 232cl, / Jerome Brunet 42-3b.

AWL Images: Walter Bibikow 14t, 136-7b; Sabine Lubenow 212.

Charles Zukow Associates: 15cr.

Chinese Historical Society: 126tl.

Coi: 34-5t.

Depositphotos Inc: Bertl123 68-9b; srongkrod481 234bl.

Disney: 69tr.

Dorling Kindersley: Neil Lukas 97crb; Andrew McKinney 170cl; Robert Vente 87bl.

Dreamstime.com: Ahfotobox 214t; Aiisha 57tr; Annalevan 200-1b; Bruno Coelho 56br; Engel Ching 224-25b; Coralimages2020 163, 227br; Debsta75 95bl; David Edelman 46br; F11photo 103b; Giovanni Gagliardi 71t; S Gibson 214bl; Enrique Gomez / *Frieda and Diego* © Banco de México Diego Rivera Frida Kahlo Museums Trust, Mexico, D.F. / DACS 2018 141cla; Yuval Helfman 47cl; Burt Johnson 13cr; Panagiotis Lambrakis 156tr; Karin Hildebrand Lau 231clb; Pius Lee 72-3; Legacy1995 197br; Meinzahn 222cra; Michaelurmann 222-23t; Minnystock 8-9; Randy Miramontez 143t; Fergal Moran 51cl; Olgashuster 44-5t; Photopictures Project 33crb; Radkol 193br; Siempreverde22 53tr; Simathers 184-5t; TobySophie 218b; Wirestock 169tr; Hakan Can Yalcin 144-5t.
Gallery of California Art, Oakland Museum of California, 2012: 222bl.

California Academy of Sciences: 192-93t, Gayle Laird 193cra

Geburtshaus Levi Strauss Museum: 183br.

Getty Images: Al Greene Archive 64clb; Sergio Amiti 26-7t; Jordan Banks 8cl; Eddie Brady 230bl; Buyenlarge 52t, / Carol M. Highsmith 196br; Christopher Chan 136-7t; Yiming Chen 213t; Bloomberg Creative 57br; Lachlan Cunningham 76bl; Jason Doiy 19, 158; Josh Edelson 138crb; Sergei Fadeichev 50tl; C Flanigan 51cr; Mitchell Funk 181tl; EyeEm / Zann Goff 35cl; Hearst Newspapers 54cr, 54bc; Hearst Newspapers / San Francisco Chronicle / Duke Downey 54-55t, / Liz Hafalia 33cla, / Gabrielle Lurie 46-47t, / Michael Macor 32-33b; Thearon W. Henderson 50tr; Adam Hester 219tr; Historical 54br; Robert Holmes 83br; Jasantiso 136bl; Jean-Pierre Lescourret 20, 172-3, 178b; Kathryn Donohew Photography 16c, 60-1; Kristine T Pham Photography 39tr; Latypova 48-49t; LimeWave - inspiration to exploration 15br; Michael Marfell 244-5t; Nicolas McComber 213bl; Jonathan Nourok 56bc; Peeterv 30br, 124-25t; Pgiam 45cr, 238-9t; Photo by Francesca Russell 27tr; Prab S 12clb; Steve Proehl 15t; Ronniechua 100-1b; sf_foodphoto 35crb; Ezra Shaw 50cl; Smith Collection / Gado 162br; Alexander Spatari 2-3; Spondylolithesis 168-169b; Justin Sullivan 57cla; Ted Streshinsky Photographic Archive 55bc; Underwood Archives 64crb; Lingxiao Xie 44bl.

GLBT Historical Society Museum: 182bl.

Getty Images / iStock: bluejayphoto 120cra, 252-53; Chinaface 13t; drserg 43br; / gregobagel / *Vaillancourt Fountain* © SODRAC, Montreal and DACS, London 2018 146-7b; Pascale Gueret 107tr; heyengel 6-7; JLWNYC 21cb, 208-09; miroslav_1 250-1b; NetaDegany 215; nevskyphoto 50bl; rudisill 24cl; Spondylolithesis 124bl; TraceRouda 4; Wallpaper101 32-33t.

Images courtesy of **Legion of Honor / Fine Arts Museums of San Francisco:** 24t, 194cra, 194crb, 196clb, 196-7, 196crb, /Steve Whittaker 196cr.

Mary Evans Picture Library: Grenville Collins Postcard Collection 64cb; Sueddeutsche Zeitung Photo 64c.

Courtesy of the Napa Valley Wine Train: 240-1b.

Robert Harding Picture Library: AGE Fotostock / Gary Moon 58-9; Frans Lanting 39br.

Courtesy of San Francisco Museum of Modern Art (SFMOMA): 138bl, 196bc, 197clb, 197bc; *The vibrant Figures with Sunset* (1978) by Roy Lichtenstein © Estate of Roy Lichtenstein/DACS 138-9t; Iwan Baan 30-31t / *Alexander Calder sculptures in the garden* © 2018 Calder Foundation, New York/DACS London 2108 141tr; Henrik Kam, 139clb, 139crb, 139fclb; Joe Fletcher 140b.

Shutterstock.com: Cdrin 204crb, Checubus 195; Kristiina Kuslapuu / *fragment of 16th Avenue Tiled Steps in San Francisco* artists www.colettecrutcher.com and www.aileenbarrtile.com 31cl; Hans Kwiotek 99br; Kit Leong 204bl; Mark Reinstein 57tl; segawa7 / Moraga Steps in San Francisco artists www.colettecrutcher.com and www.aileenbarrtile.com 31crb.

SuperStock: Age Fotostock / Kobby Dagan 50cr; Design Pics / Yves Marcoux 17bl, 90-1.

TopFoto.co.uk: AP 95cb; Underwood Archives / The Image Works 54tl, 65clb.

Front flap
Alamy Stock Photo; Stockimo / Leelocke cla; The Picture Pantry br; Michael Warwick bl; **Depositphotos Inc:** Bertl123 tc; dell640 cb; **Getty Images:** peeterv cra.

Sheet Map Cover
Getty Images: Moment / vns24@yahoo.com

Cover images:
Front and spine: **Getty Images:** Moment / vns24@yahoo.com.
Back: **Alamy Stock Photo:** Danita Delimont c; **Getty Images:** Moment / vns24@yahoo.com b; **Getty Images / iStock:** Spondylolithesis tr; **SuperStock:** Design Pics / Yves Marcoux cla.

Illustrators: Arcana Studios, Dean Entwhistle, Nick Lipscombe

First edition 1994

Published in Great Britain by Dorling Kindersley Limited,
20 Vauxhall Bridge Road,
London SW1V 2SA

The authorised representative in the EEA is
Dorling Kindersley Verlag GmbH. Arnulfstr.
124, 80636 Munich, Germany

Published in the United States by DK Publishing,
1745 Broadway, 20th Floor, New York, NY 10019, USA

25 26 27 28 10 9 8 7 6 5 4 3 2 1

A CIP catalog record for this book
is available from the British Library.

A catalog record for this book is available
from the Library of Congress.

ISSN: 1542 1554
ISBN: 978 0 2417 8407 5

Printed and bound in China.

www.dk.com

MIX
Paper | Supporting responsible forestry
FSC™ C018179

This book was made with Forest Stewardship Council™ certified paper – one small step in DK's commitment to a sustainable future.
Learn more at **www.dk.com/uk/information/sustainability**

A NOTE FROM DK

The rate at which the world is changing is constantly keeping the DK travel team on our toes. While we've worked hard to ensure that this edition of San Francisco and the Bay Area is accurate and up-to-date, we know that opening hours alter, standards shift, prices fluctuate, places close and new ones pop up in their stead. So, if you notice we've got something wrong or left something out, we want to hear about it. Please get in touch at travelguides@dk.com